IMPROPER NAMES

IMPROPER NAMES

COLLECTIVE PSEUDONYMS FROM THE LUDDITES TO ANONYMOUS

MARCO DESERIIS

UNIVERSITY OF MINNESOTA PRESS
Minneapolis · London

QUADRANT

Quadrant, a joint initiative of the University of Minnesota Press and the Institute for Advanced Study at the University of Minnesota, provides support for interdisciplinary scholarship within a new, more collaborative model of research and publication.

Sponsored by Quadrant's Global Cultures group (advisory board: Evelyn Davidheiser, Michael Goldman, Helga Leitner, and Margaret Werry) and the Institute for Global Studies at the University of Minnesota.

Quadrant is generously funded by the Andrew W. Mellon Foundation.

An earlier version of the Introduction was published as "Improper Names: Collective Pseudonyms and Multiple-Use Names as Minor Processes of Subjectivation," *Subjectivity* 5, no. 1 (2012): 140–60. doi:10.1057/sub.2012.3. An earlier version of chapter 4 was published as "'Lots of Money Because I Am Many': The Luther Blissett Project and the Multiple-Use Name Strategy," in *Cultural Activism: Practices, Dilemmas, and Possibilities*, Thamyris/Intersecting: Place, Sex, and Race 21, ed. Begum O. Firat and Aylin Kuryel, 65–93 (Amsterdam: Rodopi, 2011).

Published by the University of Minnesota Press
111 Third Avenue South, Suite 290
Minneapolis, MN 55401-2520
http://www.upress.umn.edu

Library of Congress Cataloging-in-Publication Data

Deseriis, Marco.
Improper names: collective pseudonyms from the Luddites to Anonymous / Marco Deseriis.
Includes bibliographical references and index.
ISBN 978-0-8166-9486-0 (hc) ISBN 978-0-8166-9487-7 (pb)
1. Anonymous writings. 2. Anonyms and pseudonyms. 3. Authorship.
4. Group identity. 5. Identity (Philosophical concept). I. Title.
PN171.A6D47 2015
412—dc23 2014043036

Printed in the United States of America on acid-free paper

21 20 19 18 17 16 15 10 9 8 7 6 5 4 3 2 1

For Miriam and Tito

To give a name is always, like any birth (certificate), to sublimate a singularity and to inform against it, to hand it over to the police. All the police forces in the world can be routed by a surname, but even before they know it, a secret computer, at the moment of baptism, will have kept them up to date.

—JACQUES DERRIDA

And Jesus asked him, "What is your name?"
"My name is Legion," he replied,
"for we are many."

—MARK 5:9 (ESV)

CONTENTS

ACKNOWLEDGMENTS

Improper Names is dedicated to all those who invented, borrowed, or stole a name in the service of a shared project or a common cause. Without them, this book would simply not exist. More concretely, I would like to thank a number of practitioners who agreed to be interviewed or consulted on specific chapters of the book. These include John Berndt, Dr. Al Ackermann, and Florian Cramer for the chapter on Monty Cantsin; and Roberto Bui, Andrea Natella, Daniele Vasquez, Eva and Franco Mattes, Corrado Magni, Fango, Algernon, and Vittore Baroni for the chapter on Luther Blissett. My gratitude also goes to Craig Saper and Gabriella Coleman for their insights on the chapters on Allen Smithee and Anonymous, respectively.

More generally, this book has been made possible thanks to the intellectual and professional support of a number of people. I am deeply grateful to my former advisors Alexander R. Galloway, Allen Feldman, and McKenzie Wark, who guided me through the early stages of my research while I was a doctoral student at New York University. I also thank the editors at the University of Minnesota Press, especially Doug Armato, for believing in this project and inviting me to present it under the auspices of the Quadrant initiative. The peer reviewers of this book (Ned Rossiter, in particular) have also provided precious feedback that helped me look at the manuscript through fresh eyes. Finally, copy editor Holly Monteith and indexer Lucas Freeman contributed important work to make this book more readable and accessible.

My colleagues Craig Robertson, Joanne Morreale, and Murray Forman in the Program in Media and Screen Studies at Northeastern University deserve special recognition for supporting me through the early stages of my academic career, and so does my friend and mentor Jack Z. Bratich. Finally, I express my deep gratitude to my parents, my lifelong partner, my son, and my close friends for all their love, the great conversations, and the intellectual and emotional support. Without you, I could never be the many who I am.

INTRODUCTION

GENEALOGY AND THEORY OF THE IMPROPER NAME

In May–June 1995, a local community radio station in Rome aired a curious live broadcast experiment. Every Saturday night, for five consecutive weeks, all participants in the program vowed to go by the same name and be the same person. By introducing themselves as Luther Blissett, anchors, correspondents and listeners embraced the confusion that ensued: "Hold on, we have a Luther calling in from the Colosseum. Hi, Luther, how *am I* doing tonight?" asked the anchorwoman. "Pretty good, and *myself*?" responded a male listener. "Not bad, not bad," replied the anchor. "Listen, a group of Luthers are converging on the Colosseum right now to organize a three-sided football match. Do you wanna help them out?"

As I was listening to the stream of gendered voices that greeted each other always in the first person, I realized that the radio show was a powerful expression of what we called the "condividual" *(condividuo)*. In the spring of that year, I had attended a few preparatory meetings of *Radio Blissett* at a friend's apartment. Back then, I had not realized that the number of individuals involved in the Luther Blissett Project (LBP) went well beyond the core circle of organizers I had met at these meetings. Thus I was caught by surprise when several dozen people—all of whom seemed perfectly comfortable with their new identity—materialized for *Radio Blissett*. Once on the air, the condividual came to life as a strange polyphonous being, a ventriloquist that could not help but speak in multiple tongues. As the only guest, listener, and anchor of the show, Blissett could merely entertain a conversation with itself, as it were.[1] At the same time, the distinctive timbre of each voice made clear that each Luther was a "dividual" that contributed to the condividual in his or her own distinctive way.[2] Blissett's voices and multiple bodies engaged in surreal but coordinated activities such as itinerant rave parties, urban drifts, three-sided football matches, and "psychic attacks" against government buildings such as the Birth Records Office, the Italian Society of Authors and Publishers, and the Provincial Office of Labor. According to Luther Blissett, these agencies were responsible of enforcing outdated notions of identity, intellectual property, and labor, respectively. As such, they deserved the wrath of the condividual.

Luther Blissett was a "multiple-use name." That is, anyone could become Luther Blissett simply by adopting the name. Launched in Bologna in 1994, the open reputation quickly spread to other Italian cities, and thanks to the Internet, it did not take long to go international. By the late 1990s, the multiple-use name had been borrowed by hundreds of individuals around the world to author media pranks, sell apocryphal manuscripts to publishers, fabricate artists and artworks, denounce media witch hunts, author best-selling novels, and conduct psychogeographic experiments, or simply as an Internet handle. Even though the wild circulation of the pseudonym made it difficult to define its exact role and function, in the intention of its creators, Blissett was meant to be a folk hero of the information age that could narrate a vast community of cultural producers into existence. In particular, the founders of the Luther Blissett Project saw the condividual as a modern Robin Hood who could seize the symbolic and material wealth accumulated by the culture industries and redistribute it to its increasingly underpaid and precarious producers.

To provide the multiple-use name with historical depth, the LBP founders inserted Blissett into a lineage of legendary and fictional progenitors. These included Monty Cantsin and Karen Eliot, two aliases that had been shared by North American and European mail artists in the 1980s to undermine the art world's need for originality and novelty; Ned Ludd, the eponymous leader invented by the English Luddites to resist the introduction of labor-saving machines during the Industrial Revolution; and Spartacus, a collective name adopted by the revolting Roman slaves in the homonymous film by Stanley Kubrick. Such genealogy can be extended, as I will do in this book, by adding case studies such as Allen Smithee, a collective pseudonym shared by Hollywood film directors to work outside of their reputation, and Anonymous, a tag shared by thousands of Internet activists to reclaim freedom of speech and unrestrained access to information technology.

Even though these pseudonymous personae are suspended between reality and fiction and operate in different historic settings, the twofold purpose of this book is to demonstrate (1) that despite their historical contingency, they share some common features, and (2) that the relations of similarity entailed by those common features do not prevail over relations of difference. In this sense, the orientation of this study is both analytical and genealogical. On an analytical level, *Improper Names* argues that sharing a pseudonym is a distinctive authorial strategy that performs specific aesthetic, political, and technical functions. On a genealogical level, this study tries to demonstrate, after Michel Foucault, that improper names are practices that "[allow] us to constitute a historical knowledge of struggles and to make use of that knowledge in contemporary tactics."[3] Although academic research may tend to ignore or disqualify such knowledge as "naive," "nonconceptual," and "insufficiently elaborated," this genealogy shows that however discontinuous they may be, these "knowleges from below" are able to address their own critical questions.[4]

Whether they have been handed down through oral accounts or encoded in different media, these pseudonyms have in fact circulated in the public domain and affected the social imagination for a long time. Furthermore, these aliases function as *processes of mediation* with a double function. On one hand, a shared pseudonym allows its users to recognize each other for the simple fact of sharing a name. On the other hand, the alias brings within the same discursive space actions and utterances that are produced by heterogeneous forms of association and organization—some of which are collectivized and institutionalized and some of which are more spontaneous and less structured.

Drawing from these preliminary observations, I propose to define an improper name as the adoption of the same alias by organized collectives, affinity groups, and individual authors. An improper name is improper not only because it lacks manners or propriety of behavior—in that case, it would only be inappropriate—but because it fails to label and circumscribe a clearly defined domain (what Michel De Certeau calls "a proper").[5] Contrary to a proper name, whose chief function is to *fix* a referent as part of the operation of a system of signs, an improper name is explicitly constructed to obfuscate both the identity and number of its referents. On one hand, the improper name embeds the shielding effect of any pseudonym, that is, the pseudonym's nominal function of protecting an individual by substituting her legal name qua marker of her identity. On the other hand, an improper name functions as an open multiplicity that can hardly be disambiguated and assigned a discrete referent.

MAIN FEATURES OF THE IMPROPER NAME

To further explore the ambivalent nature of this obfuscation, I shall briefly unearth the etymological meaning of the term *condividual.* A derivative of the Italian *condivisione* (sharing as "dividing together"), the condividual does not necessarily presuppose a community but only a concatenation of parts. In fact, the users of a shared pseudonym may not be bound by anything but their temporary homonymy. Yet my wager is that improper names stretch across a continuum that goes from highly centralized and planned usages (collective pseudonyms) to decentralized and idiosyncratic appropriations (multiple-use names).

To situate an improper name in this continuum, it is necessary to analyze its *authorizing context,* which determines how a pseudonym is to be used and by whom. Authorizing contexts include social movements, unions, art and political collectives, and Internet-based communities. Although such contexts may initially succeed in controlling the range of possible usages, as soon as the alias is released in the public domain, it can be easily appropriated for unforeseen purposes. In other words, *collective pseudonyms* and *multiple-use names* denote two attributes of the improper name in terms of varying degrees of control.

Although improper names have been created in the most disparate social, political, and cultural milieux, I maintain that they share three common features and functions:

1. empowering a subaltern social group by providing a *medium* for identification and mutual recognition to their users
2. enabling those who do not have a voice of their own to acquire a *symbolic power* outside the boundaries of an institutional practice
3. expressing a *process of subjectivation* characterized by the proliferation of difference

This means that improper names function as assemblages of enunciation that are common and singular, impersonal yet individuated. Although these aliases retain the formal features of a proper name, their multiple and unpredictable iterations in the public sphere put into crisis the referential function of the proper name.

I will deepen the relationship between the improper name and the proper name later in this introductory chapter. For now, I shall just notice that improper names emerge from a crisis in established forms of political and aesthetic representation. The five case studies analyzed in this book—Ned Ludd, Monty Cantsin (and Karen Eliot), Allen Smithee, Luther Blissett, and Anonymous—are all situated at critical historic junctures, such as the emergence of modern industrial capitalism, the shift from Fordism to post-Fordism, and the emergence of the information society. If these socioeconomic upheavals upset established forms of political and aesthetic representation, improper names express this instability by denoting assemblages of enunciation that are visible yet obfuscated, nameable but difficult to identify.

THE SYMBOLIC POWER OF SINGULARITIES

Improper names are never entirely secret or centralized, but they always imply a certain degree of publicity, dissemination, and loss of control. It is through circulation in the public sphere that the use of an alias becomes a process of subjectivation whereby those who do not have a voice of their own seek to acquire a symbolic power outside the boundaries of an institutional practice.

The French sociologist Pierre Bourdieu has defined symbolic power as the magic power to act on the social world through words. Drawing from J. L. Austin's reflections on the conditions of felicity of an utterance, Bourdieu argues that "the real source of the magic of performative utterances lies in the mystery of ministry, i.e. in the delegation by virtue of which an individual—king, priest or spokesperson—is mandated to speak and act on behalf of the group, thus constituted in him and by him."[6] Collective pseudonyms and multiple-use names are forms of symbolic power in their own right. But rather than being exercised through an institution, the symbolic power of an improper name is directly managed by the community of its users. This does not mean that such power is equally distributed among the users. For instance, the creator(s) of an improper name may try to retain some exclusive rights over the pseudonym. But such an attempt would not go unchallenged, as improper names often conceal divergences in opinion over their finality and function. An analysis of these divergences is essential to grasping the improper not as a process of simplification and *reductio ad unum* but, on the contrary, as a singular process of subjectivation characterized by the proliferation of difference.

The concept of singularity stems from a long tradition of political ontology that dates back to European theologians such as Duns Scotus and Nicholas of Cusa and continues in modern times with the philosophies of Baruch Spinoza, Friedrich Nietzsche, Gilbert Simondon, Gilles Deleuze, and, more recently, Jean-Luc Nancy, Rosi Braidotti, Paolo Virno, Michael Hardt, and Antonio Negri, among others. Here I shall limit myself to following Hardt and Negri's elegant observation that the notion of singularity differs from that of identity in that it is linked to multiplicity in three respects. First, singularity is defined "by a multiplicity outside of itself"; second, "singularity points to a multiplicity within itself"; and third, it "is always engaged in a process of becoming different—a temporal multiplicity."[7]

This threefold nexus between singularity and multiplicity is a distinctive feature of the improper name. Improper names do not engage dialectically with an outside, that is, they do not tend to divide the social space into two symmetrical, opposed fields. On the contrary, by making themselves available to unforeseen appropriations, they let the outside slip into the inside, and vice versa. This means that improper names do not designate fixed identities. Rather, they are heterogeneous assemblages in which the whole (the ensemble of an improper name's iterations) is unable to unify and totalize the parts, among which, nevertheless, it establishes relationships and paths of communication.[8]

In temporal terms, an improper name may take unforeseen turns as it is appropriated by different individuals. For instance, in its circulation across different regions of England, the name Ned Ludd came to be associated with a variety of demands that were not only related to resistance against industrial machinery. Allen Smithee, the pseudonym coined by the Directors Guild of America (DGA) for Hollywood film directors who want to disown a film, has also been adopted by screenwriters, actors, and film producers outside of the DGA's oversight. And multiple-use names such as Monty Cantsin, Karen Eliot, Luther Blissett, and Anonymous are all "open reputations" that purposefully lend themselves to multiple uses.

This means that behind an improper mode of subjectivation there exists an assemblage of bodies that cannot easily be integrated into members of a class. Thus the eminently political process whereby a multiplicity constitutes a collective subject of enunciation ("We, the People . . .") is displaced here by a heterogeneous composition that disturbs the smooth articulation of the many into the one. In this sense, the notion of the improper suggests that between the formation of the Western modern individual and forms of collectivism organized under the banner of the Party, the Union, the Corporation, and the Church, there exists a third, minor strand of subjectivity that does not conform to either side of this polarity but recombines the I and the We in a highly unstable, elusive assemblage. Such elusiveness points to the unrepresentable character of a multitude, a subject that escapes political unity and refuses to transfer authority to a sovereign. Theorized by Spinoza in the seventeenth century, and expunged by Hobbes and Rousseau from the horizon of modernity in favor of the People, the multitude is today regaining center stage at every level of social and political life. Unabashedly plural and multitudinous are the forms of cooperation, linguistic games, and affective flows that inform the life on the screen in a turbulent media environment such as Web 2.0. And so are the new forms of activism experimented by the embodied social movements that have been inundating the streets and squares of the Middle East, southern Europe, and North and South America since February 2011.

Yet contemporary theorizations of the multitude rarely address the concrete processes of subjectivation whereby these multitudes express themselves in the public sphere of communication. This work tries to fill this gap by delving into the complex dynamics and negotiations modern and contemporary multitudes undertake as they build up their own symbolic power while keeping its exercise open to the becoming of the social. It also suggests, especially in the chapter on Anonymous, that this becoming increasingly includes nonhuman actors, which follow a *techno-*logic of their own.

A GENEALOGY OF IMPROPER NAMES IN MODERN TIMES

As noted, the first distinctive feature of improper names is to provide anonymity and a medium for mutual recognition to their users. By failing to designate an identifiable referent, improper names make it difficult for authorities to track down specific individuals while enabling participation in social and political activities on an informal basis. It is no accident that many improper names emerge in rural societies where forms of organized resistance are unconstituted and illegal. For instance, the historian John Maddicott has suggested that the legend of Robin Hood may originate from the attribution of the same alias to notorious English thieves in the early fourteenth century.[9] And the French peasants who rose in arms against the nobility and clergy of the Beauvais in the Great Jacquerie of 1358 derive their name from their leader Guillaume Caillet, popularly known as Jacques Bonhomme. In other circumstances, peasants and farmers were not named after an eponymous leader but deliberately chose to share a personal name to conspire against the authorities. Such is the case of Poor Konrad, the collective pseudonym adopted by the Swabian peasants of southern Germany during their rebellion against taxes in 1514; Captain Swing, a pseudonym employed by impoverished English farmworkers in the riots that swept the southeast of England and led to the destruction of thousands of mechanized threshing machines in 1830; and Rebecca, the name shared by the tenant farmers of southwest Wales to attack toll gates between 1839 and 1843 as a form of resistance against rents, tithes, and the enclosure of common lands.[10]

The Rebecca and Swing riots were preceded (and presumably inspired) by the Luddite riots of 1811–17, with which improper names make their appearance in England, the first modern industrialized society. By relying on the recent publication of the *Writings of the Luddites*—a transcription of dozens of letters, ballads, and declarations written by the Luddites themselves—in chapter 1, I trace the initial baptism and usage of the eponym Ned Ludd as it migrated from Nottinghamshire (home to Robin Hood) to Yorkshire and the booming cotton districts around Manchester.[11] In this migration, Luddite discourse shifts from an initial narrow focus on the new, "obnoxious" labor-saving machines to a wider set of economic and political issues—including high food prices, low wages, rising unemployment, ineffective labor acts and regulations, and the legitimacy of monarchic power. Thus, on one hand, Ned Ludd became a medium and a catalyst for a disparate, if contradictory, set of demands. On the other hand, as we shall see, the Industrial Revolution had created a veritable rift between the workers of the traditional wool trades in central England and the new factory workers of the cotton industry in the Northwest.

If the Luddites shared the same pseudonym as part of a mythmaking strategy that amplified the symbolic power and the material effects of machine breaking, the name Ned Ludd did not have per se an economic value. The rise of the first modern culture industry—the nineteenth-century Victorian publishing industry—changes this state of affairs as a whole new political economy of the signature takes shape. By understanding that the curiosity of a fast-growing readership in the identity and lives of literary authors lent itself to commercial exploitation, late-Victorian publishers such C. H. Clarke and T. F. Unwin built successful editorial operations through novel series such as The Pseudonym Library and the so-called Anonyma series.[12] In this way, young publishers who did not own large capital were able to sign relatively unknown and therefore less expensive authors. At the same time, they brought together under the same imprint writers and literary genres that would have otherwise had little in common.

The idea that an alias can function as the lynchpin of works authored by multiple individuals resurfaces in France with Nicolas Bourbaki, a pseudonym shared by a collective of French mathematicians for more than six decades. Founded in 1934, and including extraordinary figures such as André Weil, Jean-Pierre Serre, Laurent Schwarz, and Alexander Grothendieck, the Bourbaki group consistently used the pseudonym to organize a series of seminars and author all its writings—including *Éléments de mathématique,* a monumental ten-volume treatise that systematized the principles of modern advanced mathematics. By overriding individual contributions and perspectives, the signature "N. Bourbaki" was meant to express the group's firm belief that mathematics is a unitary field held together by the axiomatic method and the invariability of mathematical structures. Such a belief was reflected in the group's consensus-based method of collaboration, which was ultimately aimed at reaching unanimous decisions and eliminating contradiction. Furthermore, the set of rules that determined membership in the Bourbaki collective (the cofounders had to retire at the age of fifty, and new members had to prove themselves in recruiting seminars) allowed new generations of mathematicians to keep the collective signature alive, in an ideal line of continuity with the founding fathers, until the late 1990s.[13]

But if the Bourbaki signature was *always* appended to the works produced by a collective, then these works may well have been signed by a collective author such as the Bourbaki Group. In other words, because it was a direct expression of the collective's unanimous decisions, the signature functioned as a proper name that designated a delineated subject of enunciation. This means that the creation of a collective pseudonym is not sufficient in and of itself to bring about an improper name. Rather, as previously noted, it is the lack of a proper domain or stable referent—that is, the instability of the relationship between signifier and signified—that puts in crisis the proper name's putative function to designate a referent in all its possible universes.

The structuralist approach of the Bourbaki group was highly influential in the 1950s and 1960s not only for mathematics but also for the social sciences. In 1949, Weil had provided an elegant algebraic solution to Claude Lévi-Strauss's classic analysis of the marriage laws and kinship structures among the Australian Murngin aborigines.[14] Beginning in the 1970s, however, the group's belief that mathematics was a unitary field proved to be increasingly untenable. Yet the crisis of structuralism did not affect the group's survival, and potential internal conflicts did not result in the circulation of competing Bourbaki texts. In this respect, it is useful to contrast the case of Bourbaki with that of Allen Smithee (or Alan Smithee), a pseudonym introduced in 1969 by the Directors Guild of America (DGA) to allow film directors to disown movies that are recut by a production company. Like Bourbaki, Smithee was initially controlled by the DGA, which required a director to undergo a strict procedure to prove that a movie had been recut without the director's consent. Unlike Bourbaki, however, the DGA monopoly over Smithee came under increasing scrutiny, and eventually the union decided to disown its own brainchild.

Chapter 2 shows how the Smithee signature was originally introduced at a time of crisis in the studio system that was marked by dwindling box-office revenues and the dismantling of the Motion Picture Production

Code—the bureaucratic and financial apparatus that had guaranteed the consolidation of the studios' oligopoly since the 1930s. From this point of view, Smithee is not a mere placeholder for a missing film director but an expression of the directors' collective ability to extend their creative control over the entire filmmaking process. Indeed, in the 1970s, directors gained a wider creative autonomy, and entire filmographies were reorganized around directors' unique visions and styles—a perspective that was pioneered by U.S. critic Andrew Sarris.[15]

By taking this perspective all too seriously, a group of scholars came together at the University of Pennsylvania in the late 1990s with the intent of studying Smithee's "oeuvre." The Allen Smithee Group drew on Derrida's theory of the signature to suggest that Smithee is an artificial author that, by linking works that have nothing in common other than their signature, denaturalizes established models of authorship figured along the masculine metaphor of the director as a film's sole and rightful father.[16] Thus, as soon as we stop considering Smithee as a simple stand-in for a missing film director and take it seriously, on a cultural level, we discover what Gilles Deleuze and Félix Guattari would call a "minor" author—an author whose oeuvre is intrinsically collective, does not have a recognizable style, and hence does not have a place of its own in the history of cinema.[17] On the level of political economy, a Smithee credit has the effect of laying bare the studio system as a money-making machine that enables the category of the director-as-auteur only to lend a face to its standardized production. As a stock of *negative cultural capital,* however, Smithee's filmography cannot be easily converted into exchange value. This means that Smithee is the improper name of what, paraphrasing Foucault, I call the *disowning-function*—a function that, by decoupling authorship into a cultural layer and an economic layer, reverses the conflation of property and propriety, ownership and reputation, set in motion by the modern culture industry.[18]

MULTIPLE-USE NAMES AND POST-FORDISM

While Smithee was introduced in an industry that was originally modeled after a Ford factory, the late 1960s mark the end of the Fordist Hollywood and the beginning of a new phase characterized by a more flexible system of production—what we might call a post-Fordist Hollywood. Within this system, the name of the director came to be associated with a distinctive *vision* through which movies could be profitably marketed. In this respect, the DGA's request to protect a director's reputation can be seen as a means for protecting a brand name that had a growing economic value for the entire film industry. This also meant that directors had to develop, as we shall see, a procedure to discriminate between legitimate requests to disown a film and illegitimate ones. In other words, as directors acquired growing stakes within the industry, they learned how to police themselves—a shift that seems to characterize the post-Fordist subjectivity in general, if it is true that, under post-Fordism, a worker invests her entire "soul" into the product of her labor, as Franco Berardi puts it.[19]

And yet the notion that a personal reputation needs to be monitored and protected can also be reversed so as to imagine what might happen if the name of a cultural producer is circulated for everyone to use. A group of mail artists in Portland, Oregon, decided to test this hypothesis when they invented the "Open Pop Star" and multiple-use name Monty Cantsin in 1977. Among the case studies analyzed in this book, Cantsin is perhaps the most unruly of all, as it was released in the public domain with virtually no instructions for use. Besides reflecting the idiosyncratic personality of many of its users, Cantsin is a figure of the distributed creativity of the Mail Art network.

In chapter 3, I trace the origins of this assemblage to early artistic experiments with the postal system in the 1960s. In particular, I show how Ray Johnson's idea of asking his addressees to "add to and return" or forward his mailings to third parties set in motion a network of correspondences that transformed the mail from a medium for interpersonal communication into a social space. The emergence of a distinctive *aesthetics of networking*—an aesthetics that shifts the emphasis from the production of objects to the manifold relations among networkers—has two major consequences for the art world. First, it restores the idea that the production and distribution of art can follow the logic—or, as Derrida puts it, the "madness"—of the gift rather than that of exchange value.[20] Second, by affirming an ethics of radical inclusiveness, it creates an autonomous sphere for the production and distribution of art that challenges traditional curatorial practices. In fact, mail artists redefined curating from a set of selective criteria aimed at separating Art from art to a collaborative effort, undertaken by the artists themselves, that brought together the manifold exchanges that made the network.[21]

This movement from Art to art is thus a movement toward the continuum of everyday life. It is no accident that by the end of the 1970s, the inclusivity of mail art meets the participatory ethics of punk in an ongoing exchange of letters, zines, tapes, and artworks through the postal system. Monty Cantsin is both an offspring and a figure of the distributed creativity of these networks. The multiple-use name embodies the possibility for *everyone* to participate in an open pop star whose fame is supposed to grow through multiple and possibly contradictory enactments. Yet, as we shall see, the fact that the name was released with no guidelines subjected it to individual appropriations and overidentifications that ultimately damaged its ability to function as a name of the common. This became clear when the improper name migrated to Canada and Europe to function as the spokesperson of Neoism—a fictitious art movement that performed the resurgence of the modern avant-garde while constantly undermining it with farcical poses and nonsensical statements.

In the final part of the chapter, I show how the emphasis on the paradoxical and contradictory character of Neoism had the unintended effect of overshadowing the power relationships that existed within the network. At the same time, Neoists such as Stewart Home and Vittore Baroni understood that the multiple-use name strategy could be improved by designing practical guidelines to protect it from personal overidentification. These included the suggestion of not using the multiple-use name in conjunction with one's patronymic and of clouding its initial baptism so that no particular individual could personally identify with it. Baroni and Home's suggestions found fertile ground in Bologna, Italy, in summer 1994, when a group of young activists decided to launch the Luther Blissett Project (LBP). Although the activists borrowed the name from a real person—namely, a British soccer player of Jamaican origins who had played an unfortunate season in the Italian Serie A a decade earlier—no one knows why the name was chosen and exactly by whom. By shrouding the origins of the project in mystery, the activists designed an elaborate mythmaking strategy aimed at turning Blissett into a figure of immaterial labor.

Chapter 4 shows how the success of this strategy was due to the interplay of at least four intertwined factors. First, because most Blissett practitioners considered themselves activists rather than artists, they had little interest in attaching their individual names to the condividual. Second, most of Blissett's interventions were coordinated through the Internet by groups operating in different cities. Thus, on an organizational level, the LBP functioned as a network whose nodes were collectively managed. Third, the LBP's innovative use of networked media was coupled with a reinvention of historic avant-garde practices such as the "psychogeographic drift"—an experiential mapping of the modern city that had been first practiced and theorized by the Lettrists and the Situationists in the 1950s and 1960s. This creative deterritorialization of the language of the avant-garde—and this is the fourth element of the LBP's strategy—was also coupled with a novel approach to the media. Whereas the Neoists' idea of launching an open pop star was hampered by the Neoists' countercultural approach—with the result that Cantsin never became famous—the LBP chose to utilize a less cryptic language and directly targeted the media. In particular, the activists devised a series of elaborate media pranks whereby they could tell their own stories both *through* the media and *against* them. These included the fabrication of satanic cults, the creation of fake artists, and the publication of a political pamphlet, which snowballed into a national *affaire* involving print publishers, server administrators, priests, magistrates, and politicians.

Finally, I elaborate a critique of mythmaking by arguing that although the authors of this strategy—in particular, the Bolognese branch of the LBP—emphasized that Luther Blissett was an open and participatory assemblage of enunciation, unspoken hierarchies made some narrative strands more powerful than others. This is evident not only from the interviews I collected with members of the Viterbo LBP but also from the cofounders' choice of announcing the seppuku (ritual suicide) of the condividual in 1999. Besides allowing the Bolognese group to move to new projects (such as the collective of novelists Wu Ming and the net art group 0100101110101101.ORG), the impromptu announcement of Blissett's suicide caught several LBP participants by surprise. By liquidating their brainchild, the cofounders of the LBP eventually reclaimed an authorship over the folk hero—an authorship they had initially rejected by clouding its origins in mystery.

IMPROPER NAMES IN THE INFORMATION AGE

Because multiple-use names are open by definition to multiple usages, they harbor potential conflicts between the early adopters of the name and the latecomers. Whereas a collective pseudonym implies the existence of a community that defines, at least initially, its purpose and function, a multiple-use name can be appropriated by communities and individuals who do not necessarily share the same ethos and objectives. As we have seen, communities and networks, collectives and affinity groups, are the authorizing contexts of an improper name. Depending on their composition, culture, and position in a wider field of forces, such contexts can adopt different norms on how an alias is to be used. The more these rules are rigidly enforced, the less the name tends to be improper—that is, the less it undergoes a transformation during the course of its life.

We have already seen that although Nicolas Bourbaki was formally a shared pseudonym, its consistent use did not make it behave differently from a proper name. Let us also briefly consider the case of Jane, an alias that was adopted by a group of feminist activists from Chicago, Illinois, to run an illegal abortion service used by thousands of women in the years leading up to the Supreme Court's landmark decision to legalize abortion in 1973.[22] If the women used "Jane" to answer the phone and make contact with other women in need of medical assistance, the illegal nature of the operation made it difficult to use the alias for speaking out in public. Thus the name functioned more as a password that disclosed access to an underground world than to set in motion a process of subjectivation characterized by the proliferation of difference. Yet if Jane would have circulated and been appropriated by other women across the country, it would have probably become an improper name.

Thus the obfuscating function of collective pseudonyms is not in contrast with the possibility that these may acquire a symbolic power and a public dimension. What enables such transformation is the encoding of the alias in a variety of media and cultural forms, such as oral and written accounts, songs, essays, novels, letters, zines, artworks, graffiti, films, e-mails, online forums, and websites. By detaching the alias from its original authorizing context and the intentions of its creators, those media allow for its dissemination across vast swaths of time and space.

The rise of the network society accelerates this process of deterritorialization. As signifiers are unhinged from their referents at an increasingly fast pace, we assist the emergence of phenomena that are improper and condividual in character. For example, the impropriety of Internet memes—such as catchphrases, image macros, viral videos, and Web celebrities—lies in the fact that those signifiers maintain recognizable features while their associated meanings are subject to continuous variation. Memes are also condividual in that they are situated at the intersection of the collective imagination and dividual iterations that are authorless yet discrete and punctual. Furthermore, as an expression of the imaginal productivity of pseudonymous and anonymous Internet forums, Internet memes can be seen as a cultural inversion of the Web 2.0 reputation economy—with its obsession with individual identity and the measurement of social preference, status, and influence.

One of the earliest and most powerful Internet meme machines is the imageboard 4chan—a forum in which users communicate by exchanging images and short texts. Launched in 2003, 4chan allows users to post anonymously and does not archive its message threads, which are erased as soon as the server capacity is reached. This feature of the software prompts users to select and reply to certain message threads to stretch their life-span. 4chan's production of memes is thus a function of a specific relationship between the attention time shared by users on a single thread and the competition among multiple threads to capture and retain that attention. Because a discussion thread is usually made of several contributions, taken as a whole, it constitutes an assemblage of enunciation in its own right.

Chapter 5 is dedicated to Anonymous, a network of hackers and activists that derives its name from the tag that marks all unsigned posts in 4chan. Initially, the problematic of Anonymous lies at the intersection of an impersonal, potentially deindividuating technology, such as the imageboard, and human subjectivity and will. Throughout the chapter, I broaden this initial claim to suggest that Anonymous expresses the convergence of a technological drive toward indetermination with the human belief that open technologies are conducive to a freer society. Anonymous emerges from the mutual constitution of these poles in an assemblage that is both indifferent to the meaning and consequence of its actions and ethically committed to them. I base this paradoxical claim on Gilbert Simondon's notion of transduction as an operation that progressively structures a domain that is filled with potentials and in a state of "metastable equilibrium."[23]

My wager is that Anonymous is itself a metastable system that undergoes multiple individuations. I particular, I show how Anonymous has undergone at least three transition phases since its inception around 2005. The first phase coincides with the transition from Anonymous as a default function of the imageboard to Anonymous as a collective assemblage of enunciation. Such individuation emerged from the confrontation of those who insisted on using personal identifiers in the imageboard and those who argued for complete anonymity as a more egalitarian mode of communication. Once Anonymous emerged as a "we," it further individuated between those who inscribed its actions within an ethical and political horizon—the so-called moralfags—and the lulzfags, who refused any justification for them. While the lulzfags organized online raids—that is, sudden assaults on websites, individuals, and organizations, which had the primary function of entertaining their participants—the moralfags began coordinating larger campaigns for political purposes.

First with a global campaign against the Church of Scientology and then with a series of operations against corporations and government agencies that restrict access to information and information technology, Anonymous's second individuation marks a transition phase toward an organized political movement. Such actions are coordinated mostly through Internet Relay Chat (IRC), a text-based chat protocol that require users to identify themselves through a handle. Thus, while the imageboard continues to function as a *smooth machine of subjectivation* in which each post both contributes to and is an expression of Anonymous—that is, each dividual transaction can be exclusively attributed to the condividual Anonymous—the IRC network sets in motion a *striated machine of subjectivation* in which pseudonymous users contribute to Anonymous as an open reputation but also grow a personal reputation through their contributions.

In the second part of the chapter, I show how the improper name is further contended between those who use it to denote secrecy and mastery of a superior technical knowledge and those who attach it to social movements that are mostly based in public space. In this third individuation,

Anonymous swings between an abstract pole for which hacking and hacktivism should be mainly concerned with technical advancement and what I call a "deictic pole," to refer to a form of hacktivism that is strongly attached to local conditions and contextual information. My wager is that this understanding of context implies an apprehension of the vulnerability of the Other—an encounter that Anonymous experiences by witnessing the risks to which Tunisian and Egyptian Anons exposed themselves during the revolutions of January 2011. This notion of human vulnerability is contrasted to the hackers' search for technical vulnerabilities in computer networks—a search that is associated with the power to hack for its own sake. I conclude that Anonymous's ability to mediate between the technical and the human may also be seen as a potential for transducting different notions of otherness, technological and corporeal velocities, finite codes, and sensuous languages. Such power may ultimately project the improper name beyond a properly human language and ethics—in a domain where humans and machines will be able to search for and affirm their freedoms only in relation to one another.

THE MINOR, THE TACTICAL, AND THE IMPROPER

Because they are open to unforeseen appropriations, improper names imply an opening of closed spaces and a constant subversion of fixed relations. In this respect, the improper can be likened to two other philosophical concepts: the notion of the minor mode, as developed by Gilles Deleuze and Félix Guattari, and the notion of tactics, as developed by Michel De Certeau. In their book on Kafka, Deleuze and Guattari describe minor literature as a literature whose language is characterized by a high degree of deterritorialization, that is immediately political, and in which "everything takes on a collective value."[24] By extending this concept to the social field, Nicholas Thoburn argues that when minorities find their movements and expressions cramped on all sides, they have to invent a new, "minor" politics—a politics in which individual concerns are *immediately* merged with the social forces and resonate with them in an intensive, continuous exchange.[25] This is not only the nomadic and queer politics of migrants and sexual minorities but also, as Stevphen Shukaitis points out, the countercultural politics of punk (with its DIY ethics and constitutive rejection of talent) and of the pseudonymous strategies discussed in this book. As a mode of creating and elaborating difference, minor politics, writes Shukaitis, refuses "to subsume individual concerns and interests . . . within a collective homogenous general interest (for the sake of the movement and so forth)."[26] Rather, such politics is concerned with the power of singularities to transform themselves in the process of transforming the territories they traverse.

Such deterritorializations often rely on tricks and clever usages of resources that are not permanently available but can be tapped to gain temporary advantages. Michel De Certeau defines these clever temporary usages as "tactical" and distinguishes them from the "strategic" power that an institution such as a state, a corporation, a city, or a university exercises over a "place that can be circumscribed as *proper (propre).*"[27] If an institution can leverage this power "for generating relations with an exterior distinct from it," a tactic "cannot count on a 'proper' (a spatial or institutional localization). . . . The 'proper' is a victory of space over time. On the contrary, because it does not have a place, a tactic depends on time—it is always watching for opportunities that must be seized 'on the wing.'"[28]

De Certeau's distinction between the tactical and the strategic presents striking similarities to Deleuze and Guattari's distinction between the minor and the major (or molar) modes. Not unlike strategies, major and molar processes consist in the standardization and fixation of a set of relations. This fixed distribution—such as that of statistical analysis—is predicated on the capacity of extracting constants from a homogenous and denumerable space. Spatialization is, in other words, the precondition of every act of mastery, or as De Certeau puts it, "it is the mastery of time through the foundation of an autonomous place."[29] On the contrary, being predicated on the lack of a proper space, minor, tactical, and improper interventions have to make do with what is at hand by taking advantage of opportunities and resources that cannot be stockpiled without becoming strategic and major in their turn.

This is why these interventions should not be identified with specific communities or minorities whose identity is constituted on the basis of structured affiliations. Rather, they should be seen as the movement of those communities and minorities that have no identity, membership, or constituency of their own—a becoming over which no one has ownership. It is this openness to the becoming of the social that makes it difficult to assign an improper name to a circumscribed subject. And it is precisely this instability of the relationship between signifier and signified that denaturalizes the synthetic function of the name as a rigid designator that fixes the referent.

As Jean-François Lyotard has shown, the proper name is a "pure mark of the designative function" that invariably refers to a subject *x* independently of the position this occupies in a sentence (as *x* can be found in the position of addressor, addressee, or referent) at different time intervals (as *x* designates the same referent at *t* and at *t* + 1) and on different levels of reality (as *x* can stand both for a referent endowed with material reality and for a purely fictional one). "This is because to name the referent is not the same as to show its 'presence,'" writes Lyotard. "To signify is one thing, to name another, and to show still another."[30] But if the proper name is merely an index and an empty link that does not have the power to endow a subject with reality (i.e., to show its existence) nor with sense (i.e., to attribute any property to it), what happens when even the indexical function of the name is destabilized? I shall try to answer this question by first discussing some contrasting interpretations of the referential function of proper names and then considering how the modern state has overcoded such a function as a technique of government.

FIXING A REFERENCE: THE PROPER NAME AS A POLITICAL TECHNOLOGY

A specific strand in the philosophy of language has discussed for a long time whether proper names designate or describe a referent. The origins of this strand date back at least to the time of the disputes among the Sophists, Socrates, Plato, and Aristotle on language's ability to accurately represent reality, the divine, and hence to convey or obfuscate the truth.

The basic terms of the dispute are already laid out in Plato's *Cratylus,* whose formal topic is "the correctness of names." Cratylus—an early philosophical influence on Plato—and Hermogenes call in Socrates as a referee to determine whether names are natural extensions of the things they describe or are determined by social conventions. Socrates first seems to side with Cratylus's naturalism as he claims that, to accurately represent the essence of things, names must share something with them. Thus names cannot be purely arbitrary. But Socrates also criticizes extreme naturalism by noting that, similar to portraits, names only provide an "outline" of the things they describe. It is only because of this approximation that names can still be distinguished from things. If the copy cannot be told apart from the original, how could we ever discern the truth from falsehood?[31]

The question of names' mimetic accuracy resurfaces in the *Metaphysics,* as Aristotle discusses Antisthenes's paradoxical claim that if we admit that each state of affairs can be described in its singularity by one, and only one, proposition ("one formula, one referent"), then contradiction is no longer possible. Although Aristotle at first dismisses Antisthenes's claim as "foolish," he then concedes that designation precedes signification in that the primary elements of a proposition cannot be defined, but only postulated—in the same way as the bricks, stones, and timbers of a house cannot be derived from this composite entity of matter and form inasmuch as they provide its basic components.[32]

Drawing from Aristotle, Lyotard notes that both the distinction between designation and signification and the isomorphism between names and objects, propositions, and state of affairs returns, mutatis mutandis, in Wittgenstein's "theory of simples." In the *Tractatus Logico-Philosophicus,* the German philosopher seeks to construct a logically perfect language by positing a fundamental correspondence between the structure of a proposition (or picture) and a state of affairs. The *Tractatus*'s project is to design an ideal language that can accurately reflect the world by relying on logical structures that cannot be said but only *shown,* insofar as propositions must share the same logical structures "with reality in order to represent it."[33] Like Aristotle, Wittgenstein maintains that propositions are composed of simple signs (called names) that "cannot be dissected any further" in the same way as states of affairs are complexes that result from a combination of objects that are irreducible to smaller parts. As Bertrand Russell notes in the introduction to the *Tractatus,* this ideal language is based on the fundamental requisite "that there should be one name for every simple, and never the same name for two different simples."[34] If the same sign is employed to designate two different objects, it must be disambiguated by showing that it belongs to two different modes of signification or that it is part of two propositions whose senses are different.[35]

Here Wittgenstein follows Gottlob Frege's famous distinction between the sense *(Sinn)* and reference *(Bedeutung)* of a proper name. To refute John Stuart Mill's thesis that proper names denote without connoting, in 1892, Frege had argued that because multiple names can be used to designate the same object (e.g., the morning star Phosphorus and the evening star Hesperus both refer to the same planet, Venus), different names correspond to different modes of presenting the same referent and thereby convey a plurality of senses.[36] Along with Russell's theory of descriptions, Frege's distinction between sense and reference came to form the so-called descriptivist theory of names.[37] On the basis of the assumption that a proper name is nothing other than an abbreviated or disguised description, the Frege–Russell view—which is nothing but a modern version of Cratylus's naturalism—dominated the philosophy of language for most of the twentieth century, until Saul Kripke struck several blows to it.

In three lectures given at Princeton in 1970, Kripke returned to Mill's theory of direct reference to argue that while the properties and sense of an object may vary across time and space, and depending on social conventions, once the existence of an object has been established, it can no longer be refuted. It follows that the different names used for describing the changing properties of the same object refer to it only under certain circumstances—and may thereby be called *nonrigid designators*—whereas the names that designate an object throughout its existence constantly refer to it and are thereby rigid. Kripke argues that the function of a rigid designator (or proper name) is to fix a referent *in all its possible universes,* independent of whether its properties may change over time. He adds that the reference is fixed through an *initial baptism,* that is to say, by an obstension or a description, or, alternatively, is "determined by a chain, passing the name from link to link."[38] These acts are social in character; that is, the name is successfully assigned to a referent insofar as there is a community of speakers that recognizes this referential relationship.

Even though, being a logician, Kripke is not interested in exploring these acts, his theory of rigid designation allows us to leave behind the dualism between denotation and signification, which Wittgenstein had tried to solve by assuming that the former precedes the latter and positing, in line with a long-standing logocentric tradition in Western thought, a fundamental isomorphism between logical structures and worldly structures. Once we recognize that the reference of a proper name does not satisfy certain properties described by the name, but rather that the referential relationship is socially constructed, we can focus on the actual communities, institutions, and practices that enable or bar the societal adoption of a proper name.

Through this line of reasoning, we can return to our previous reflection on symbolic power and the institutionalization of naming. If within familial and tribal structures proper names are passed from link to link, through a communication chain, the emergence of molar institutions such as the church and the state entails an inscription of the name into a birth register. Whereas in the great civilizations of antiquity, such as the Persian, Roman, and Chinese empires, names were registered mostly for tax purposes and for the determination of available military manpower, with the emergence of the modern nation-state, the birth name becomes a political technology that enables the scientific management of a population.

Michel Foucault has argued that the development of the modern science of government—what he calls "governmentality"—would have not been possible without the political usage of statistical analysis. Beginning in the eighteenth century, statistics, writes Foucault, "discovers and gradually reveals that the population possesses its own regularities: its death rate, its incidence of disease, its regularities of accidents"[39]—and also, and perhaps preconditionally, its birthrate, for which the birth record is the elementary unit. By becoming legal, the proper name enters a whole network of apparatuses (demographic records, criminal records, fiscal records, voting records, immunization and health records) through which the state can both identify an individual and effect calculations and operations whose domain is the population. From the state's standpoint, fixing a reference—that is, ensuring that a legal name identifies one and only subject—is thus an essential precondition of modern politics. It is through the legal codification of the initial baptism that a government gets to know its people and can target either specific individuals through the security apparatus or segments of the population through the leverage of political economy. Paraphrasing Wittgenstein, we may say that this double operation—which is both selective and extensive, individuating and massifying—is predicated on the assumption that there should be one name and only one name for every subject and never the same name for two different subjects.

COLLECTIVE ASSEMBLAGES OF ENUNCIATION

As noted in the opening pages of this introduction, the main distinctive feature of improper names is to provide anonymity and a medium for recognition to their users. By failing to designate clearly identifiable referents, improper names make it difficult for authorities to track down specific individuals while enabling individuals to participate in social and political activities on an informal basis. The primary political function of improper names is thus to challenge the governmental techniques whereby an individual is classified as a subject of knowledge, a patient, a criminal, a taxpayer, and so forth. Because the state apparatuses produce the subject as a political, epistemological, and biological unit that is always fundamentally *in place,* those subjectivities that cannot be properly located pose a fundamental threat to state power.

As previously noted, the secondary political function of the improper name is to mediate between heterogeneous practices and organizational methods. Such mediation is possible precisely because the designating function of the proper name is indifferent to heterogeneity and change. Kripke's theory of rigid designation assumes in fact that the distinctive feature of the proper name is to designate a referent regardless of its changing properties. Slavoj Žižek has taken Kripke's antidescriptivism one step further by noting that "this guaranteeing the identity of an object in all counterfactual situations—through a change of all its descriptive features—is *the retroactive effect of naming itself.* It is the name itself, the signifier, which supports the identity of the object."[40]

Responding to Žižek, Ernesto Laclau recognizes that, in the sociopolitical field, some signifiers empty themselves out of their attachment to a particular referent and give unity to an object by representing a heterogeneous assemblage of actors and demands. Yet Laclau adds the important proviso that "the reverse movement also operates: [empty signifiers] can never fully control which demands they embody and represent."[41] From this angle, if a proper name establishes the unity of the designated object retroactively, a shared alias can designate such unity *only to refer to the ensemble of the name's uses.* As soon as we consider individual and contingent uses (e.g., *a* Luther Blissett, *some* Monty Cantsins), heterogeneity and difference resurface. My wager is that rather than expressing heterogeneity *or* homogeneity, difference *or* totality, the improper is a mode of mediation between these two poles. This mediation is evident not only in the passage from the one to the many (and vice versa) but also in the relation between signifying and a-signifying practices within the assemblage.

To illustrate this point, let us consider the case of the Luddite assemblage. Luddite subjectivation emerges from the breakdown of a traditional order (the Guild system) and the abrupt appearance of a network of illegal practices (machine breaking) and linguistic expressions (threatening letters, ballads and declarations) that do not stand in a referential relationship to one another. In the Luddite assemblage, machine breaking is the pragmatic side of a sophisticated rhetorical strategy in which threats acquire the force of action and actions endow threats with performative force, even though the destruction of machinery is distinct and relatively independent from Luddite discourse. This means that the subversion of the proper name as a political technology of the state is set in motion by a collective assemblage of enunciation that has the faculty of speech and the power to act on things *without letting its words represent its deeds.*

As a collective assemblage of enunciation, an improper name is thus an articulation of linguistic and nonlinguistic expressions—what Deleuze and Guattari call a semiotic system and a pragmatic system—between which "there is neither a relationship of correspondence nor a cause-effect relationship nor a signifier-signified relation" but only reciprocal presupposition and "piecemeal insertions."[42] This impersonal notion of the assemblage allows us to think of actions without a human subject that is formally in charge of them. For example, the Allen Smithee filmography is an assemblage of movies whose author is a nonhuman agent, a ready-made signature that performs a specific function within the film industry, namely, to solve labor disputes between film directors and film producers. And, as we shall see, the software used by Anonymous's hackers and activists to coordinate street protests, denial of service attacks, and hacking operations often follows a logic of its own, which precedes and conditions human agency and will.

To sum up, in this introductory chapter, I have examined the notion of the improper name as the expression of a process of subjectivation that is neither collective nor individual but rather condividual, that is, simultaneously collective and individual. Although improper names encompass both collective pseudonyms and multiple-use names, the distinctive feature of the improper name is to be opened to unforeseen appropriations and third-party usages—something that may not pertain to all collective pseudonyms. Even though the mode of disposition and usage of a collective pseudonym may be initially defined by an authorizing context, to be thought as improper, a name has to undergo a certain level of dissemination in the public sphere. The historic conditions under which an improper name is introduced and circulates are by definition subject to change. In modern and premodern times, as a collective assemblage of enunciation—that is, an ensemble of semiotic and pragmatic expressions that enjoy a relative autonomy from one another—the improper name challenges the modern state's invention of the legal name as a political technology of identification. As the name of the author acquires an economic value, the improper name challenges the conflation of property and propriety that is set in motion by the emergence of the modern culture industry. Finally, with the rise of the information society, the accelerated destabilization of the relationship between signs and referents sets in motion assemblages of enunciation that reverse Web 2.0's obsession with identity, reputation, and status.

In the conclusion, I return to the contention that improper names are singular processes of subjectivation that cannot paradoxically be attached to a subject to deepen the relationship between the improper, the common, and the community. After revisiting a recent philosophical debate on the negative, "inoperative," and "unavowable" character of the community, I suggest that improper names can be read, following Simondon, as the transductive actualization of a potential *and,* following the deconstructive tradition, as the expression of a community that assumes the impossibility of being completely transparent to itself. Even more, I suggest that improper names allow us to bring together immanence and deconstruction, monist and dualist philosophies, by advancing an impersonal politics that shuttles between the constitution of a subject from within and its ongoing effacement from without. Such shuttling ultimately points to the improper as a mode of mediation that is strictly connected to the common, increases or decreases its power depending on usage, and opens up the subject onto the many it is.

1

NED LUDD, THE MACHINE BREAKER

On March 11, 1811, a large demonstration of framework knitters gathered at the Nottingham marketplace. The knitters reclaimed higher wages and lamented the growing employment in the hosiery and lace trades of the region of new labor-saving machines known as wide frameworks. The demonstration was quickly dispersed by the military. On that same night, sixty wide stocking frames were destroyed in Arnold, a large village northeast of the city, "by rioters who took no precautions in disguising themselves and who were cheered on by the crowd."[1]

Historians identify the Arnold riots with the onset of Luddism, an insurrectionary movement that broke out in the midst of the Napoleonic Wars, threatening the very basis of social order in England. The movement peaked in 1811–12, a biennium of generalized social unrest marked by food riots, arms robberies, and other disorders in every corner of the country. Although machine breaking was by no means an invention of the Luddites and continued throughout the nineteenth century, the last episode associated with the Luddite movement dates to April 1817, when six Luddites were executed at Leicester Gaol for a raid against a Nottinghamshire lace factory.

The Luddites acquired their name only few weeks after the Arnold riots, as the destruction of knitting frameworks spread from Nottinghamshire to the neighboring counties of Leicestershire and Derbyshire in the Midlands. Apparently, the Luddites named themselves after a Ned Ludlam, an inexperienced apprentice stocking-frame knitter of Anstey, a village near Leicester. Having been criticized by his master for making his hose too loose and instructed to "square his needles"—namely, to adjust the mechanisms of his frame—Ludlam allegedly took the instruction literally and hammered the needles into a heap.[2]

If the story may be apocryphal, it is curious that the framework breakers of the Midlands borrowed their name from an individual whose gesture could hardly be considered heroic, according to their own proud and long-standing tradition of craft. Framework knitting was in fact sanctioned and regulated by the Worshipful Company of Framework Knitters, a livery company that had been incorporated by Oliver Cromwell in 1657 and reissued a royal charter by King Charles II in 1663. Whatever the reasons for choosing this name may have been, they proved to be quite effective, if it is true that in early 1812 an abridged version of the eponym ("Ned Lud" or "Ned Ludd") surfaced in the West Riding of Yorkshire and in the Northwestern cotton districts surrounding Manchester (Lancashire, Cheshire, northern Derbyshire, and Flintshire) in conjunction with machine breaking. As we shall see, in each of these regions—the Midlands, Yorkshire, and the Northwest—the Luddites adopted a variety of tactics stemming from specific productive histories and responded to local political conditions.

Despite these regional differences, two recurrent features characterize the Luddite movement as a whole. First, contrary to popular identification of Luddism with technophobia, the Luddites targeted only the manufactories and the machines that downsized the workforce and drove down wages by facilitating the employment of untrained workers. Thus the framework knitters or "stockingers" of the Midlands wrecked only the new wide frameworks that produced cheap "cut-up" stockings, gloves, sandals, and socks, while leaving intact the traditional knitting machines, which stitched the articles with proper loop selvages and a lacy seam.[3] In the West Ring of Yorkshire, the clothworkers or shearmen of the woolen industry (also known as "croppers") opposed the introduction of shearing frames and gig mills, which reduced the number of work hours necessary to raise and sheer a woolen cloth—a process called "finishing."[4] And the cotton weavers of the Manchester area sought to eliminate the steam-powered looms that were believed to drive down the wages in the cotton trade.

The second common feature is that the Luddites conducted their attacks within what E. J. Hobsbawm has described as a strategy of "collective bargaining by riot."[5] Lacking legal means to redress their grievances, the Luddites often sent threatening letters to manufacturers to remove the new machines from their workshops—and frequently destroyed them when they did not comply. In this respect, the Luddite strategy had a pragmatic side and a rhetorical side. While the two complemented each other, they were also relatively independent from one another. In fact, Luddism proper is defined by machine breaking as much as by a significant body of texts authored by the Luddites themselves—including ballads, chalkings, declarations, manifestos, and the ubiquitous threatening letters. Not only did these texts target the manufacturers who introduced the new machines and the authorities who protected them but they also addressed a wider set of economic and political issues, including high food prices and food shortages, low wages, rising unemployment, ineffective labor acts and regulations, and the legitimacy of monarchic power.

As Adrian Randall notes, the strategy of sending threatening letters signed by the same person was particularly effective "because Ludd's imprimatur suggested the presence of a coordinated force whose ultimate strength could not be easily discerned."[6] The letters were alternatively signed Ned or Edward Ludd (or Lud), often preceded by aggrandizing appellations such as "General," "King," and "Captain," which were meant to enhance their performative force. Ludd's name appears also in poems and ballads celebrating the gestures of this new folk hero created by popular imagination. As we shall see, some of these ballads explicitly compared Ludd's exploits to those of another mythic hero of Nottinghamshire, Robin Hood. And some of the threatening letters claimed to be sent from the legendary Sherwood Forest. On one hand, this mythological stratification buttresses the argument of those scholars who claim that Luddism is part and parcel of a premodern web of communal relationships. On the other hand, the wild circulation of the pseudonym across regions with different productive histories suggests that Luddism was a hybrid movement that included both modern and premodern elements.

This chapter explores this tension between the original association of Ludd with machine breaking and the progressive detachment of the eponym from its originating context. It does so by examining the composition of labor in different regional contexts against the backdrop of the Industrial Revolution. Furthermore, by analyzing both the pragmatic side and rhetorical side of Luddism, it asks whether Ned Ludd was capable, as an improper name, of articulating the resistance of traditional wool workers to the new industrial machines with the economic requests of the industrial workers of the cotton industry and other demands of political reform. Although the wide circulation of the eponym in 1811–12 suggests that Ludd could have become a signifier for a generalized struggle against modern industrial capitalism, the social composition of these workers was fundamentally different. As we shall see, the Luddites of the Midlands and Yorkshire directed their rage against the new means of production—what Marx would later describe as "capital's material mode of existence."[7] On the contrary, the cotton workers of the Manchester region largely saw the new machines as a source of wealth and soon oriented their struggle toward other objectives.

In this respect, and anticipating part of my conclusion, the name Ned Ludd designates two asymmetrical forms of struggle. On one hand, Ludd expresses the resistance of the last guild masters and apprentices against industrial capitalism. On the other hand, as it enters the Northwest, it comes to designate the emergence—albeit still in embryonic form—of a modern form of class struggle all internal to the capitalist mode of production. The goal of this chapter is to understand whether the improper name enabled the articulation of social and productive forces that coexisted in time while de facto belonging to different temporalities or whether its symbolic power was appropriated locally without leading to the constitution of durable alliances. Drawing from a rich historiographical debate, the chapter also discusses whether Luddism contributed to the development of a modern working-class consciousness in England.

THE REGIONAL DYNAMIC OF LUDDISM

As previously noted, the multifaceted character of Luddism is rooted in preexisting productive histories and customary traditions (or lack thereof), which can be analyzed on a regional basis. In particular, whereas in the Midlands and Yorkshire, the advent of industrial production revolutionized the wool trade, which had existed since the Middle Ages, the cotton industry of the Manchester region did not graft itself to a preexisting trade and organization of labor. Before reviewing how historians have tackled the differential relationship the Luddites entertained with modern technologies, I shall quickly recapitulate the development of Luddism on a regional basis.

In the Midlands, the movement kicked off in March 1811, paused in the summer, and peaked in the winter with the destruction of several hundred frameworks. By summer 1812, it was ebbing a second time for at least four reasons: first, most of the hosiers had agreed on raising wages; second, several thousand troops were stationing in the region; third, Parliament had begun discussing a bill to make framework breaking a capital offence; and fourth, the United Committee of Framework Knitters of Nottingham was trying to introduce a bill into Parliament to limit the use of wide frames in the industry.[8] After the constitutional attempts to improve the knitters' condition failed, the destruction of machinery in the Midlands resurfaced in 1814 and 1816—albeit at a much slower pace than in 1811–12. Most of the Midlands Luddite documents refer to the 1663 charter of the Company of Framework Knitters. As we shall see, the stockingers considered the charter as the legal and moral foundation of their actions, recurred less than other Luddites to an insurrectionist rhetoric and Jacobin threats, and composed songs and ballads that celebrated General Ludd's military prowess and sense of justice.

In the West Riding of Yorkshire, the first attacks on gig mills and shearing frames begun in January 1812 and continued amid food riots, arms raids, and robberies until January 1813. Because the number of workshops that still employed gig mills and shearing frames quickly declined after the first riots, Luddite strikes became more predictable. In April 1812, an attack against the Rawfolds Mills of William Cartwright met armed resistance for the first time, and two Luddites were killed. This setback radicalized the movement. William Horsfall, a factory owner who had made himself known as an active pursuer of Luddites, was assassinated at the end of the month, while repeated food riots and arms robberies attracted a massive military presence to the region. In January 1813, after a few men were convicted and executed for the Horsfall murder and other riots, troops were withdrawn from the region. Writings of the Yorkshire Luddites are generally more violent than those of the Midlands Luddites, are less supportive of petitions and parliamentary initiatives, and frequently target local magistrates.

In Lancashire, and in particular in the booming cotton towns of Stockport, Oldham, Bolton, Middleton, Rochdale, and Wigan, around Manchester, Luddism took on peculiar and mixed features, crossing boundaries between machine breaking, widespread food riots, arms robberies, and support for political reform. The cotton weavers and spinners were the most active Luddites of the region. The attacks on power-looms began in Stockport in March 1812 with the assault on the factory of William Radcliffe (the inventor of the dressing machine) and continued in other towns of Lancashire and Cheshire until the summer. Like in Yorkshire, the bloodiest event of Lancashire Luddism occurred in April 1812, when at least ten people were killed in the riots following an attack on a power-loom mill in Middleton. Although the Luddite riots in the Manchester region are of an exceptional intensity, *machine breaking proper did not last more than four weeks.* All major disorders in the Manchester region came to an end in summer 1812.

According to E. P. Thompson, Northwestern Luddism was divided between a constitutionalist wing and a revolutionary wing and changed tactics at a faster pace than in other regions. Thompson contends that, on one hand, the presence of a strong Irish immigration colored the pre-existing Jacobin propaganda with revolutionary overtones. On the other hand, oath taking and republican agitation mixed with initiatives tied to political reform, such as the April 8 riots at the Manchester Exchange, which broke out after the Prince Regent chose to appoint a conservative cabinet.[9]

The language of Northwestern Luddism reflects this ambiguity. As Kevin Binfield points out, Lancashire Luddite writings support petitions, address economic issues of various nature, and frequently employ Jacobinic language. While in the Midlands and Yorkshire, Luddism was rooted in local traditions and mostly targeted local manufacturers and authorities, Northwestern Luddism "tended to look at the top, to those locations where power in a larger sense was more likely to reside. Threats to the Prince Regent, for instance, are more common from Manchester-area writers than Nottinghamshire writers."[10]

The difficulty encountered by historians in grasping the essence of Northwestern Luddism reflects a larger historical problem. Luddism has been so identified in popular imagination with a violent reaction against machinery as to become a common name for machine breaking.[11] At the same time, historians have shown how this practice was by no means an invention of the Luddites. For example, the Spitalfields silk weavers of the East End of London had already targeted and destroyed the looms that were being introduced into their manufactories in the 1760s. And as the Industrial Revolution accelerated the mechanization of multiple branches of the textile industry, attacks against looms and spinning jennies continued throughout the country. To be sure, the 1810s were the first decade in which machine breaking became widespread and systematic. But is it fair to identify Luddism *exclusively* with machine breaking? Did the Luddites play a role in other social movements of their time? And did they have a political agenda, or were their grievances and objectives strictly confined to industrial matters? To answer these questions, I first review the rich historiography on this fascinating subject.

THE HISTORIOGRAPHIC DEBATE

The study of Luddism has produced a significant body of literature. If historians generally agree on the facts associated with the appearance and rapid eclipse of the movement, contrasting interpretations have emerged, especially since the 1960s, over the historical significance of Luddism for the labor movement. These interpretations can be roughly grouped into three distinct strands.

First, a current of liberal and progressive historians, which includes John Lawrence and Barbara Hammond and Malcolm Thomis, among others, treat Luddism as an apolitical movement that relied on unsophisticated and ultimately ineffective tactics to further a lost cause. Second, unorthodox Marxist historians such as Eric J. Hobsbawm and Edward P. Thompson read Luddism as an original movement, capable of inventing new forms of collective bargaining and of contributing to the formation of a working-class culture and consciousness. Third, historians and sociologists such as Norman Simms and Craig Calhoun see Luddism as an exclusively regional phenomenon—an offspring of the tensions manifested in local contexts within particular social structures and traditions. Before addressing how these strands relate to one another, we shall first review those historical accounts that reflect on the phenomenon without a polemical intent.

Nineteenth-century histories of Luddism are either firsthand accounts or oral histories that limit themselves to a general reconstruction of the events or focus on specific regions.[12] The first history of Luddism based on documentary evidence is J. L. Hammond and Barbara Hammond's *The Skilled Labourer*. By making extensive use of the Home Office Papers—the largest single archive for the study of Luddism—this couple of progressive historians treats Luddism in a systematic manner, rooting it in different regional and productive histories. Arguably, the most important insight of this work is to link the rise of Luddism to the demise of customs and legal protections that had formerly guaranteed the livelihood of textile workers for at least a couple centuries.

For example, in looking at the causes of Luddism in the West Riding of Yorkshire, the Hammonds show how the Yorkshire croppers had long been established and enjoyed a high status within the woolen trade, primarily because their work was essential to adding value to woolen clothes. This high status had been legally codified through a series of statutory protections. A statute dating back to Edward VI's times had prohibited for more than two centuries the use of gig mills. A second one, included in the Elizabeth code (5 Eliz., c. 4), enforced a seven-year apprenticeship in the woolen trade. A third statute limited the number of looms a clothier could possess to one.[13] The Hammonds show how the advancing mechanization of the textile industry in Yorkshire and Gloucestershire rendered these legal measures increasingly ineffective, thus threatening the status of cloth dressers. By 1802, the regulation of apprenticeship had fallen into disuse, and as the Industrial Revolution kept advancing, the norms against concentration were simply ignored by manufacturers, while local magistrates no longer enforced them. Thus, in the first decade of the nineteenth century, the croppers built a coalition with other shearmen from the Southwest of England to petition Parliament and pass a bill that would have reintroduced serious checks on the labor-saving machines. These attempts failed, and in 1809, Parliament officially repealed some of the statutory protections. This progressive but seemingly inexorable disenfranchisement pushed the croppers toward a radicalization of their struggle and into adopting some of the Luddite tactics that had been initially successful in the Midlands.

If *The Skilled Labourer* does an excellent job in delineating the social context from which Luddism arose, the Hammonds' interpretational bias emerges in their tendency to downplay the revolutionary and conspiratorial character of the movement. As E. P. Thompson points out, by depicting the claims made by the authorities as exaggerated and maintaining that the riots were frequently instigated by agents provocateurs, the Hammonds implied that Luddism "was without ulterior aims, and was either a matter of spontaneous riot (Lancashire) or an action with strictly limited industrial objectives."[14]

It is only in the late 1950s, and in particular with E. J. Hobsbawm's *Primitive Rebels,* that a different perspective begins to emerge.[15] By distancing himself from a rationalist (Marxist) historiography that tended to read rural and urban revolts against modern capitalism as backward looking phenomena, the British historian initiated a work of rehabilitation of popular movements and plebeian politics, banditry and spontaneous riots, that led him to publish three other volumes: *Labouring Men* (1964), *Bandits* (1969), and, along with his friend George Rudé, *Captain Swing* (1969). In the first chapter of *Labouring Men,* Hobsbawm attempts to bridge the gap between labor history à la Hammond and Hammond and the study of Luddism as an issue of public order by coining the often cited expression "collective bargaining by riot."[16] Hobsbawm argues that far from being an antimodern reaction against technological progress, selective machine breaking was a bargaining strategy whereby highly skilled workers tried to retain control over the labor market in the early phases of the Industrial Revolution.

In the same years, E. P. Thompson's *The Making of the English Working Class* sealed this new tendency in Marxist historiography to read into Luddism something more than a residual movement of resistance to modernization. According to Thompson, Luddism was an expression of an emerging "working-class consciousness" whereby the working classes began to see their struggles as related to one another. This process of unification, argues the British historian, was not linear and resulted from the combination of several, sometimes contradictory, ideologies, such as the popular Radicalism stemming from the Jacobin agitations of the 1790s, Irish nationalism, the writings of Thomas Paine and Thomas Spence, Methodism, and the ambiguous radicalism of William Cobbett.[17] In other words, Luddism acquired a political character when groups of English Jacobins, Painites, and Spenceans, who had been operating underground since the early 1790s, were brought into association with the illegal unions operating in Lancashire and Yorkshire.

The encounter between the Jacobins and this secret industrial tradition was prompted by the convergence of two elements. First, under the government of William Pitt the Younger, the British Parliament had passed a repressive antirepublican legislation, which included the suspension of the habeas corpus for eight years (1794–1801) and the Combination Acts

(1799–1800), which banned all forms of collective bargaining and labor association. According to Thompson, these laws had the unintended effect of bolstering a secret tradition of union organizing that had been active in England since the late eighteenth century. Second, as we have seen, Parliament had dismantled the paternalist legislation that regulated the system of apprenticeship and the use of machinery in the textile sector. Like the Hammonds, Thompson notes that stockingers, croppers, and weavers repeatedly petitioned Parliament to prevent the repeal of such regulations. But the popularity of Adam Smith's economic theory of laissez-faire among Tories and Whigs alike condemned these attempts to failure.[18]

To sum up, Thompson argues that the combination of three elements—that is, the illegalization of unions, the dismantling of the paternalist legislation, and the extension of labor-saving machinery to a growing number of manufactures—created an explosive mixture. To initiate it were a series of bad harvests, which raised the price of provisions to famine level between 1809 and 1812. Finally, Napoleon's continental blockade on British trade, in effect between 1806 and 1814, also had negative effects on textile exports and on British imports of food.[19] In this context, it is no surprise if Luddism overlapped with food riots, arms robberies, and a period of generalized social unrest.

Thompson and other historians agree that the distinctive cultural trait of Luddism was the moral outcry for the twilight of customs and legal protections, which had guaranteed a livelihood even to the lower ranks of textile workers for centuries. Yet although, until the publication of *The Making of the English Working Class,* historians saw Luddism as a traditionalist and antimodern movement, Thompson was the first to argue that the Luddites' defense of a traditional moral economy had a progressive and positive function:

> On the one hand [Luddism] looked back to old customs and paternalist legislation which could never be revived; on the other hand, it tried to revive ancient rights in order to establish new precedents (including) the control of the "sweating" of women or juveniles; arbitration; the engagement by the masters to find work for skilled men made redundant by machinery; the prohibition of shoddy work;

> the right to open trade union combination. All these demands looked forward, as much as backwards; and they contained in themselves a shadowy image, not so much of a paternalist, but of a democratic community, in which industrial growth should be regulated according to ethical priorities and the pursuit of profit be subordinated to human need. . . . The Luddites were some of the last Guildsmen, and at the same time some of the first to launch the agitations that led to the 10 Hour Movement. In both directions lay an alternative political economy and morality to that of the *laissez-faire.*[20]

Thus Thompson reads Luddism as a Janus-faced movement that lays the ground, on one hand, for the foundation of the modern trade unions (with their constitutive struggle for the shortening of the workday) and Chartism. On the other hand, he contends that

> while finding its origin in particular industrial grievances, Luddism was *a quasi-insurrectionary movement,* which continually trembled on the edge of ulterior revolutionary objectives. This is not to say that it was a wholly conscious revolutionary movement; on the other hand, it had a tendency towards becoming such a movement, and it is this tendency which is most often understated.[21]

Thompson's bold reading had the effect of illuminating the debate over the actual nature of the movement. The first response came from progressive Australian historian Malcolm Thomis. In *The Luddites,* Thomis argues that collective bargaining by riot and resistance to technological change contributed little to the formation of a working-class culture and to the powerful trade unions that were to secure new labor rights in the following decades. By contesting the reliability of Thompson's sources (mostly oral history accounts), Thomis contends that the connections between the Luddites and the political agitators both of their times and of the following decades are undemonstrated. If they ever occurred, they were more an expression of personal support by individual Luddites to specific campaigns than the result of an organic relationship.[22]

Second, Thomis maintains that Luddism was a highly diversified movement that should be studied on a regional basis and from a strictly industrial perspective. Besides resisting the introduction of labor-saving machinery and the decline of wages, it pursued neither reformist nor revolutionary political objectives, nor it was able to achieve any substantial, tangible improvement of the workers' condition. Thomis concedes that the Luddites were well organized and enjoyed a vast support among the populace. But their moral appeals to customs would show that they were "a voice of the residual crafts and not that of groups more central and vital to the carrying-forward of the Industrial Revolution."[23] Moreover, the notions of working-class culture and consciousness are for the Australian historian vague and difficult to assess from an historic standpoint.

Thomis has been in turn criticized for his "compartimentalist approach," that is, for drawing a sharp line between industrial action and political agitation, and between the legalistic side of the movement and its violent fringes. In a regional study on "Luddism and Politics in the Northern Counties," J. L. Dinwiddy argues that there is enough evidence to demonstrate that among the northern working classes were men with revolutionary aims, that those men were "loosely" in contact with the underground republican network Thompson described, and that "the crisis of 1812 was of some importance in the process whereby discontent in the northern counties acquired a major political dimension."[24] In another study on the socioeconomic structure and mentality of the West Riding of Yorkshire, Adrian Randall shows how the Jacobin ideology "against kingcraft, lordcraft and priestcraft," and the republican "Painite ideal of petty-producer independence," found a conducive home in a region in which the small master clothiers were proud of their capacity for self-government and identified taxes and tithes as the causes of their poverty.[25] By noting how, in Yorkshire, the combinations were powerful and well equipped to undertake strike action, Randall rebuffs Thomis's claim that "where trade unionism was strong enough it could effectively achieve its aims without resort to violence"[26] and contends that violence was part and parcel of late-eighteenth-century trade unionism:

> We must firmly resist a simplistic imposition of nineteenth- or twentieth-century models of "appropriate" trade union behaviour upon the actions and activities of eighteenth-century combinations regardless of their very different context and culture. Machine wrecking, arson, violence, or threats of such, represented some of the

> most easily and most frequently implemented industrial sanctions available to an eighteenth-century trade union. Violence was in no way alternative to Thomis' "labour approach" but a major weapon of the trade unions, reflecting the organization, culture and community from which they developed.[27]

If the compartimentalist approach may not stand up to scrutiny—at least in Yorkshire and the Northwest—*The Making of the English Working Class* has been criticized not only by labor historians such as Thomis but also by sociologists such as Craig Calhoun. In *The Question of Class Struggle,* Calhoun argues that the roots of Luddism lay in a local web of communal relations and traditions and that radical movements of the time acted on this basis, and not on the modern, rationalistic notion of class. "The people they mobilized," writes Calhoun, "were knit together through personal bonds within these communities much more than they were unified as a class. As such movements attempted to go beyond local communities in their mobilization or objects, they foundered."[28] Calhoun's contention is that one has to wait until the 1830s to see a "discontinuous shift from communally based mobilizations toward more rationalistic mobilizations founded on formal organizations."[29]

Even if Calhoun's book lends itself to criticism for being a polemicist attack on *The Making of the English Working Class* largely based on social theory rather than on a thorough evaluation of historical sources, it had the merit of stimulating a trend toward the study of Luddism as a community phenomenon. For example, historian and sociolinguist Norman Simms situates the Luddite uprisings within archaic forms of English communal justice dating back to the times of Robin Hood and Jack Straw.[30] Simms argues that Ludd was the mythic figure through which the villagers asserted and renewed their "juridic right to violence" against external forces, embodied in the past by feudal landlords, ecclesiastic functionaries, and magistrates and now by the new labor-saving machines that threatened the independence of the leading craftsmen and the integrity of the craft communities. Simms contends that by facilitating the employment of unskilled workers—including women and children—the new machines undermined the traditional gender division of labor and the patriarchal family. Thus the possible bastardization of gender roles called for an act of purification, which was performed in a ceremonial, ritualistic form. By relying on Frank Peel's description of a major Luddite attack on the Rawfolds Mills in Yorkshire, Simms notes that the rebels disguised themselves by blackening their faces, wearing masks, and in some cases dressing up as women. This carnivalesque inversion has for Simms a double function. On one hand, it demonstrates that the men "are made women by the introduction of the new frames (their skilled jobs can be performed by untrained women, they are now out of work and depend on the womenfolk to earn their bread)."[31] On the other hand, it allows men to identify precisely "with the women most affected by the breakdown of the village economy (the women, also, who were so much in evidence in the bread riots associated with the Luddite outbreak)."[32]

There is indeed scattered evidence that gender play was not foreign to Luddism. In the same days of the attacks on the Rawfold Mills, two men claiming to be "General Ludd's wives," and dressed in women's clothes, led a crowd in Stockport, Lancashire, to assault a large powered-loom manufactory. In August and September 1812, the food riots that broke out in Leeds and Nottingham, respectively, were apparently led by a woman who was carried on a chair and given the name "Lady Ludd." Finally, as we shall see, one threatening letter sent from Manchester to a manufacturer was signed by the female eponym "Eliza Ludd." Nonetheless, this circumstantial evidence may not be sufficient to prove that cross-dressing was a systematic Luddite practice nor that it had the symbolic function described by Simms. Although Simms's folkloric reading is undoubtedly suggestive, it may be more pertinent to rural revolts, such as the Swing riots of 1830, which frequently broke out, as Hobsbawn and Rudé have shown, during the preparation of communal ceremonial functions held in occasion of annual and seasonal festivities.[33]

Luddism, on the contrary, had an unmistakably urban character. To be sure, in the small centers of the Midlands and Yorkshire, knitting, cropping, and shearing were handed down according to long-established and relatively sheltered traditions. Yet the massive migrations set in motion by the Industrial Revolution disrupted the insularity and *longue durée* of folk culture. Beginning in the 1760s, urban centers such as Nottingham and Manchester, and their satellite towns, knew a demographic boom that undermined the survival and renewal of archaic forms of communal justice. Furthermore, stockingers, weavers, and croppers petitioned Parliament to redress their grievances, showing an awareness of the national implications of their actions. This does not mean that local traditions could not be reinvented, as shown by several Nottinghamshire writings that praised Ned Ludd as the honorable heir of Robin Hood. Yet if the roots of Ludd's mythic persona undoubtedly lie in folk culture, the eponym did not *function* along the lines of a rural folk hero. In particular, what seems doubtful is the existence of a ritualistic basis for the set of narratives that constructed Ludd's myth.

I shall return to this point. For now, I limit myself to observing that subsequent studies by John Bohstedt, Adrian Randall, Alan Brooke, and Lesley Kipling have continued to analyze Luddism as a community phenomenon by focusing on specific regions.[34] These works cannot be easily compared, either because they focus on different time frames, they rely on different types of sources, or they are inserted within research projects that exceed the study of Luddism. It was only in the mid- to late 1990s that Kirkpatrick Sale and Brian Bailey published two new comprehensive studies.[35] Whereas the latter is more a chronology than a history, the former has the limit of reducing Luddism to a rebellion against machinery, thereby contributing to the narrow perception of the Luddites as technophobes.

To sum up, as with any historiographical dispute, the debate on the significance of Luddism is a litmus tests that tells us as much about the subject of study as it does about the political positions of the observers. As we have seen, liberal historians such as Hammond and Hammond, Thomis, and others read Luddism as a residual kind of struggle and an aberration of modern industrial relations—residual as it did not affect "the nature of working-class participation in industrial or political affairs in the future,"[36] aberrant as it was an exasperated reaction to a repressive regime that operated under exceptional historic circumstances (the Napoleonic war, rapid industrialization, bad harvests, and so forth).

On the latter point, liberal historians find themselves in agreement with E. P. Thompson, who reads the 1811–12 unrest as a symptom of the increasingly antagonistic character of class relationships in England. Thompson, however, assigns to Luddism a positive function for the development of the working-class movement by noting how the convergence of political and economic demands resurfaces in the formation of the

Chartist movement in the 1830s and 1840s and of the general trade unions in the following decades. Thus, whereas Thompson considers Luddism as a significant moment in the *constitution from within* of a working-class consciousness, the liberals downplay or deny this aspect while agreeing with him on the *constitution from without* of the movement, that is, on its essentially reactive nature. Finally, the sociological strand tends to agree with the liberals either by denying any significant continuity between Luddism and the modern working class (Calhoun) or by highlighting the folkloric origins of the movement (Simms).

Although it is true that the very notion of class consciousness is difficult to assess from a historical standpoint, it is also true that historians can now rely on a significant body of primary and secondary sources that allow them to make increasingly systematic assessments of Luddite language and rhetoric. Hence we shall now pause on an emerging strand of historiography that, by analyzing Luddism as a form of discourse, will allow us to advance in our inquiry on the alias's ability, or lack thereof, to link different demands and forms of struggle.

LUDDISM AS A RHETORICAL STRATEGY

Until recently, historians based their interpretations of Luddism on primary sources, such as the anonymous threatening letters archived in the Home Office Papers and the Radcliffe Papers, the reports of local newspapers such as the *Nottingham Review* and the *Leeds Mercury,* and oral history accounts collected by nineteenth-century historians. By doing so, they necessarily emphasized certain sources over others, leaving the reader with the difficult task of assessing their interpretational biases.

From this point of view, the recent publication of *Writings of the Luddites,* a collection of texts edited by Kevin Binfield, is an important contribution to the study of Luddism in that it allows the lay reader to access a comprehensive body of Luddite literature without having to pay lengthy visits to the archives. To be sure, verbatim reproduction of documents that are sometimes unclear or illegible still implies interpretation. Yet Binfield has done a meticulous job in transcribing the originals as faithfully as possible, including struck words and intercalations, footnoting unclear terms, reproducing different versions of the same document, and introducing each writing with headnotes that provide precious contextual information on lettering, postmarks, and related historical facts.

Even though the writings are organized on a regional basis, and encompass a wide range of rhetorical styles, Binfield maintains that Luddite discourse presents "a small number of centralizing features," such as anonymity, threatening language, and its recurrent association with resistance to oppressive industrial practices.[37] Whereas, as Thompson has shown, before the advent of Luddism, threatening letters containing social grievances were by and large anonymous, the introduction of Ned Ludd had the effect of linking and amplifying the force of each threat.[38] Thus, as Binfield points out, "despite the variety, Luddite discourse can be understood as a more or less continuous practice deriving from *one* forceful exercise of naming—the creation of the eponym 'Ned Ludd.'"[39]

But from where is this exercise of naming deriving its force? Should the performative force of Luddite threats be seen as a mere linguistic extension of the organized practice of machine breaking? Or can Luddite discourse be considered a practice in its own right—something that is at least partially independent from machine breaking? And if that is the case, what are the authorizing contexts from which such a practice draws its legitimacy?

To answer these questions, we have to consider that resistance to labor-saving machinery preexisted and continued to exist independently of Luddism even in the 1810s. Not all attacks on machinery made claims on Ludd's name. Conversely, Ludd's signature was appended to documents denouncing unfair hiring practices, declining wages, high food prices, and the corruption of monarchic power. But if Luddite discourse is not entirely coextensive with machine breaking, this is because the eponym acquired a life of its own as it migrated from Nottinghamshire to Yorkshire and the Northwest. In each of these regions, Binfield notes, the eponym fulfills different functions:

> In Nottinghamshire, Ned Ludd was a force generated wholly from within the framework knitting trade that perceived itself as constituted and sanctioned, although threatened. In Manchester, Ludd was a fairly unified set of resistances that could provide a focus for constituting new laboring populations in the cotton trades into a cohesive body capable of expressing its will to industrialists and a magistracy

> that sought to keep it unconstituted and weak. In Yorkshire's West Riding, General Ludd was a combination of law and local power that could be mapped onto a trade that had recently lost its statutory protections but that had not yet become impotent.[40]

Through a close reading of the Luddite texts, we shall now situate Luddite discourse in each of the three regions, focusing on the relationship between each authorizing context and the rhetorical function of the eponym.

THE GRAND EXECUTIONER OF THE MIDLANDS

The most striking aspect of Luddite writings from the Midlands is that they share so many rhetorical features with the official documents produced by the Worshipful Company of Framework Knitters that the very distinction between lawful and illegal writings appears here problematic. Both Luddite letters and lawful addresses to hosiers and manufacturers often refer to "the Trade" as the ultimate legitimating authority of the knitters' actions—thereby signaling the existence of a trade consciousness that transcended local and communal issues to encompass all knitters across the nation.

As we have seen, the charter that had instituted the Worshipful Company of Framework Knitters had been dispensed by King Charles II to prevent the migration of textile production overseas. As in the mid-eighteenth century, the center of stocking manufacture began moving from London to Nottingham and the Midlands, the document remained a fundamental reference for the profession. "Migration from one community to another was one method by which the knitters participated in the new industrial economy, but the charter moved with them from one community to others and was invoked periodically as the binding force of the trade," writes Binfield.[41] This binding force stemmed from the constituent character of the charter, which provided a legal foundation and allowed the trade to add texts such as wage agreements and the Company Rule Books. Such a body of documents was constantly updated according to custom and trade usage to regulate the knitting techniques, the procedures for wage negotiations, and the determination of frame rents, as well as the mechanisms "for prosecuting those selling substandard goods or undercutting prices."[42]

But as the advancing mechanization and laissez-faire threatened this customary legality, the knitters blended violent tactics and legal initiatives to defend it. As previously noted, this ambiguity can be evinced from the Luddite texts, which often borrow figures of speech from the official Company documents and sometimes even appropriate the rhetorical style of government documents. To make an example, "By the Framework Knitters, a Declaration," a text dated January 1, 1812, and signed "Ned Lud's Office, Sherwood Forest," appealed to the authority of King Charles II to justify frame wrecking:

> Whereas by the Charter granted by our late Sovereign Lord Charles the Seacond by the Grace of God of Great Britain France and Ireland the Frame Worck Knitters are Impowre'd to breake and Distroy all Frames and Engines that fabricate Articles in a fraudilent and Deceitfull manner and to destroy all Frameworck Knitters Goods Whatsoever that are so made—And Whereas a number of Deceitfull Unprincipled and Intriguing Persons did Attain An Act to be passed in the twenty Eighth Year of our preasent Sovereign Lord George the third Whereby it was enacted that Persons, Entring by Force into any house Shop or Place to Breake or Distroy frames should be Adjudged Guilty of Feloney, and as we are fully Convinced that such Act was Obtain'd in the most Fraudilent Manner Interesting and Electioneering manner and that the Honorable Parliment of Great Britain was deceived the Motives and Intentions of the Persons Obtained such Act we therefore the frame worck knitters do hereby declare the aforesaid Act to be Null and Void to all Intents and Purposes, Whatsoever, as by the passing of this Act Vilinous and Impassing persons are Enable to make Fraudilent and Deceitfull Manifactory's to the discredit and utter ruin of Our-Trade.[43]

The use of adverbs such as "whereas" and "hereby" signals that the declaration is meant to function as a paralegal text having the force of action.[44] As Binfield points out, the declaration aims at demonstrating that the constituent power emanating from the charter is so great that it can even nullify an act of Parliament—namely, the law that had made frame breaking a capital felony. Since this self-regulatory power was under threat, the framework knitters claim the legality of frame breaking and offer in the end a compensation of one thousand pounds to anyone who will provide information about the "Gangs of Bandittys" who have committed various robberies in the region under the pretense of acting as frame breakers.[45]

Thus Ludd appears here as a modern Robin Hood who defends the community from both the social injustices coming from without (the "fraudulent and deceitful" legislation) and the threats to peaceful coexistence coming from within (the robberies). Yet, unlike Robin Hood, Ludd does not only protect the community—that is, he is not only a paternalist figure. Rather Ludd is invested here with *executive power by a community that sees the Charter as its constitutional foundation, the Company as its deliberative branch, and the Company Rule Books and other regulations as its body of laws.*[46] This modern political structure, which marks a departure from the paternalist tradition, is clearly articulated in "General Ludd's Triumph," a text cited by several historians and sometimes referred to as the "Luddite anthem." Divided into six stanzas, the ballad is a eulogy of sorts, which begins with a comparison between Ludd and Robin Hood:

> Chant no more your old rhymes about bold Robin Hood,
> His feats I but little admire
> I will sing the Atchievements of General Ludd
> Now the Hero of Nottinghamshire
> Brave Ludd was to measures of violence unused
> Till his sufferings became so severe
> That at last to defend his own Interest he rous'd
> And for the great work did prepare.

After eulogizing the general's military prowess, the ballad praises Ludd's sense of justice and grounds his authority in a vote of the Trade:

> The guilty may fear, but no vengeance he aims
> At [the] honest man's life or Estate
> His wrath is entirely confined to wide frames
> And to those that old prices abate
> These Engines of mischief were sentenced to die
> By unanimous vote of the Trade
> And Ludd who can all opposition defy
> Was the grand Executioner made.[47]

Ludd's role as "grand Executioner" surfaces in another renowned Midlands document, "Declaration; Extraordinary," dated November 1811 and addressed "To our well-beloved Brother, and Captain in Chief, Edward Ludd." Having determined the guilt of master Charles Lacy, responsible for accumulating wealth through the production of "fraudulent Cotton Point Nett," the assembled "General Agitators" determine a penalty and put Ludd in charge of executing it:

> In default whereof, we do command that you inflict the Punishment of Death on the said Charles Lacy, and we do authorize you to distribute among [the party] you may employ for that purpose the Sum of Fifty Pounds, we enjoin you to cause this our Order to be presented to the said Charles Lacy without Delay.
>
> November 1811—By Order Thos Death.[48]

By adopting legalistic expressions such as "whereas, it hath been represented to us," "it appeareth to us," and "in default whereof," the text mimics the language and even the lettering of legal writs and governmental proclamations.[49] Above all, the declaration reveals the determination of the community to enforce the customary legislation through which the knitters had traditionally levied fines or forfeitures against those trade members, usually masters, who violated the trade's rules. Because the manufacturers were now ignoring trade customs and usages—with the tacit consent of national and local authorities—the knitters assess matters of jurisdiction, judgment, forfeiture, and punishment to invest Ludd with the mandate of enforcing their decisions as well as bringing renewed attention to a charter that was falling into obscurity. My wager is that such an investiture was nothing less than a *transfer of symbolic power* from the community to a leader effected by means of a set of performative utterances.

As we have seen, Pierre Bordieu argues that symbolic power ultimately rests with a ministry who is authorized by the community to act on the social words through words and magic gestures. In our case, the Worshipful Company of Framework Knitters transfers its institutional power to a representative (Ludd) who in turn mediates between the group and the social world at large.[50] If the *constituent movement* from the institution to the ministry is well evident in the texts analyzed here, the second movement of *mediation* between the workers and the social world transpires from the Luddite texts of the other regions.

THE GENERAL OF THE ARMY OF REDRESSERS

The situation in Yorkshire presented similarities and differences with the Midlands. The West Riding cloth dressers or croppers enjoyed a great deal of power within the wool trades, which had been sanctioned by three statutory protections regulating apprenticeship and limiting the use of gig mills and other finishing machines. Unlike their Midlands counterparts, however, croppers and shearmen could not rely on a constituent document such as the charter. Thus, in the two decades leading up to Luddism, they had explored both legal and illegal avenues to contrast the progressive erosion of their statutes, which were eventually repealed by Parliament in 1809.

In 1796, the clothworkers had founded the Brief Institution, an organization that built on their local societies with the purpose of preventing the hiring of "illegal" workers. As Adriall Randall notes, the Brief Institution

> provided the means, far better than before, of scrutinising recruitment to the trade by issuing membership cards, of enforcing closed shops, and of regulating the tramp system. It enabled information on disputes to be diffused more completely than before and, most important, it ensured that any employer standing out against his workmen's demands faced the weight and financial resources not only of the local cloth dressers but of all the region.[51]

In other words, the Brief Institution provided a basic organizational structure that allowed croppers to share information and enforce their statutes when manufacturers tried to raise above them. Between 1799 and 1804, cloth dressers destroyed two gig mills in Holbeck and Huddersfield and forced a manufacturer to take down a third one in Leeds. Until 1809, this combination of legal and violent tactics proved quite successful in limiting the introduction of new labor-saving machines. Moreover, although the Brief Institution was unsanctioned by the Crown, it brought the West Riding cloth dressers into closer cooperation with their peers in the West of England, teaching them that "neither their problems nor their solutions were entirely local."[52] But when the national petitions to introduce serious checks on gig mills and shearing frames failed, and Parliament repealed their statutes, the croppers lost faith in the possibility of improving their condition by legal means and reverted to the violent methods that had yielded some results at the turn of the century.

The recognition of the complicity between the industrial capitalists who sought to control the labor market and the government is apparent in the Luddite writings of Yorkshire. Such documents are generally more political than the Midlands' counterparts at least in three respects. First, they tend to target not only manufacturers but also local authorities and magistrates, who were held responsible for carrying out the government repression against the machine breakers. Second, they have an expansive character in that they try to establish links with other workers both inside and outside the wool trade and to wield these relationships into a national struggle against the government (usually identified with the "corrupt" figure of the Prince Regent). Third, they frequently employ Jacobin discourse and Paineite motifs, occasionally advocating a kingdomwide revolution.

In regard to the latter point, Adrian Randall notes that the West Riding's decentralized productive structure—also known as the Domestic System—was particularly conducive to the Painite ideals of a democratic community of small, independent producers. "The ethos of the Domestic System," writes Randall, "reflected a society of small capitalists, conscious of personal rights and liberties and jealous of any encroachment by the large merchant capitalists whose role, they believed, should be confined solely to selling and not manufacturing cloth."[53]

The Yorkshire document that best exemplifies this expansive movement from the local to the national, the interdependence of economic and political issues, and the rejection of undemocratic political systems is a letter addressed "To Mr Smith Searing Frame Holder at Hill End Yorkshire" on March 9 or 10, 1812. Signed by the "General of the Army of Redressers Ned Ludd Clerk," it begins with the usual warning: "Information has just been given in that you are a holder of those detestable Shearing Frames, and I was desired by my Men to write to you and give you a fair Warning to pull them down."[54] After threatening to burn Smith's manufactory to ashes, the writer mentions the existence of a local popular force, "the Army of Huddersfields," composed of "2782 Sworn Heroes," ready to "perish" in the act of redressing their grievances.[55] The uprising, the General ensures, will not be an isolated initiative:

> By the latest Letters from our Correspondents we learn that the Manufacturers in the following Places are going to rise and join us in redressing their Wrongs Viz. Wakefield, Halifax, Bradford, Sheffield, Oldham, Rochdale and all the Cotton Country where the brave Mr Hanson will lead them on to Victory. the weawers in Glasgow and many parts of Scotland will join us the Papists in Ireland are rising. . . . But we hope for assistance from the French Emperor in shaking off the Yoke of the Rottenest, Wickedest and most Tyranious Government that ever existed; then down come the Hanover Tyrants, all our Tyrants from the greatest to the smallest. and we will be governed by a just Republic, and may the Almighty hasten those happy Times is the Wish and Prayer of Millions in this Land, but we won't only pray but we will fight, the Redcoats shall know that when the proper time comes We will never lay down our Arms. The House of Commons passes an Act to put down all Machinery hurtful to Commonality, and repeal that to hang Frame Breakers. But we. We Petition no more that won't do fighting must.[56]

In a few sentences, the letter unveils the existence of an underground network linking the West Riding Luddites to the Northwestern cotton districts, invokes the demise of a corrupted monarchic line and the advent of the republic, and declares the end of petitioning as a viable instrument for the redressing of grievances. In other words, the emphasis shifts here from *constitution* to *mediation,* which enables the General to coordinate different Luddite initiatives across the country. Furthermore, the source of Ludd's power seems to stem from the numeric force of his army rather than from a legal document such as the charter. Such a shift can be explained partly with the fact that Yorkshire Luddism was more violent than in the Midlands and partly with the fact that Ludd had already been constituted in Nottinghamshire. By the time it reached Yorkshire, the eponym was already "charged" with a certain symbolic power, which was appropriated by the croppers without having the need to ground it in a formal authorizing context such as the charter.

This argument needs to be qualified in two respects, first, by noting the existence of songs that celebrate machine breaking (along with the unruly attitude of the croppers), that is, the existence of a specific, self-referential subculture that was autonomous and self-sufficient.[57] Second, I examine a curious letter, archived in the Radcliffe Papers, sent from

"Peter Plush, Secretery to General Ludd" to "Mr Edward Ludd Market Place Huddersfield."[58]

The letter, the only known document sent from a Ludd to a Ludd, is dated May 1, 1812, three days after the assassination of William Horsfall in Yorkshire. Since the text does not mention this topical event, E. P. Thompson speculates that the letter was written by a "freelance Nottinghamshire Luddite" who may not have heard of the murder yet.[59] This hypothesis is validated by the fact that the only concrete information conveyed by the writer is a report on the status of Luddite activism in Nottinghamshire. After professing Luddite potency and expressing regret for the death of two Luddites in the attack on Rawfolds Mills, Plush, writing on behalf of General Ludd, states that although his troops are currently idle, they are "devising the best means for a grand attack" and "dispatching a few individuals by pistel shot."[60] The letter has no postmark, and Thompson argues that it was "more intended to alarm the authorities than to communicate with Yorkshire Luddites."[61]

In his analysis of the letter, Binfield seems to agree with Thompson. However, he does not exclude "the possibility that the letter was intended for an internal audience . . . of machine breakers."[62] If this is true, then the document would support Thompson's general classification of the anonymous threatening letters published in *The London Gazette* between 1750 and 1820 on the basis of two distinct types of recipients: an audience of employers and rich superiors; and an audience of fellow workers and social equals. While until the 1790s the letters largely fall in the first group, after 1790 the second group, consisting mostly of handwritten placards and handbills, enlarges.[63] Plush's letter clearly belongs to this second group, thus revealing the possibility that the Luddites might have employed the improper name not only to threaten manufacturers and authorities, but also to communicate internally across the country.

Contacts among Luddite delegates from different regions are indeed reported by the authorities and are documented in the Home Office Papers. For instance, in April 1812, a handbill addressed "To Whitefield Luddites" appears in Prestwich, Lancashire, requiring them "to be ready on the shortest notice to join our army."[64] There is only scattered evidence, however, that the name Ned Ludd was consistently used for organizational purposes. More likely, when intended for an internal audience, the eponym had a concentrating and mythmaking function, that is, of offering a focal point to a disparate set of narratives of resistance.

NORTHWESTERN WRITINGS

This concentrating function is particularly evident in the Northwest, where Luddism blends disparate discourses—including wage complaints, opposition to labor-saving machinery, distress caused by high food prices, and frustration at the government. According to Binfield, the spurious character of Northwestern Luddism is due to the lack, among the laboring populations of the cotton districts, of "long-standing traditions of collective activity, organic identity, and social practice that would have been imparted by an ancient and communitarian trade."[65] In fact, the nineteenth-century cotton trade did not stem from craftsmanship and was largely a by-product of the Industrial Revolution. Until the 1760s, cotton was essentially carded and spun by hand in the spinners' own houses and woven at hand looms by the weavers. But the automation of weaving ignited by the invention of the flying shuttle (1733) and the opening of new markets in Europe and the Americas spurred a considerable growth in the demand for yarn, leaving the weavers wanting more than the spinners could supply. This growing demand stimulated in turn the invention of new machines that automated the spinning process. These included the spinning jenny (1764), the water frame (1769), the spinning mule (1779), the power-loom (1884), and the dressing frame (1803). As a result, "by 1830 hand-spinning was dead and all the processes previous to weaving were carried on by complicated machinery in factories, whilst weaving was partly done in factories, by power-looms worked by girls, but partly still by hand-loom weavers in their own houses."[66]

The opening of new markets and the output increase of suitable cotton yarn attracted to the Manchester region a soaring population of weavers and spinners, affecting dramatically labor (and power) relationships within the trade. Until the 1760s, the Manchester small-ware and check-weavers had tried to resist the uncontrolled influx of untrained labor by securing legal enforcement of apprenticeship. But lacking a well-established trade, their attempts were quickly defeated. Meanwhile, the exponential growth in productivity due to technological change made the British exports so competitive that new jobs were constantly created. Thus, between 1788 and 1803, a period described by William Radcliffe as the "great golden age of this trade," the booming cotton industry afforded prosperity even for the lowest ranks of the profession—the journeymen weavers.[67]

Nonetheless, the soaring output of machine yarn disguised a more essential loss of status for the category. Within a completely deregulated labor market, the old artisans were quickly assimilated into the scores of new workers—displaced farmers, former soldiers, and Irish immigrants—who entered the lower ranks of the profession with little, if any, training. Thus as soon as the Napoleonic Wars set off a gradual but steady decline in the exports wages also decreased, as manufacturers were able to keep them at recession level.[68] Furthermore, as wages were beaten down, the number of weavers continued to grow, supplying a considerable reservoir of workforce. Moreover, the Combination Acts curbed the weavers' bargaining power, making their position even more defenseless.

In March 1800, the journeymen weavers of Chester, York, Lancashire, and Derby petitioned Parliament demanding a regulation of their wages. The weavers did not call for the fixation of a standard price but for the possibility of opening up a bargaining process directly with the manufacturers.[69] In response, the Pitt government gave them the Cotton Arbitration Act (1803), a piece of legislation that instituted a complicated arbitration process for the settling of disputes over wages. The law provided that each party could appoint an arbitrator. If the arbitrators could not reach an agreement, either of them had the power to require the intervention of a Justice of the Peace, whose decision would be final. But although the act empowered the arbitrator, it did not *compel* him to act. As soon as the manufacturers discovered this flaw, they "amused themselves by appointing an arbitrator living in London or some other distant place who had no intention of acting, with the result that the arbitration went no further."[70]

Having verified the failure of the Arbitration Acts to protect their interests, the weavers began organizing along different lines from stockingers and croppers. Whereas the latter relied on charters and statutes, the weavers had to earn their legal protections from scratch. Thus, in 1807 and 1811, the Lancashire and Cheshire weavers petitioned Parliament, demanding the introduction of a minimum wage bill. In 1808, despite the Combination Acts, they organized a large strike in the Manchester area. But both minimum wage petitions were rejected, and the strike had a limited effect. Shortly thereafter, the bad harvests of 1809–11 made the price of provisions soar. Increasingly desperate, the weavers begun adopting Luddite tactics, which quickly blended with food riots and other forms of political agitation.

Even though it does not make explicit use of the eponym, this anonymous letter addressed to the factory owner of the Holywell Twist Company, a large cotton works located in Holywell, Flintshire, in May 1812, draws an explicit link between the low salaries and the high costs of food:

> Sr. If you do not advance the wages of all your workmen at Holywell, you shall have all your mills burnt to the ground immediately. it is harder upon many of us here than upon those who receive parish relief. we are starving by inches by reason of our small wages & provisions so high. You had better be content with a moderate profit, than have your mills destroyed. You know how it is with Burton & Goodier & many others. It will be the same with you in a few days, if you do not advance all hands. All the Miners and Colliers are ready to join us. 3000 men can be collected in a few hours
>
> The poor cry aloud for bread
> Prince Regent shall lose his head
> And all the rich who oppress the poor
> In a little time shall be no more
>
> Take care you be not in the number of the oppressors. we cannot wait but a very few days, we are ready for blood or bread, anything is better than starving by inches.[71]

Besides providing a rare example of an anonymous letter containing lines of verse, the text explicitly threatens the mills' destruction as a response to the low wages and high food prices, questions unbounded profit making, foreshadows the gathering of an army, and links these economic demands and the possible show of force to the Jacobin celebration of the sovereign's beheading. According to E. P. Thompson, this mix of industrial demands and political claims reflects the peculiar composition of Northwestern Luddism. As previously noted, Thompson's argument is that the Combination Acts had unwittingly brought into association the weavers agitating for a minimum wage with small groups of republicans and radicals operating in Lancashire since the 1790s. "Thus when Luddism came to Lancashire it did not move into a vacuum," writes Thompson. "There were already, in Manchester and the larger centers, artisan unions, secret committees of weavers, and some old and new groups of Painite Radicals, with an ebullient Irish fringe."[72]

Even if Thompson's analysis has been questioned by those historians who tend to emphasize the local and apolitical nature of the movement, his reading of Northwestern Luddism as a hotbed of political radicalism is sound and can be verified through a rhetorical analysis of Manchester-area documents. As Binfield points out,

> three types of discourse surround Manchester Luddism. The first is petition. The second is a language of economic analysis that, although not macroeconomic in any real sense, does consider economic issues that extend beyond the rather confined purview of any particular trade. The third is Jacobin language. Luddite rhetoric blended with each of these discourses, but all of them have in common a hierarchical perspective . . . in other words they tended to look to the top, to those locations where power in a larger sense tended to reside.[73]

In regard to the first discourse, Binfield notes how, in the years leading up to Luddism, different petitions were sent to Parliament from Manchester and other cotton towns but very few, if any, from the weaving cotton trade as a whole. The lack of a trade history and trade institutions in charge of setting professional standards and bargaining protocols was not conducive to the development of a trade awareness. Furthermore, as John Bohstedt has shown, the Manchester authorities were conservative, unable to cope with the rapid growth of the cotton industry, and unwilling to include working-class Mancunians in negotiations.[74] Given such a gap between the elites and the working classes, it is no surprise that the weavers preferred to look outside of their communities for relief rather than to their employers.

In some circumstances, Luddite writers express an awareness of the larger political implications of their actions by denouncing the autocratic nature of the British government and engaging in curious exercises of comparative political science. Such is the case of the only known Luddite letter signed by a woman, Eliza Ludd, and addressed to a Manchester factory owner named Mr. Simpson:

> Sir,
>
> Doubtless you are well acquainted with the Political History of America, if so you must confess that, it was ministerial tyranny that gave rise to that glorious spirit in which the British Colonies obtain'd their independence by force of arms, at a period, when we was ten times as strong as now!—if bands of husbandmen could do this, in spite of all the force our government was then able to employ—cannot such an action be accomplish'd here, now the military strength of the country is so reduced—Consider Sir, what a few troops there is at present in England,—remember that none can be call'd home; because that would relinquishing the little we have gain'd to the fury of the enemy—little indeed to have coss'd so much money and such torrents of blood, yes British blood!——————let me persuad you to quit your present post, lay by your sword, and become a friend of the oppress'd—for curs'd his the man that even lifts a straw against the sacred cause of Liberty.[75]

It is unclear why the writer chose a female pseudonym, but, as we have seen, there are a few documented episodes in which the Luddites staged inversions of gender roles. For sure, the letter is quite sophisticated both stylistically and in its ability to link opposition to the wars (a theme shared by many Northwestern writers) to sincere patriotism, or in decoupling "ministerial tyranny" from true British nationalism. The meaning of this distinction can be better grasped against the backdrop of the new political climate created by the April 8 riots at the Manchester Exchange.

Although, until early 1812, the Prince Regent was generally considered a supporter of the Whigs and of political reform, his choice of confirming Spencer Perceval (a conservative and a former prosecutor of Thomas Paine) as prime minister in a moment of social unrest made him suddenly unpopular. The riots at the stock exchange—which saw a high participation of young weavers—marked a turn in the public feelings toward the Crown and a revamping of Jacobin initiative. Previously to April 8, "Church-and-King was the favourite cry and hunting 'Jacobins' a safe sport," one old reformer later recalled. "But we had no Church-and-King mobs after that!"[76]

Two weeks later, the city of Middleton became the theater of the bloodiest events associated with Luddism. On April 20, 1812, a crowd of several thousand people attacked Daniel Burton's power mill. Like William Cartwright's mill in Yorkshire, the power mill was defended by armed guards, who killed three people during the attack. The following morning, a larger crowd gathered and burned down Burton's house. Here, writes Thompson, it was met by the military, "at whose hands at least seven were killed and many more wounded."[77] After this episode, the attacks on machinery in the Manchester region declined, but several informants report an increase in oath taking, arms raids, and other insurrectionary preparations in the following months. In other words, throughout spring and summer 1812, Jacobin and Luddite agitations seemed to overlap in the Manchester region, as illustrated by the recurring presence of Jacobin and Painite motifs in the Luddite writings of the period.

The convergence of industrial, economic, and political protest is also quite visible in the wide range of pseudonyms adopted by Northwestern Luddites. While in Yorkshire and the Midlands the name Ned Ludd is frequently preceded by aggrandizing appellations such as "General," "Captain," and "King," which bestow on him executive and military power, in the Northwest the eponym is interspersed with eccentric variations, such as Eliza Ludd, alternative pseudonyms, such as "General Justice," "Falstaff," and "Thomas Paine," or curious Latin denominations, such as "L . . . Teoxperorator," "Iulius—Lt. de Luddites," and "Ludd finis est."

This wide gamut of signatures and writing styles, and the frequent use of Latin expressions and literary references, raises questions about the education of Northwestern writers.[78] "Perhaps," writes Binfield, "the figure of General Ludd is a 'transclass bridge' (effective because imported from another region) between a systemic awareness and the expression of basic human suffering."[79] Here Binfield seems to follow Thompson's contention that in the Northwest, industrial grievances, economic struggles, and political campaigns entered, if only for a short time, a relationship of contiguity and mutual exchange. According to Binfield, Ludd was the name of this relationship, functioning here as a metonym rather than as an eponym organically growing out of its own subculture.

To assess the cogency of Binfield's distinction between Ludd as eponym (in Yorkshire and Notthinghamshire) and Ludd as metonymy (in the

Northwest) that links different struggles, I first draw a distinction between the reductionist properties of metonymy and the expansive properties of synecdoche. Then I rely on a rhetorical analysis of Luddite discourse to advance a new political reading of Luddism.

SYNECDOCHE, HEGEMONY, NED LUDD

Russian linguist Roman Jakobson was the first to describe metaphor and metonymy as the fundamental "poles" of language, operating respectively along the axes of similarity (in absentia) and contiguity (in presentia). While the former allows one to apprehend a phenomenon figuratively by replacing a term or expression with another term drawn from a different semantic field (in Greek, *metaphor* means "to transfer, to carry over"), the latter replaces a term with another to which it is closely associated (in Greek, *metonymy* means "name change").[80] Drawing from Jakobson's original insight, linguists have classified a whole range of metonymic substitutions, including the cause for the effect, the material for the thing, the agent for the act, or the container for the content. When a term denoting a part of something is used to denote the whole thing, we encounter a synecdoche, a trope usually defined as a specific typology or class of metonymy.

Hayden White has advanced an alternative and suggestive analysis of the relationship between synecdoche and metonymy. Metonymic substitutions, argues White, remain confined within the same semantic field. For instance, if the expression "fifty sails" is used to denote "fifty ships," "it is suggested that 'ships' are in some sense identifiable with that *part* of themselves without which they cannot operate."[81] But if we use the expression "he is all heart," writes White, "the term 'heart' is to be understood figuratively as designating, not a part of the body, but the *quality* of character conventionally *symbolized* by the term 'heart' in Western culture."[82] White contends that the movement from part to whole characteristic of metonymy gives way in this case to a movement from microcosm to macrocosm, in which the former undergoes *a qualitative transformation*. It follows that synecdoche is not just a type of metonymy but a *hybrid trope* that combines metonymic reductions with the figurative aspects of metaphor.

My wager is that when the eponym Ned Ludd migrated to the Northwest, it underwent a qualitative transformation, which, from a rhetorical standpoint, is akin to the hybrid properties of synecdoche outlined by White. On one hand, especially in the Midlands and Yorkshire, Ned Ludd is strictly associated with machine breaking, thereby functioning as a metonymical substitution of the agent for the act or as someone who destroys the obnoxious machines on behalf of the community. On the other hand, especially in the Northeast, the name functions synecdochically by integrating economic and political demands into a wider struggle for social justice and political reform. If this is true, then the question is whether Ludd articulates each demand into a whole that is more than the sum of its parts or whether the improper name resurfaces within different discursive practices (the agitation for higher wages, for the republic, against unregulated apprenticeship, and so forth) without articulating them into a new whole, and therefore without constituting the social groups behind these demands into a unified subject of enunciation.

In the latter case, Ned Ludd would be an ambiguous signifier, floating between different signifieds without affecting or transforming their substance. In the former case, the improper name would function as what Ernesto Laclau calls an "empty signifier," a sign that empties itself out of its attachment to a particular signified (in our case, machine breaking) to represent a signifying system in its totality.[83]

Drawing on Marx, Laclau argues that the empty signifier is a general equivalent of sorts that encompasses differential identities that are not "strong enough" to have a signifier of their own. In the social field, it functions as a semantic conveyor belt by enabling a group or a class "to present itself as realizing the broader aims either of emancipating or ensuring order for wider masses of the population."[84] In *Hegemony and Socialist Strategy,* Laclau and Mouffe call "this relation, by which a certain particularity assumes the representation of a universality entirely incommensurable with it . . . a *hegemonic relation.*"[85] Subsequently, Laclau has added the important proviso that "the presence of empty signifiers . . . is the very condition of hegemony."[86]

In Marxian terms, the empty signifier can be compared to the money form in that it establishes a relation of equivalence among different terms (exchange value) by overriding and subverting their differential characters (use value). Laclau argues that this principle of equivalence is not predicated on a positive foundation, an ultimate ground that would be the source of all societal differences. Rather, following de Saussure, he maintains that "1) each identity is what it is only through its difference from the other ones; 2) that the context has to be a closed one—if all identities depend on the differential *system,* unless the latter defines its own limits, no identity would be finally constituted."[87] It follows that the differences internal to the context are not constitutive but receive their meaning and identity from something that by standing *outside* of the system traces its boundaries. In other words, the system has no essence of its own, as it is defined by a "radical otherness" that both constitutes and threatens it from without.[88] Yet, because the system needs to manifest in the symbolic field, argues Laclau, it will do so through particular signifiers, which contingently assume the function of representation. An empty signifier is thus a signifier that makes "its own particularity the signifying body of a universal representation," in the same way as gold has both a use value and an exchange value or Jesus is both a human being and the incarnation of divine essence. In the political field, the empty signifier hegemonizes the differential identities internal to a system by setting itself in opposition to the Other that defines the boundaries of the system and threatens its existence.[89]

Now, to understand whether Ludd was an empty signifier articulating multiple demands and social groups in a hegemonic relation or an ambiguous signifier floating among different signifieds without integrating them into a new whole, I shall first return to E. P. Thompson's definition of class consciousness. Then I compare and contrast his position to other interpretations of Luddism and reach my conclusion.

THE LUDDITE ASSEMBLAGE AND THE QUESTION OF CLASS CONSCIOUSNESS

Thompson's definition of class consciousness revolves around three key elements. First, he broadly defines class consciousness as the way in which the class experience is handled in cultural terms: "If the experience appears as [economically] determined, class-consciousness does not."[90] Second, as we have seen, Thompson claims that class consciousness is not a given but the result of a long, tortuous *process of unification* whereby different sectors of the working class begin to understand their interests as common. Third, because "class is a relationship, and not a thing," this process is of an *antagonistic nature*; that is, the working people feel the identity of their own interests inasmuch as they have to confront employers and rulers, who also behave as a class.[91]

As we have seen, Luddism was not only an antagonistic movement of direct action against machines, the manufacturers, and the magistrates who withdrew from a web of communal relations but also a distinctive subculture within the popular Radicalism of the early nineteenth century. Its unifying force is apparent from the fact that the eponym spread across regions marked by different productive histories and demographics. If Luddism was exclusively, as Calhoun and others have suggested, a phenomenon growing out of community roots, it would have remained confined within a craft community or a trade. In this sense, the reading of Luddism as a community phenomenon is limited and needs to be supplemented with an analysis that situates Luddism at least within a national framework.

A first approach, shared by liberal and Marxist historians, is that Luddism was a popular response to an authoritarian regime, which had dismantled the old paternalist legislation, forestalled unionization, and stifled political liberties at a time in which the Napoleonic Empire threatened the very basis of monarchic power in Europe. In this repressive climate, collective bargaining by riot immediately acquired a political significance. Because every attack on machinery was in a sense an act of defiance against the constituted order, it is plausible (if difficult to prove) that Lancashire and Yorkshire Luddites sided with the Radicals who were conspiring against the monarchy. Simply put, Thompson's political reading of Luddism is a compelling hypothesis because textile workers and republicans shared the opposition to a common enemy.

In a way, this reading of Luddism resembles Rosa Luxemburg's analysis of the Russian Revolution of 1905.[92] Commenting on Luxemburg's text, Laclau notes that if the mass strike had become the most popular form of struggle of the time, it is because it was able to connect partial struggles, economic and political demands, in their opposition to the tsarist autocracy.[93] Thus these partial demands form a chain of equivalence not because they share something positive but because an external, negative force (the tsarist regime, in this case) flattens their differences by frustrating them all. It follows that when this force is lifted or absent—as in the case of democratic regimes that allow for a "healthy" development of class conflict and the exercise of political liberties—the differential identity of each demand should resurface.

This is precisely what happened in England after the end of the Napoleonic Wars and the Luddite riots. As previously noted, the repeal of the Combination Acts (1824–25) paved the way both to the eight-hour working day movement and Chartism. Whereas the former signaled a shift from the attacks on machinery to an intensification of the struggle over wages, the latter created the conditions for the integration of the working class in the democratic political system. This possible "return" of economic and political struggles to their differential identity allows us also to shed a fresh light on the aforementioned ideological battle underlying Luddite historiography.

As we have seen, liberals, sociologists, and Marxists agree on the fact that Luddism expressed a popular and exasperated reaction against a repressive regime that crushed every form of dissent. Yet while the liberals and the sociologists would probably describe Ludd as an ambiguous signifier that shifted among different grievances and demands without establishing a durable and transformative relationship among them, Thompson would argue that the movement had at least the potential of becoming an empty signifier capable of articulating a hegemonic relation between a particular practice (machine breaking) and a general struggle for social justice. According to Thompson, if this relationship did not solidify a hegemonic bloc, it is not because the British political system suddenly became more democratic but because machine breaking did not prove to be a viable tactic, especially in the Northwest, where the attacks on power-looms lasted only few weeks.

Thompson notes that in comparison to the stocking and shearing frames, "the power-loom was a costly machine, only recently introduced, employed only in a very few steam-powered mills, and not to be found scattered in small workshops over the countryside."[94] Thus the attacks on this kind of machine became extremely predictable, and more likely to meet an armed resistance, as demonstrated by the tragic events of Middleton. Furthermore, whereas in the Midlands and Yorkshire the new labor-saving machines supplanted traditional machinery, the power-loom had been introduced at a time in which the cotton industry was booming, making it appear as a source of wealth rather than a threatening, obnoxious technology. Thus "there must have been very many (and probably a majority) of weavers who doubted of the efficacy of resistance to the new machines as such."[95]

Thus if machine breaking quickly declined in the Northwest, it is because the workers chose to prioritize other forms of conflict, namely, the struggle over wages. This is precisely Marx's argument in *Capital,* where he claims that in its early stages, the workers' struggle against capital takes the form of a struggle against machinery. After briefly mentioning the Luddite riots in the context of the repressive measures adopted by the British government, Marx writes,

> It took both time and experience before the workers learnt to distinguish between machinery and its employment by capital, and therefore to transfer their attacks from the material instruments of production to the form of society which utilizes those instruments. The struggles over wages within the manufacturing system presuppose manufacture, and are in no sense directed against its existence. The opposition to the establishment of manufactures proceeds from the guild-masters and the privileged towns, not from the wage-labourers.[96]

On one hand, Marx's reading of Luddism seems to support the progressives' argument on the regressive character of Luddism. But on the other hand, the reference to machine breaking as an early manifestation of the struggle between labor and capital is not incompatible with Thompson's reading of the movement as a primeval form of class consciousness. What is more relevant to our analysis, the antagonism set by Marx between the guilds and the manufacturing system is neither equivalent nor symmetrical with the struggle between waged labor and capital. Whereas the former is a manifestation of a systemic antagonism between the feudal and the capitalist modes of production, the latter points to a conflict that takes place *within* the capitalist mode of production.

As previously noted, the three strands of scholarship share the vision that Luddism was a popular reaction to an authoritarian government that did not allow collective bargaining and other forms of democratic participation. Yet this superficial agreement conceals a more fundamental disagreement. If the liberals see Luddism as a manifestation of a *systemic opposition* between capitalism and the remnants of the feudal order, the Marxists see it as something that, although originating from such an antagonism, can prepare the ground for a class struggle *internal to the capitalist system*. In fact, for Thompson and Hobsbawm, the continuity between these two kinds of antagonisms lies in the continuity of laboring practices.

This shifting of antagonism from the outside to the inside of the capitalist system is reflected by the aforementioned shift in Luddite discourse. If in the Midlands and Yorkshire, Ludd is metonymically anchored to a specific signified—namely, the destruction of machinery on behalf of the community—in the Northwest, Ludd loses this material reference and floats among different signifieds. In a context in which labor has already been subsumed by capital, Ludd is no longer confronting the capitalist system as Other but has to engage with a complex set of demands and positions that do not stand in a relation of absolute exteriority to industrial capitalism. To be sure, even in the Northwest, the eponym personifies the strife of the poor, opposition to the monarchy, and the manufacturers' greed. But it cannot articulate these differential identities hegemonically—that is, it cannot articulate them in a relation of equivalence—insofar as the limits of the system are set here not by capitalism but by an authoritarian regime that bars the unfolding of a truly democratic (capitalist) dialectic. In Yorkshire, conversely, opposition to the government conceals a more fundamental antagonism between the highly regulated Domestic System inherited from the Middle Ages and capitalism. Finally, the systemic antagonism between the two modes of production emerges in its "pure form" in Nottinghamshire and the Midlands, where Ludd is least politicized.

In *Hegemony and Socialist Strategy*, Laclau and Mouffe argue that hegemony presupposes the existence of an open social field in which antagonistic forces struggle for the articulation of floating identities in a plurality of political spaces (local and national elections, industrial relations, rural and urban economies, etc.). These complex formations are typical of advanced capitalist societies. Conversely, a social formation whose boundaries are rigidly determined and in which identities are assigned a fixed position does not allow for the articulation of a hegemonic practice: "We will therefore speak of *democratic* struggles, where these imply a plurality of political spaces, and of *popular* struggles where certain discourses *tendentially* construct the division of a single political space in two opposed fields."[97]

In this light, Luddism can be seen as a mixed movement that embeds elements of both a popular struggle and, especially in the Northwest, a democratic struggle. This ambiguity can also be grasped in rhetorical terms. In the Midlands and Yorkshire, the name Ned Ludd is assigned a fairly stable symbolic function by means of a metonymic exchange between agent and act. In the Northwest, Ludd moves toward abstraction by establishing, if only for a short time, a synecdochic link between a material microcosm (machine breaking) and an immaterial macrocosm (the demand for social justice, as envisioned by a plurality of subjects). But ultimately Luddism *fails* to constitute a durable hegemonic link among different social forces—or in Gramscian terms, to constitute a hegemonic bloc—insofar as machine breaking was inadequate to bring together subjects that were unified by their common opposition to an authoritarian government but not necessarily to the capitalist system per se. Or, to put in positive terms, whereas some Luddites rejected industrial capitalism en bloc, other Luddites were ready to overthrow the government and negotiate higher wages.

It is worth remarking that in the Northwest, the improper name circulated in a number of instances detached from the original practice or signified for which it stood. We have seen how this movement toward abstraction is already under way in Yorkshire, where the collective appointment of Ludd as the agent–spokesperson for the community (originally performed in Nottinghamshire) is taken for granted and does not need to be formally repeated. But it becomes fully manifest only in the Northwest, where, by entering an open social field, the eponym takes a life of its own. One wonders, however, whether to acquire a new meaning within an open social field such as the Northwest, the initial baptism of the eponym did not have to be renewed or reformulated on a new basis.

Such a dilemma informs the entire problematic of the improper names discussed in this book. If the initial baptism of a collective pseudonym is always a constituent act, the circulation of the alias inevitably subjects the name to unforeseen appropriations, thereby weakening its original performative force. At the same time, the distinctive feature of the improper name is precisely to eschew fixation by incorporating a plurality of usages that cannot easily be reduced to one. From this angle in migrating from Nottinghamshire to Yorkshire to the Northwestern cotton districts, Ludd changed in nature and became a "multiple-use name"—a term that emphasizes a more decentralized use of a pseudonym. This shift signals that, while in the Midlands and Yorkshire, Ludd was endowed with a symbolic power that expressed the internal unity of knitters and croppers, once it entered the Northwest, the eponym catalyzed a set of demands that were too heterogeneous to be articulated as one.

Thus, drawing from Deleuze and Guattari, we can say that as it enters the Northwest, Luddism functions as an *assemblage of enunciation,* that is, a network of pragmatic actions and semiotic expressions that are connected but also enjoy a relative autonomy from one another.[98] These actions (machine breaking, strikes, riots) and texts (letters, declarations, manifestos) are linked to one another, presuppose each other (e.g., the request for higher wages cannot really be advanced in the context of an autocratic state), but are also clearly distinct from one another, as became clear in the ensuing decades with the parallel development of Chartism and the eight-hour movement. (As we have seen, political and economic demands enjoy a relative autonomy within a democratic political space.) Deleuze and Guattari maintain that assemblages are dynamic formations that are caught up in a double movement of territorialization and deterritorialization, or, as Nicholas Thoburn puts it, "are determined as much by what escapes them as by what they fix."[99] In this respect, Northwestern Luddism functions as the line of flight that, by attaching itself to the deterritorializations brought about by the Industrial Revolution, opens up the Luddite assemblage to modern, democratic forms of class struggle.

Thus the question of whether Luddism contributed to the development of a modern working-class consciousness can be answered positively by adding the important proviso that it could do so *only by becoming something other than itself.* If we follow Thompson's definition of class consciousness as a nonlinear process of unification, then Luddism was certainly a significant stage in this process. Its heterogeneous character suggests that such consciousness was internally divided into multiple consciousnesses, some of which looked backward, at the defense of traditional political economies, and some of which looked forward, at forms of class struggle that existed only in an embryonic form in the 1810s.[100] From this angle, Ned Ludd is the improper name of the fault line where the customary laws regulating the traditional world of craft are about to be swallowed and the new world of modern industrial relations has not yet emerged. And this is not only because the eponym was adopted by workers who happened to be contemporaries while de facto belonging to different temporalities. If the Luddite assemblage linked singular and incongruent processes of subjectivation, it is also because each appropriation of the name *could not be integrated into the assemblage without transforming it from within.* In this sense, the circulation of the eponym across different regions opened it up to molecular and idiosyncratic usages that ultimately undermined its ability to function as an empty signifier representing a system in its totality. (This does not mean, however, that the pseudonym lacked such potentiality. I will return to the tension between multiplicity and identity, constitution from within and constitution from without, potentiality and actualization, in the conclusion.)

Finally, in retrospect, we can say that Ned Ludd exceeds *by far* the historic conditions of Luddism and acquires a whole new significance with the emergence of the modern culture industry. The next chapter discusses in fact the introduction of a new collective pseudonym for bargaining purposes. But rather than being associated with illegal practices and social unrest, Allen Smithee materializes within the hyperregulated world of Hollywood labor relations at a critical historic juncture for the film industry. Perhaps, in lieu of the analysis of Luddism advanced in this chapter, it is not surprising if the authorizing context of this pseudonym was an organization, the Directors Guild of America, whose name and mission evoke the self-regulation of a qualified craft. Yet, as we shall see, the accumulation of negative reputation in a shared pseudonym had unpredictable effects for its parent organization.

2

ALLEN SMITHEE, THE ANTI-AUTEUR

MATTERS OF PROPERTY AND MATTERS OF PROPRIETY

If the Luddite texts amplified the symbolic power of machine breaking and brought a diversified set of demands within a common discursive space, the name Ned Ludd did not have an economic value in itself. Not only did the Luddite texts hardly fit the literary canon of their time but the notion that an author's name could have a monetary value was foreign to a society whose book publishing market was still in its infancy. Yet with the mid- to late-nineteenth-century expansion of the Victorian publishing industry, a whole new political economy of the signature began to emerge. In particular, technical advances in the printing process, the decline of paper costs, fast-growing literacy rates, and the enforcement of modern copyright law all set the conditions for the professionalization of authorship and for the rapid decline of the patronage model that was still in vogue in early modern Europe.[1]

As Mark Rose has convincingly argued, until the late seventeenth century, literary ownership was associated with the material act of writing, copying, or printing a book and not with the immaterial activity of conceiving it. While the author was perceived as a father to his text and the book was tied to his honor and reputation, "the concept of an author owning a book did not quite fit the circumstances of literary production in the traditional patronage system."[2] Certainly authors could be protected, rewarded, and even accorded special printing privileges for their state service. But because publishers were usually licensed by the monarch to print copies of the original manuscript, they were the ones who reaped the profits of bookselling—whether or not they had previously secured the author's consent.[3]

Scientific authorship in early modern Europe was also entirely dependent on patronage. As Roger Chartier has pointed out, scientific experiments had to be validated by a princely or aristocratic testimony to be guaranteed the force of truth. The foundation of learned societies in mid-seventeenth-century Europe depersonalized patronage by creating institutional bodies that incorporated authors and legitimated scientific research. Even though the sovereign remained the ultimate guarantor of the truthfulness of knowledge, the verification of scientific claims was now entrusted with "gentlemen scientists" whose testimony was considered reliable precisely because *unconditioned by economic interest*. Thus, similar to literary authorship, the construction of scientific discourse was more concerned with matters of *propriety*—that is, of honor and reputation—than with matters of *property*.

The notion that personal economic gain could compromise the honorable and disinterested activity of writing and researching began to be challenged only in the middle of the nineteenth century. This is particularly clear if we consider that, until the 1850s, anonymity had been standard practice in the Victorian periodical press. Because journalists were believed to have a mentoring role and speak the moral values of society, there was no need for them to sign their articles—the publisher's name was more than sufficient to seal their authority. Beginning in the 1860s, however, a number of influential authors, such as Thomas Hughes, John Morley, G. H. Lewes, Antony Trollope, and J. Boyd Kinnear, began to argue that signatures were necessary to foster personal responsibility and manliness among journalists, to allow readers to make informed choices about who and what to read, and to enable a free market of cultural products.[4]

The rise of bourgeois authorship, however, came at a cost. The growing literacy rates and anonymous authorship had had, in fact, the unintended effect of enabling access to writing for those subjectivities who had been historically excluded from the order of the discourse, most notably women. As Alexis Easley and others have pointed out, by writing anonymously or under a pseudonym, many women had been able to address large audiences and conventionally masculine sociopolitical issues on the thriving periodical press of the mid-nineteenth century.[5] Through such practice, some of them started successful literary careers. Thus, as soon as signed publications became synonymous with reliability and high culture—and conversely, anonymous publications were relegated to second-class status—women found it more difficult to gain access to the broad audiences and subject matter they had addressed as anonymous writers.

This emphasis on the importance of individual authorship was accompanied by the booming market of fiction books and the rising popularity of Victorian novelists. Whether or not these authors relied on pseudonyms to author their works, by the late nineteenth century, the notion that writing was a profession rather than a disinterested moral activity had become widely accepted among the Victorians. Thus, as publishers competed to contract emerging and established writers, the name of the author acquired an immediately economic value. This also meant that the cultural significance and the economic value of cultural products now tended to coincide and find their identity in the marketplace. In this respect, to Foucault's famous theorization of the "author-function" as a set of authenticating procedures that contain the transgressive nature of writing by attributing it to identifiable subjects, we might add that for the modern culture industry, such authentication functions also as a *dispositif* for including and excluding and is mostly relevant for its economic implications.[6]

Once a modern publishing market is established, publishers and authors become aware that the name of the author functions like a two-sided virtual currency: on the side of propriety and reputation, the name value is determined by its exposure and circulation in the public domain, the cultural products to which it is linked, and the author's ability to protect its integrity from plagiarism, misattribution, and misinterpretation; on the side of property and ownership, the name value is determined by the size of the market, copyright law, and the contractual conditions each author is able to negotiate on the basis of her reputation.

This means that if positive reputation can be leveraged to increase an author's exchange value, negative reputation can have the opposite effect. From this angle, the obfuscating function of a pseudonym is also double-sided. On one hand, an author can consistently use an alias to spark interest in her own identity and engender a specific *effect* in the reader's mind—namely, to distinguish between the author as a function of literary discourse and the author as a physical person. (Gérard Genette calls this mental bifurcation the "pseudonym-effect.")[7] On the other hand, an author can adopt a pseudonym to work outside of her reputation. In this case, the pseudonym's negative function is to allow the author to freeze the symbolic capital associated with her given name by creating an alternate persona.[8]

The case of Allen Smithee—a pseudonym introduced by the Directors Guild of America (DGA) for Hollywood film directors who wished to disown movies that had been recut by third parties—allows us to explore the pseudonym's obfuscating function from the perspective of political economy. In this chapter, we will see how, as an accumulated stock of negative symbolic capital, Smithee suspends the conflation of property and propriety, ownership and reputation, that characterizes the discourse of modern authorship. As the alias was adopted over the course of three decades by dozens of directors, it came to author a spurious filmography. While such a corpus may carry little economic value, the signature that kept it together accumulated over time an increasingly symbolic charge. In this respect, it is no accident that Smithee was liquidated at the moment at which its growing notoriety threatened to compromise the commercial viability of the films with which it was associated. But before discussing the historical circumstances of Alan Smithee's demise, I should first address those of its initial baptism.

THE BIRTH OF ALLEN SMITHEE

In 1969, Universal Pictures released *Death of a Gunfighter,* a Western in which a gunfighter turned lawman has outlived his historical function of enforcing a code of frontier justice in a turn-of-the-century Texas town. Twenty-five days into the film shooting, clashes between director Robert Totten and Hollywood star Richard Widmark prompted the former to quit. To complete the film, Universal contracted the former director of *Invasion of the Body Snatchers,* Don Siegel, who finished shooting and editing in only ten days. As the film was about to be released, however, neither Totten nor Siegel wanted to take credit for it. Caught in a potentially disastrous impasse, Universal turned to the DGA for a solution. Recognizing that *Death of a Gunfighter* did not represent the creative vision of either director, the DGA chose the pseudonym "Allen Smithee."[9]

Since then, and until 1999, Allen Smithee (or Alan Smithee) became the official pseudonym the DGA set aside for those disgruntled directors who could prove, to the DGA's satisfaction, that their movie had been manipulated or recut by a third party.[10] In those three decades, the nom de plume was used to sign more than fifty motion pictures, made-for-TV films, and TV series episodes. The "highlights" of Smithee's filmography include the TV drama *City in Fear* (an ABC production that launched Mickey Rourke in 1980), the TV version of David Lynch's *Dune* (1988), Dennis Hopper's *Catchfire* (1990), and episodes of popular TV series such as *The Twilight Zone, MacGyver, Red Shoe Diaries,* and *The Cosby Show.*[11] In all cases, the Smithee credit was used "quietly," to alert Hollywood insiders that something had gone wrong with the film production. Such discretion was necessary to allow for the movie to be released without damaging its reputation.

In 2000, the DGA discontinued the use of the pseudonym, assigning to director Walter Hill a non-Smithee credit (Thomas Lee) for *Supernova* (2000), a sci-fi horror film distributed by Metro-Goldwyn-Mayer. Although no official explanation was provided for this decision, DGA board member John Rich has suggested that the release of *An Alan Smithee Film: Burn Hollywood Burn,* a Disney production that satirized the Smithee phenomenon, may have contributed to it.[12] Another element that may have played a role is the lawsuit British director Tony Kaye filed against the DGA for *not* allowing him to take a Smithee credit for *American History X* (1998). Furthermore, in 1997, a collective of film scholars, the Allen Smithee Group, was formed at the University of Pennsylvania to study Smithee as an author in its own right. Thus, by the late 1990s, Smithee became overexposed and begun to takes a life of its own.

As we shall see, the DGA could not welcome this development for three distinct reasons. First, the studios had allowed the use of the shared alias only insofar as it did not compromise a movie's commercial success. Second, parodic and anomalous uses of Allen Smithee suggest that the signature could be appropriated by different parties to signal forms of abuse and conflict that cast a negative light on the DGA's role as a representative of the directors' interests. Third, Smithee's hybrid filmography stood in many ways at odds with the kind of authorial model the DGA had been trying to promote since its very foundation in the 1930s. This authorial model had first come true in the late 1960s, when the crisis of the studio system granted unprecedented power and creative control to Hollywood film directors.

THE END OF HOLLYWOOD'S GOLDEN AGE

Besides marking the birth of Allen Smithee, 1969 is a notable year in the history of Hollywood as it also marks the first year of full implementation of the current film-rating system, which replaced the obsolete Motion Picture Production Code. Originally introduced in 1930, to hold in check the tendency of the eight Hollywood studios to produce salacious or sensational films every time box-office revenues dwindled, the Motion Picture Production Code (or Hays Code) was terminated by the Motion Picture Association of America in 1968 after repeated violations had shown its untenability.

Enforced since 1934, the Hays Code incorporated a form of preemptive censorship in various stages of the production process. Its first administrator, Joseph Breen, "had the power to halt or delay the production of a film . . . since, until he offered the promise of a certificate, producers could not secure the banks' production loans."[13] Besides limiting the cultural offer, the Hays Code protocol was a powerful standardizing force that reinforced the studios' oligopoly. In fact, until the 1950s, each Hollywood studio was modeled after a Ford factory, vertically integrating the entire filmmaking process, from preproduction to production and distribution in studio-owned theaters nationwide.

It is only in 1948, with the antitrust case *United States v. Paramount,* that the Supreme Court forced the film majors to divest from their distribution chains.[14] Film historians usually identify this ruling as one of the two major causes to the end of Hollywood's Golden Age—the other being the rise of television. The dismantling of the Hays Code in 1968 set the last nail in the coffin of the Fordist organization of the studio system.[15] By the late 1960s, the studios were in dire financial shape. According to *Variety,* in 1971, at the end of a three-year slump, attendances hit an all-time low of 15.8 million a week—nearly 80 percent down from the 1946 all-time high of 78.2 million.[16] Furthermore, the unexpected success of movies whose narrative structure was opaque or that explicitly defied old morals—including *Blow-Up* (1966), *Point Blank* (1967), *Bonnie and Clyde* (1967), and *The Graduate* (1967)—convinced studio executives that survival was dependent on their ability to take chances and open up to the countercultural ferments that were brewing within society.[17]

On a productive level, the restructuring efforts that began in the late 1960s all went in the direction of creating a more flexible production structure. On one hand, this "post-Fordist Hollywood" was characterized by lighter facilities; lower overheard costs; and a major emphasis on the sale of TV rights, horizontal integration, and the full exploitation of ancillary rights. On the other hand, the studios' efforts to build large film libraries with the goal of extracting value from their global distribution—an effort pioneered by Universal Picture's CEO Lew Wasserman—had the effect of revitalizing independent productions.[18] Frequently founded by emerging directors such as George Lucas, Francis Ford Coppola, and, later on, Steven Spielberg, these production companies relied on the studios for distribution, while they guaranteed directors the creative freedom they could not enjoy under the studio system.

Thus it is by seizing on this moment of industrial crisis, in which studios' interference and censorship were significantly weakened, that directors were able to gain the creative autonomy they had been striving for for several decades. In fact, the Screen Directors Guild (SDG; renamed DGA in 1960) had been trying to expand directors' control over screenplays, editing, and casting since its very foundation in 1936. As compared to the Screen Writers Guild and the Screen Actors Guild—the two other unions that organized Hollywood's creative workers—the SDG was much more hesitant to call on strikes and other forms of labor agitation. As Douglas Gomery points out, "money was never the issue; the SDG wanted participation in the preparation of scripts, and the same requirement for cutting of the final release."[19]

In 1964, under the direction of George Sidney, the DGA drafted its first Bill of Creative Rights, a collective bargaining platform that reclaimed the right for directors to control the movie's final cut and receive final credit in the main titles. Predictably, the notion that the directors, rather than the producers, were responsible for a movie's final version was not easily accepted by the Motion Picture Association of America (MPAA). It first took the DGA a long round of negotiations to get the director's cut into its 1964 contract and significant vigilance to ensure that the contract would be enforced in the following years. The success of the DGA's bargaining strategy became fully evident only in the 1970s, when a new generation of cineastes such as Martin Scorsese, Robert Altman, and Brian De Palma—as well as the aforementioned Coppola, Lucas, and Spielberg—enjoyed an unprecedented level of creative freedom within Hollywood.

THE POLITICS OF THE AUTHORS AND ITS AMERICAN ADAPTATION

The directors who came to age in the 1970s were primarily inspired by the French New Wave's capacity to elevate cinema to a form of art in its own right through a specific aesthetic program. Nouvelle Vague directors such as François Truffaut, Jean-Luc Godard, Éric Rohmer, Claude Chabrol, and Jacques Rivette had first entered the world of cinema by writing for the prestigious *Cahiers du cinéma* in the 1950s. Truffaut, in particular, was the first to argue that cinema should reflect a director's personal vision and style. In an influential article titled "A Certain Tendency of the French Cinema" (1954), he decried the so-called tradition of quality in French cinema, which tended to rely on screenplays that simplified French literature to serve a narrow political agenda. To this tendency, he counterposed the works of directors such as Jean Renoir, Jacques Tati, and Robert Bresson, among others, who wrote or edited their screenplays and had developed a distinctive filmmaking style.[20]

Truffaut's call to found a new *politique des auteurs*—a program or policy of the authors that would put a director's vision at the center of a film—was not only endorsed by film critics and theorists such as Alexandre Astruc and *Cahiers* director André Bazin but directly inspired the up-and-coming New Wave directors. More importantly, at least for the subject of this chapter, the policy of the authors had an echo in the United States, where it was imported, with some adjustments, by film critic Andrew Sarris. In "Notes on the Auteur Theory in 1962," Sarris adapted the French debate to the American context by arguing that the commercial nature of Hollywood cinema had forced U.S. directors to express their personality through visual style rather than adaptations of literary materials. In defining a great director as someone who is technically skilled, stylistically recognizable, and able to bestow an "interior meaning" upon his material, Sarris laid the foundations for the critical hierarchization of American cinema.[21] He proceeded himself to do so in *The American Cinema: Directors and Directions 1929–1968*, an influential book that reorganizes the history of cinema on the basis of directors' oeuvres.[22]

As we have seen, 1968 is also the year in which the Hays Code was terminated. If we situate the end of the Code-based censorship and Sarris's emphasis on personal style against the backdrop of the counterculture's critique of the consumer society and corporate culture, we can see how the DGA's efforts to emancipate directors from the studios were not only timely but historically necessary. From this angle, the end of the 1960s is the historic juncture at which Allen Smithee—the seeming anti-auteur—becomes a necessary possibility precisely because the crisis of the film industry set the conditions for the emergence of the director as artist and auteur. Thus the DGA's ability to turn the *Death of a Gunfighter* accident into a durable bargaining strategy is to be inscribed within historical conditions that allowed directors to gain unprecedented contractual power within the film industry.

And yet, the apparent success of the *politique des auteurs* also coincides with the rise of the marketable director-as-auteur, that is, with Hollywood's renewed ability to extract a profit from the directors' creative freedom. If in its Golden Age Hollywood had been able to lend a human face to its standardized production process by elevating actors to stars, the post-Fordist Hollywood of the 1970s added the director as "a kind of brand-name vision that precedes and succeeds the film."[23] Such a development implied that the studios' corporate authorship had to cede some rights to directorial authorship—a concept the DGA had first laid down in its 1964 Bill of Creative Rights. As we have seen, it took several years for the producers to fully accept the director's cut. In this respect, the introduction of Allen Smithee in 1969 signals that the studios had begun to recognize that a "brand-name vision" was valuable symbolic capital that could be protected by allowing individual directors to work outside of their reputation.

ALLEN SMITHEE AS A FUNCTION OF THE FILM INDUSTRY

As soon as the studios conceded these new rights, as the directors' bargaining body, the DGA was called to verify that its members would exercise them within certain boundaries. Because the removal of a director's name from the film credits represents a fundamental problem for the directing model the DGA intends to advance, the DGA does not allow its members to take their names off films for just any reason and replace them with just any pseudonym. Allen Smithee is the only pseudonym sanctioned by the DGA, which exercises absolute authority over its use. Thus, to receive a Smithee credit, a director had to prove his case before a DGA panel, which asked pointed questions about the filmmaking process:

> "It's like going to court," said one such [anonymous] director who recently went to the process. "They ask a lot of hostile questions. If they suspect you want to remove your credit because you're embarrassed by your own work or because the studio re-cut a scene, they tell you to piss off."[24]

Many of these questions are listed in the DGA's *Creative Rights Handbook* and range from the specific ("Did you participate in all casting?" "Did all notes to cast and crew come directly from you?" or "Did you get your cut without interference or 'cutting behind'?") to the general ("Were you consulted about *every* creative decision?").[25] Jeremy Braddock notes that the "Creative Rights Checklist"—the main section of the *Handbook*—and the accompanying Basic Agreement repurpose Foucault's author-function into a "director-function," which legally defines the director as a bureaucratic and managerial figure rather than a cultural or artistic entity.[26] In this sense, the checklist "is haunted by the unnamed, yet everywhere implicit specter of Smithee," so that "despite the DGA's best intentions, Allen Smithee is the director that best exemplifies these guidelines, for each description refers completely to the work done by the name and in the name of Allen Smithee."[27]

If the DGA verification protocols were meant to ensure that only those directors whose work had been manipulated could reclaim a Smithee credit, they also had the pragmatic function of solving complicated labor disputes. From this point of view, the DGA shares a common interest with the studios in ensuring that when such controversies arise, a film is properly signed so that it can be released. As Jonathan Eburne points out,

> although it is easy to think of Smithee as a pseudonym "standing in" for a missing film *auteur,* that is, as a name that marks incompleteness, it seems more productive to consider him quite literally as the figure nominated by the film industry to *complete* a film. Without

> necessarily making a film watchable, Smithee spares a company considerable financial losses by making a film *releasable,* allowing the company to cut its losses and to stave off further expenditures, losses, and potential lawsuits.[28]

If this is true, argues Eburne, then Allen Smithee should be understood as "an automatic auteur," that is, as a discursive function of the film industry rather than as a signifier of a Romantic gesture of refusal. In this sense, Smithee is both a ready-made that fulfills the industrial function of lending a director's name to a film and the alias that transforms a mass-produced object *into* a ready-made ("An Allen Smithee Film"). But because such ready-made denotes prevarication of a director's role, a Smithee credit predictably foreshadows a negative outcome at the box office. "In doing so," writes Eburne, "[Smithee] demonstrates how the production of films can be understood not just as the assembly line of moving pictures, but as a vast industry for producing meaning and opinion which can be studied and manipulated independently of the actual commercial product."[29]

Thus, on one hand, Smithee functions as an index of failure after the rise of the director-as-auteur within a post-Fordist Hollywood. On the other hand, Smithee may well have been the name of a *whatever director* within a Fordist organization of the studio system, that is, of any director who just executes the producers' directives. In this sense, as Braddock points out, the name of Allen Smithee invokes "the history of Hollywood-as-factory, the studio system that impersonally employed directors as if they were only of slightly more importance than the cinematographers, writers, editors, actors, casting agencies, and so forth, all of them equally and relatively anonymously involved in the making of the same movies."[30]

The conceptual tension between Allen Smithee as an interchangeable cog of the film industry (a whatever director) and Allen Smithee as a ready-made signature for a missing film auteur (an anti-auteur) can be explained historically with the transition from a Fordist Hollywood to a post-Fordist Hollywood. If Smithee-the-whatever-director insists on the level of property (which demands just a signature for a movie to be released), Smithee-the-anti-auteur concerns the level of propriety (which demands that a movie be signed by its supposedly real author). Whereas the DGA had originally introduced Smithee to signal impropriety, the increasing centrality of the film director to the production process led the DGA to progressively identify the director with the product that carries his name. Thus, as directors acquired important stakes in the film industry, the DGA came to inscribe directorial authorship within the economic rationality of film production. This meant that if, until the 1960s, directors could blame the studios for denying their creative vision, within a post-Fordist Hollywood, they had to ensure that protecting such vision would not jeopardize the movie's commercial viability.

TONY KAYE GOES TO HOLLYWOOD

The complicity between the DGA and film producers is evident if we consider that the DGA required directors who applied for a Smithee not to publicize their differences with the production company. For this reason, Smithee had to remain a carefully guarded secret, a keyword that allowed Hollywood insiders to recognize the violation of a director's rights without damaging the film before its release.

The compromising character of this provision became apparent when *American History X*—a movie directed by Tony Kaye and starring Edward Norton in the lead role of a Californian neo-Nazi—was about to hit the theaters in 1998. A cutting-edge British director of TV commercials at his first experience in Hollywood, Kaye applied for a Smithee credit with the DGA, claiming that the production company, New Line Cinema, had allowed Norton to change the final quarter of his film. While Kaye might have had a right to a Smithee under the DGA's protocol, his disagreements with New Line had received wide publicity *before* the movie's completion. Kaye had in fact run nearly forty full-page ads in trade papers such as *Variety* and *The Hollywood Reporter* denouncing both New Line and Norton.[31] On this ground, the DGA rejected his request. At this point, to make clear that the producers had ruined his film, Kaye asked to sign it as Humpty Dumpty. The DGA rejected this second request as well, offering him instead a choice of six "neutral" pseudonyms. Kaye refused to choose and filed instead a $275 million suit against the DGA and New Line for not allowing him to use Humpty Dumpty.[32] Commenting on the dispute, DGA president Jack Shea said, "The right to a pseudonym is not absolute or subject to unilateral determination by the DGA. Our agreement with the producers places certain obligations and conditions upon directors which they must meet in order to obtain a pseudonym."[33]

The Kaye–DGA clash is significant because it reveals the discursive structures that underpin the production of authorship in the film industry. By denying Kaye the use of Smithee and Dumpty, the DGA made clear that Kaye's alias was to be understood as a screen name to protect a personal reputation rather than as a commentary on a dispute between authors and producers. Smithee (or Humpty Dumpty) would have made that conflict explicit, thus fulfilling a positive function rather than a merely obfuscating one. Because the DGA had centralized a series of gestures of refusal under the same alias for nearly three decades, Smithee had in fact become a moniker for the DGA's own bargaining power, fulfilling a clearly delineated function within the MPAA–DGA negotiating process.

It is significant, however, that the DGA decided to prioritize this function—which was meant to protect the movie's commercial viability—over Kaye's right to criticize the production company. Kaye had in fact not only attacked New Line but had also failed to deliver the final director's cut within a reasonable amount of time. Because the DGA had always assured the studios that higher directorial control came with higher responsibility, it was hesitant to back a first-time director who had no contractual right to a director's cut and who had failed to meet Hollywood's standards of efficiency.[34] In this respect, the DGA made clear that a director had a right to access the authority and force of collective authorship only insofar as he was able to put his creativity at the service of a highly regulated production process.

Kaye's creativity, however, refused to be constrained by rules and regulations. In fact, Kaye saw his filmmaking as an extension of his mid-1990s "Hype Art," a series of conceptual "investigation[s] into the value of art." These included the hiring and exhibition of a homeless man at the Tate art gallery of London *(Roger, by Tony Kaye)* and the hijacking of a Damien Hirst exhibition of medical equipment by means of blaring ambulances driving around the gallery's block *(Empty Vessels Make the Most Noise)*.[35] According to New Line producer John Morrissey, Kaye "began to treat the movie like Hype Art" as soon as the first divergences with his company emerged. "And like all of Tony's work, he was its subject. The ads in the trades and all the controversy he created—it was all a giant conceptual art piece about him."[36] Determined to end the controversy, the producers decided to allow Kaye to use Smithee after all. But, according to Craig Saper, the DGA rejected New Line's request, prompting Kaye's suit.[37]

DECONSTRUCTING THE AUTEUR-FUNCTION

Soon after Kaye filed suit, one of his lawyers contacted Craig Saper as an expert witness on the trial. A film scholar, Saper had taught the graduate seminar *Auterism* and Artificiality in Film Studies at the University of Pennsylvania in 1997. The seminar had inspired the formation of the Allen Smithee Group, a collective of film scholars that embarked on the project of analyzing Smithee's work as a corpus in its own right, a real filmography whose consistency is guaranteed by a unifying signature rather than a unifying aesthetics or vision.

By noting how 1968 is the year in which both Sarris published his taxonomy of film auteurs and Roland Barthes famously proclaimed the death of the author, paving the way to deconstruction and demystification of bourgeois authorship, the group came to a consensus that the case of Allen Smithee "provides the best opportunity to apply the insights of poststructuralism to the trope of the *auteur*."[38] Since Sarris's adaptation of French auteur theory had proved functional to Hollywood's restructuring, the group focused on those dissonant voices within the French debate on auterism that provided fodder for alternative readings of the auteur-function.

In 1957, *Cahiers du cinéma* director Bazin had distanced himself from the more extreme auteurist positions by arguing that what made classical Hollywood films "admirable" was "not only the talent of this or that director, but the genius of the system, the richness of its ever-vigorous tradition, and its fertility when it comes into contact with new elements."[39] The group noted that as a signature that "requires no human author in order to function,"[40] Smithee is certainly a by-product of this genius and an excellent case study to operate a critical shift from auterism to "signateurism."[41] Saper refers to this shift as "artificial *auteurism*," noting that such theory

> allows for the study of the role of the director as a socioeconomic structure, the function of naming and names in Hollywood films.

> This figurative dimension of *auteurism* allows one to study it as a language system, or what Wittgenstein calls a "language game." How do we speak this language and defamiliarize it enough so that we can see it as a language—to see its figurative potential? How do we invoke its ability to be neither just another myth to demythologize, nor another natural fact to accept unproblematically, nor even an alternative to Hollywood, but to function as a way of writing that uses this structure as a generative procedure?[42]

One such generative procedure is the theory of the signature developed by Jacques Derrida in works such as *The Truth in Painting, Signsponge,* and *Glas.* Taking a descriptivist approach to the theory of naming, Derrida developed a method for interpreting an author's writing by retrieving latent connotations embedded in his name. Rather than functioning as marks of authentication, origin, and closure, signatures contain for Derrida phonetic and semantic connotations that can be mobilized *in association with* the texts in which they are embedded. Thus, in *Signsponge,* Derrida shows how, with a simple slippage, the name Ponge becomes *éponge* (sponge), a term that describes the "medusant character" and spongelike quality of Francis Ponge's poetry.[43] In other texts, Derrida follows the movement of antonomasia—by which a proper name slips into a common noun—to offer a critique of authors such as Hegel (which slips into *aigle,* or "eagle"), Genet (broom flower), and Kant (border or edge).[44]

Extending the movement of antonomasia across different languages, Christian Keathley notes that Smithee shares the same root with the word *blacksmith,* which is associated in English with the profession of shaping hot iron (thus bringing order, function, and identity to an object). In French, however, the blacksmith is known as a *forge,* a term that shares something with the opposite activity of counterfeiting and subverting the identity of an object:

> With this, we see clearly why Smithee is appropriate for our study, for the meaning of the name both implicates the act of signing, and calls it into question: precisely the issues at stake in *signateurism.* . . . The variation that a "Smithee" works on the process of forging is part of the inversion of value that occurs in the move from *auteurism* to *signateurism*: rather than signing a fraudulent work that he has

> produced with another's name that is itself associated with value, the Smithee forger offers an impostor's name to an authentic object, but one that is, according to the dominant system, without value.[45]

Thus Smithee is caught in a contradictory movement between forging as imparting order and identity and forging as counterfeiting. If Smithee-the-blacksmith allows a studio to release a film, thus completing an unfinished product, Smithee-the-forger denotes prevarication and failure, thereby voiding the symbolic capital attached to the auteur's name. I shall return to this contradiction—which I have previously referred to as the tension between Smithee-the-whatever-director and Smithee-the-anti-auteur—toward the end of this chapter. For now, I shall just note that if Smithee is a forger, there is no guarantee that the signature will perform the function the DGA designed it for. In fact, the Allen Smithee Group has noted that, in a number of instances, the *alias appears in the wrong place* in the film credits. It is by following this cue that we can trace the transformation of Smithee from a collective pseudonym that expresses the symbolic power of a formal organization like the DGA to an improper name that expresses multiple, sometimes contradictory, instances.

ANOMALOUS USES OF ALAN SMITHEE

For example, in *Student Bodies* (1981), a parody of the late-1970s slasher horror film subgenre, producer and codirector Michael Ritchie decided to remove his name from the film credits. But instead of replacing his directing credit with Smithee's, he left writer and codirector Mickey Rose to sign the film on his own and inserted a Smithee credit in the list of producers. The rationale of Ritchie's choice has never been made public, however, the appearance of Smithee as a producer undermines the assumption that the pseudonym symbolizes the authorial voice of Hollywood directors, pointing instead to a failure or glitch within the industrial filmmaking process.

The anomalous usage of the pseudonym is even more apparent in the case of *The Twilight Zone: The Movie* (1983), a four-part film in which the name "Alan Smithee" appears as a second assistant director credit in the segment directed by John Landis. (The other three directors were Steven Spielberg, Joe Dante, and George Miller.) The film is best known for a helicopter crash that caused the death of lead actor Vic Marrow and two child actors, Myca Dihn Le and Rebee Shinn Chen, during the shooting of a highly realistic night scene that simulated the bombing of a Vietnamese village. In the ensuing federal trial against Landis and four codefendants, the second assistant director Anderson House was granted immunity in exchange for his testimony. Subsequently, House decided to remove his name from the credit list and replace it with Alan Smithee.

Jessie Labov convincingly argues that the trial was a serious test case for the auteur theory on a legal and cultural level.[46] If directors had been claiming (and gradually obtaining) the right to oversee the entire production process, *The People v. John Landis et al.* was the first trial in which a director was indicted for an accident on a film set. Symbolically, the grand jury's indictments of Landis and the four codefendants for involuntary manslaughter were unsealed on the same day the movie opened, June 24, 1983. Furthermore, the DGA had to face a negative press campaign. In a long article published in the *New York Times Magazine,* Stuart Black charged that the DGA had taken steps to forestall proposals that would have given safety officials the final say over a director's decisions on the set.[47] This criticism was echoed by Randall Sullivan in a controversial article published by *Rolling Stone.* Linking auteur theory to Landis's role on the film set, Sullivan wrote, "What we have here is the auteur theory of homicide. . . . The question is whether credit has another side, an obverse angle, a yin for its yang; that is, responsibility."[48]

It is in this climate that Anderson House decided to dissociate himself and testify against Landis. As a second assistant director—a figure that usually functions as a liaison between the set and the production office—House was one of the few crew members who was fully aware of the potential danger associated with the filming of the incriminated scene. Because the bombing of the Vietnamese village involved the use of pyrotechnic explosions—whose premature ignition may have caused the helicopter crash—more than once during preproduction, he objected to the use of child actors and suggested replacing them with dolls or midget stunt doubles. But Landis insisted on keeping real actors on scene to obtain a more realistic effect, despite that industry regulations prohibited the use of underage actors after 6:30 P.M.[49]

The trial eventually led to the codefendants' acquittal and to an overhaul of the regulations involving the use of children during the shooting of risky scenes. It also created a rift within the film community, if it is true that camera operators and other crew members who had cooperated with the prosecution reported being "blackballed" in the months following their depositions.[50] House, who was at his first experience in a high-budget feature film, never worked in Hollywood again. Although it is impossible to verify the workers' claims in a period of high unemployment in the film industry, Labov argues that testifying against a Hollywood director automatically triggered memories of the role played by informers during the McCarthy era. Thus he poses the challenging question of whether House's choice to take a Smithee credit can be read as an attempt to dissociate himself not only from the film but also from "the equally career-damaging label of 'informer.'"[51] Such a question becomes the departure point for a meditation on the relation between Smithee and the use of pseudonyms in the blacklist era.

NAMES THAT CANNOT BE NAMED

The Hollywood blacklist was formally instituted by studio executives on November 25, 1947, the day after a group of writers and directors known as the Hollywood Ten were cited for contempt of Congress (and subsequently tried and incarcerated) for their refusal to testify before the House Un-American Activities Committee (HUAC). Created under the aegis of the MPAA to demonstrate that Hollywood was able to self-police communist infiltrations and political radicalism, the blacklist not only failed to stop the HUAC investigations but also generated a black market for screenplays in which independent producers sought the opportunity to purchase high-quality scripts at a lower cost. On their side, underpaid blacklisted writers had to struggle with the hardship of increasing their compensation when working through fronts or writing under pseudonyms that had no previous history.

As Jeffrey Smith has shown, Dalton Trumbo, the best known screenwriter of the Hollywood Ten, devised a sophisticated set of pseudonymous strategies that increased his asking price and contributed to breaking the blacklist by showing its untenability.[52] In 1957, to prevent Michael Wilson, another blacklisted writer of the Hollywood Ten, from winning an Oscar for *The Friendly Persuasion* (1956), the Academy enacted a bylaw that made a blacklistee ineligible for an Oscar. Unexpectedly, however, Trumbo won the

Best Original Story award for *The Brave One* (1956)—a script he had penned under the pseudonym Robert Rich. Because the film had not performed well in theaters and no one really expected it to win, the award created an embarrassing incident at the Academy Awards ceremony. Because nobody was approaching the stage to reclaim the Oscar (Trumbo was watching the ceremony on TV at home), the vice president of the Screen Writers Guild, Jesse Lasky Jr., rushed to the stage to accept the award on Rich's behalf, claiming that Rich was at the hospital for the birth of his first child.[53]

The press did not take long to realize that the name was an alias and quickly turned to Trumbo for confirmation. Furthermore, the incident had immediate repercussions for the production company, King Brothers, which now faced plagiarism suits, with different people claiming that Rich had stolen their idea for the script. Asked by the production company to give an interview to CBS's newsman Bill Stout, Trumbo neither confirmed nor denied his identification with Rich.[54] Instead, he suggested that because Michael Wilson was barred from winning an Oscar for *The Friendly Persuasion,* he might have written *The Brave One* so he would "have something to show for his year's work."[55]

Besides causing a national sensation, and embarrassing the Academy, the Stout interview allowed Trumbo "to dissociate himself from bad films he had written while, at the same time, linking himself to excellent films with which he actually had no connection."[56] In other words, it allowed him to capitalize on the symbolic value associated with some successful pseudonyms while detaching himself from less successful ones. It is in this reputational strategy of claiming or disowning a pseudonym that the first traces of Allen Smithee can be recognized.

In December 1957, given the notoriety acquired by Robert Rich—with CBS planning a comedy loosely based on the Academy Awards incident—Trumbo devised an elaborate plan to employ the pseudonym as a publicity stunt for *Mr. Adam,* a new script he had written for the King Brothers. The idea was to use two unknown pseudonyms during the period of cutting and advanced publicity of the film and switch them to Robert Rich on the opening night of the film. In a letter to his lawyer, Trumbo wrote that after identifying himself as Rich, he would have used "the best publicized writer's name in the world motion picture history" to claim the Oscar for *The Brave One* from the Academy, "and if they didn't come through with it, bring suit against them" and "laugh this fucking blacklist out of existence."[57] In the end, *Mr. Adam* was never produced because it failed to pass the test of the Motion Picture Production Code. But in the following years, blacklisted writers, such as Nedrick Young, Carl Foreman, and Michael Wilson, continued to embarrass the Academy by winning Oscars for *The Bridge on the River Kwai* (1957) and *The Defiant Ones* (1958). After this series of incidents proved the untenability of the blacklist, Dalton Trumbo became the first blacklistee to obtain a film credit for Stanley Kubrick's *Spartacus* (1960).

Aside from its all-star cast (Kirk Douglas, Laurence Olivier, Jean Simmons, Charles Laughton, and Peter Ustinov), *Spartacus* is known for the climatic scene in which the revolting slaves captured by Crassus are asked to identify their leader in exchange for leniency. Instead of complying, the slaves stand up and shout out, one by one, "I am Spartacus!" thus sharing their leader's fate. In light of Trumbo's personal experience, I believe that this scene can be read as an allegory of the Hollywood Ten's refusal to give the names of suspected communist sympathizers to the HUAC and their willingness to go to jail. (Besides inspiring similar scenes in cult movies such as *I Am Cuba* [1964] and *Malcolm X* [1992], as we shall see in the next chapter, this scene also became a pop culture reference for the Luther Blissett Project.)

There are several reasons why the blacklist came to an end. Some of them—such as the end of the Korean War and the decline of McCarthyism in the late 1950s—are broadly historical and supersede the world of cinema. If we stick to the internal dynamics of the film industry, however, there is no doubt that Trumbo's clever manipulation of the pseudonym-effect played a role in breaking the blacklist. With the Academy Awards ceremony being televised since 1953, screenwriters' names and faces had become integral to the Hollywood spectacle. As such, they inevitably attracted a great deal of media attention. It is by carefully exploiting the contradiction of names that could not be named at the very heart of the film industry—an industry whose secrets are constantly exposed to the public—that Trumbo and his allies won the consensus necessary to break the blacklist.

And yet for every Robert Rich, there are dozens of pseudonymous scripts and missing film credits that were never claimed insofar as they were attached to flops or ordinary films that simply were not worth being claimed. In 1991, Larry Ceplair asked several ex-blacklistees whether it any longer mattered who wrote what:

> Abraham Polonsky answered: "Yes it matters, no it does not matter." If it is a good movie, an award-winning movie, or a history-changing movie, then he thinks it matters. For the ordinary run of movies, however, it does not."[58]

Labov notes that Allen Smithee shares something with the pseudonymous authorship of this ordinary run of movies, namely, "the capacity to absorb failure and reconstitute an author's good name."[59] But whereas the pseudonyms of the blacklist era were "use and throw," Smithee serialized and congealed this capacity to absorb failure into a standardized *disowning-function,* which operates in many ways as the obverse of the author-function outlined at the beginning of this chapter.

THE DISOWNING-FUNCTION AND THE DEMISE OF ALLEN SMITHEE

As previously noted, when an author manipulates an alias to claim successful works and spark curiosity in her actual identity, the pseudonym accumulates a symbolic capital (a socially recognized competence) that can be easily converted into exchange value. Certainly the use-and-throw pseudonyms of the blacklist era did not live long enough to build a reputation of their own. By contrast, the Smithee signature has accumulated over time a negative symbolic capital (a socially recognized *in*-competence) that can damage the commercial success of a film.

Thus it is not the sheer accumulation of disowned movies that determines Smithee's depressing effect on the box office but the concrete risk that the signature's true meaning can be exposed to the general public. Such exposure can occur through multiple channels. If the *American History X* controversy had the effect of publicizing Smithee more than the DGA and the MPAA ever intended, in 1998 Disney released a film based on the case of Alan Smithee—a move that eventually forced the DGA to discontinue the pseudonym. Meant to be a satire of the Smithee phenomenon, *An Alan Smithee Film: Burn Hollywood Burn* tells the story of a director whose real name is Alan Smithee and who desperately tries to disassociate himself from a film that has been brutally recut by the producer. As soon as he realizes that he cannot do it—because the only pseudonym allowed by the DGA is precisely Alan Smithee—he steals the film and goes on the run, threatening to burn it.

Despite the original screenplay, a $10 million budget, and cameo appearances by film stars such as Sylvester Stallone, Whoopi Goldberg, and Jackie Chan, the film was a spectacular fiasco, grossing only $45,779 at the box office.[60] Furthermore, it fell victim to its own plot when director Arthur Hiller objected to writer and producer Joe Eszterhas's recutting of the film, demanding a Smithee credit. Finally, consistent with the bad reputation that was preceding every Alan Smithee film, *Burn Hollywood Burn* received exceptionally negative reviews and won more Golden Raspberry Awards than any film before it, including the award for Worst Picture of 1998.[61] From this angle, it is ironic that the DGA's decision to get rid of the name was motivated as a consequence of the "irreparable damage" inflicted by Eszterhas to Smithee's reputation.[62] In fact, it is hard to imagine a more appropriate way for Smithee to crown a thirty-year-long career than with a disastrous film that exhibits in its very title the ready-made mark of failure.

Thus, by 1998, the meaning of Alan Smithee had shifted from a Hollywood inside joke to an open secret. If Kaye had tested the legal boundaries of the DGA's monopoly over the alias and the Allen Smithee Group had claimed that Smithee was an author in its own right, *Burn Hollywood Burn* signaled that the film studios were no longer willing to recognize Smithee's function. My wager is that these legal, conceptual, and political challenges turned an alias that was meant to protect an author's reputation into an improper name that explicitly denoted conflict within the film industry. To be sure, the growing visibility of Allen Smithee meant that its symbolic power kept increasing. And yet the DGA renounced the opportunity to exercise such power insofar as the name now compromised the producers' interests.

It is worth remarking that if Smithee became an openly contended alias only in the late 1990s, its negative reputation had grown slowly and organically through a filmography that, by linking works that had nothing in common other than their signature, destabilized a model of authorship figured along the masculine metaphor of the director as a film's sole and rightful father. Ironically, *this is precisely the model of authorship the DGA had been advocating since the 1960s.* Thus we face here the paradox by which the authorizing context that controls access to Smithee has set in motion a filmography of mixed parentage, which undermines the ordering function of bourgeois authorship—and this despite the industry's best efforts to reduce Smithee to nothing other than a mere placeholder for a real director.

As previously shown, as soon as modern copyright replaced aristocratic patronage, authorship came to conflate property and propriety, ownership and reputation. As the cultural and economic values of intellectual products tend to find their identity in the marketplace, reputation becomes critical in determining the value of an author's name. By removing the auteur from the film credits and exposing Hollywood as a machine designed to produce commodities for profit, not art, Alan Smithee decouples authorship into a cultural layer and an economic layer. Thus, as soon as we stop considering Smithee as a name that simply "stands in" for a missing film auteur, on a cultural level we discover a filmography of mixed parentage. On an economic level, the studio system is laid bare as a money-making machinery that enables the trope of the auteur only to lend a human face to its standardizing procedures and impersonal style.

I refer to this decoupling, which suspends the amalgamation of ownership and reputation set in motion by modern authorship, as the *disowning-function.* If Foucault introduced the author-function to refer to the author as a function of discourse that embeds a set of authenticating procedures, the disowning-function can help us think through a subtractive strategy that delegitimizes not only a cultural product but also and foremost the discursive structures that govern the culture industry. Slavoj Žižek's notion of "violent subtraction" from a hegemonic field of operation is of some use here. Žižek argues that a violent subtraction does not attempt to attack and destroy a ruling power dialectically (as in the case of a purely destructive, "terrorist," negation), nor does it limit itself to fleeing society to create a new space on the outside (as in the case of a New Age meditative withdrawal). Rather, an effective subtraction from a field of hegemonic relations

> violently *affects* this field itself, laying bare its true coordinates. Such a subtraction does not add a third position to the two positions whose tension characterizes the hegemonic field. . . . This third term rather

> "denaturalizes" the whole hegemonic field, bringing out the underlying complicity of the opposed poles that constitute it.[63]

In our case, the film industry's hegemonic field is constituted by the MPAA and the DGA—two organizations that are in an antagonistic relation yet also share an interest in ensuring that films are released. Although Smithee was originally introduced to serve such interest, as soon as it was *recognized* as denoting abuse of a director's vision, it brought to the surface "the underlying complicity" of the poles that constitute Hollywood's order of the discourse. In this perceptual shift from Smithee's normalizing function to Smithee's destabilizing potential, we can recognize what Žižek defines as

> the art of a "politics of minimal differences": to be able to identify and then focus on a minimal (ideological, legislative, and so on) measure which, *prima facie,* not only does not question the system's premises, but even seems to merely apply its own principles to its actual functioning and thus render it more consistent with itself; however, a critico-ideological "parallax view" leads us to surmise that this minimal measure, while in no way disturbing the system's explicit mode of functioning effectively "moves underground," introduces a crack in its foundation.[64]

That this perceptual shift is not merely subjective but "is always-already inscribed into the perceived object itself," as Žižek refers to the parallax view in Lacanian terms, is evident from the fact that as soon as Smithee becomes contended, it takes a life of its own.[65] In fact, each iteration of the Smithee credit not only occurs before a different economic, historical, and political background but is itself generative of displacements that ultimately undermine the ability of its progenitor to contain the virtuality of the alias within the hegemonic field of labor relations.

Such displacements of Smithee's original function are evident in at least three distinct circumstances. In the case of the Kaye–DGA controversy, Smithee is the absent cause that sets in motion a legal dispute over who has the right to control the name of the author in Hollywood. In the case of the second assistant director of *The Twilight Zone: The Movie,* rather than expressing the directors' moral force and bargaining power, Smithee comes to signify the refusal to be blacklisted *by* the film community and to partake in its self-absolving rituals. Finally, this dissociation of Smithee from itself is also evident in *Burn Hollywood Burn*, where Smithee's secret normalizing function as a ready-made signature is rendered public as it is turned into the subject of a major Hollywood production. In all these circumstances, Smithee comes to express disputes and unauthorized appropriations that cannot be properly integrated within the regulated field of labor relations, thus "disturbing the system's explicit mode of functioning."[66]

In sum, in this chapter, I have traced the transformation of Allen Smithee from a collective pseudonym that was originally meant to express a compromise between the organized interests of Hollywood film directors and those of Hollywood producers to an improper name that exposes Hollywood's order of the discourse. On a first level, such a transformation was made possible by Smithee's slow but constant accumulation of negative symbolic capital, that is, of a recognized and, above all, recognizable incompetence that threatened to undermine the valorization cycle of a motion picture. The withdrawal of the director's signature was all the more significant because it concerned a professional figure that had become central to the post-Fordist Hollywood. (As we shall see in chapter 4, autonomist–Marxist theorists such as Mario Tronti and Antonio Negri see the withdrawal of labor as a motive force in capitalist restructuring.) On a second level, Smithee's exposure was fueled by conflicts that could not be productively regulated by the film industry. Such conflicts had the effect of turning Smithee into a positive assemblage of enunciation whose overt political function could not be reconciled with the DGA's efforts to carve out a greater creative autonomy for film directors in exchange for greater efficiency and productivity.

As previously noted, the DGA was hardly a radical union. Among the three unions that organized Hollywood's creative workers (screenwriters, actors, and directors), the DGA was the one that placed the greater emphasis on the creative aspects of the profession. Since the constitution of the Screen Directors Guild in 1936, Hollywood directors understood their guild as a bargaining body whose function was primarily to ensure that the profession could be performed according to certain self-determined standards. In this sense, the DGA revived the customary legality of the textile guilds and trades that we encountered in the previous chapter. From this angle, Smithee shares with Ludd the function of expressing a guild's aspiration to bring under its purview every aspect of a profession, including the regulation of apprenticeship, safety measures, and the adoption of specific technologies. But whereas Ludd was created at a time in which the customary legislation of the guild system was in decline, Smithee was forged at a time in which the power of film directors was on the rise.

It is precisely the success of the DGA's auteurist model that gave Smithee the visibility that eventually put this very model into crisis. This is particularly clear if we consider that after the DGA officially discontinued the alias, Smithee remained in use as a self-parodic commentary, mostly to author films and video that have little artistic merit.[67] It is worth underscoring, once again, that the DGA had introduced a verification protocol to regulate the mode of disposition and usage of the alias precisely to prevent directors from disowning movies they were simply embarrassed by. Thus, by disowning a pseudonym that embodies the very act of disowning, the DGA removed the only authorizing context whereby Smithee's iterations could be articulated as a collective practice. In this respect, if the DGA's monopoly over Smithee lends itself to criticism, the lack of a more or less formalized context whereby collective decisions regarding the access to a shared pseudonym can be made is also problematic as it can weaken the alias's symbolic power. As we shall see in the next chapter, the artists who launched Monty Cantsin soon came to realize that the lack of clear guidelines concerning the pseudonym's use unleashed internal conflicts that could not be easily mediated and solved.

3

MONTY CANTSIN, THE OPEN POP STAR

Neoism is a state of mind. This is why it transforms itself according to the situations it encounters. Neoism applies itself to everything, and yet it is nothing; it is the point at which all opposites collapse.

—THE UNKNOWN NEOIST

To repeat is to behave in a certain manner, but in relation to something unique or singular which has no equal or equivalent.

—GILLES DELEUZE

At the end of the previous chapter, I noted how Allen Smithee and Ned Ludd share, from a discursive standpoint, several features. First, the myths of origin surrounding both aliases are associated with accidents and breakdowns in laboring practices. Second, both Smithee and Ludd were employed for collective bargaining purposes in times of industrial crisis. Third, the notoriety accrued by both aliases undermined their creators' ability to control and fully leverage their symbolic power for such purposes. Thus, in taking a life of their own, Ludd and Smithee evolved from collective pseudonyms to *multiple-use names*—a term that denotes a more decentralized use of a pseudonym.

But what happens when a pseudonym is not created to confront a counterpart or to represent a defined professional category but simply as a name anyone can borrow? Shall this strategy still be considered collective? And is it possible (and desirable) for the users of such names to introduce norms that can regulate their mode of disposition and usage?

The case of Monty Cantsin, an "open pop star" created by a group of mail artists in Portland, Oregon, in 1977, provides a useful starting point for addressing these questions. In fact, Monty Cantsin is to my knowledge the first experiment in which a pseudonym was released in the public domain with virtually *no guidelines or instructions for use.* In other words, whereas only textile workers and film directors initially had access to Ned Ludd and Allen Smithee, respectively, anyone could adopt the name

"Monty Cantsin" from the beginning, with no further requirements. In this respect, the Monty Cantsin strategy can be elegantly summarized in one simple statement: "The name is fixed, the people using it aren't."[1]

And yet the creation and circulation of the multiple-use name within the Mail Art network and the artistic fringes of the punk movement confined its potentially unlimited uses to a specific milieu. While such milieu had ramifications in many countries, its participants shared common interests and a set of practices, and in some cases even an ethos and a lifestyle. This does not mean that the Monty Cantsins were in agreement on how the name was to be used and to what ends. Furthermore, as we shall see, Monty Cantsin was only one of the shared pseudonyms that circulated within the Mail Art network.

In this chapter, I explore the tension between the semantic chaos that can be theoretically generated by a proper name available to anyone for any use and the existence of a shared ethos among some of the actual users of the name. In particular, Monty Cantsin stems from a community of practice, the Mail Art network, that habitually subjected the names of senders and recipients to pseudonymous permutations to turn them into the very subject of the mailed object. As we shall see, this sociopoetic dimension of mail art was rooted in a gift economy that embedded a set of ethical norms underpinning the exchange and possible exhibition of mail art.

My wager is that with the invention of Monty Cantsin, the inclusive, participatory, and selfless ethos of mail art came unwittingly into conflict with a cognitive nihilism that aimed at destroying all truth-claims. Embodied by Neoism—a pseudo-avant-garde that became strictly associated with the multiple-use name—this nihilistic approach claimed to eschew all categorizations.[2] Yet it could also not determine how Cantsin was to be shared by a community of users. In this sense, as an improper name, Cantsin came to express a conflict between those who saw it as an epitome of insoluble cognitive contradictions and those who tried to endow it with a political function in the wake of avant-gardes such as Dada, Fluxus, and the Situationist International.

Among the latter is certainly the British novelist, pamphleteer, and cultural activist Stewart Home. Perhaps the person who has contributed the most to the development and historicization of the multiple-use name concept, Home was one of the first persons to understand that without guidelines (and thus without an ethos), the multiple-use name strategy was doomed to fail. Thus, along with other mail artists who had tinkered with similar practices and concepts, he used the lessons of the Monty Cantsin experiment to advise the new generation of activists who were to launch the Luther Blissett Project in the 1990s.

According to Home, the first to play with the idea that a name could be shared by many individuals for artistic purposes was the group Blitzinformation. Cofounded by British mail artists Adam Czarnowski and Stefan Kukowski in the mid-1970s, Blitzinformation circulated a leaflet that invited all readers to become Klaos Oldanburg. By filling out a form and mailing it back to the artists, participants were assigned a progressive Roman numeral (e.g., Klaos Oldanburg XXIII, prev. John Smith).[3] In this way, the name accumulated symbolic capital every time someone borrowed it for creative purposes. Home criticizes the use of numerals and the reference to the user's legal name for retaining traces of the individuals behind the alias—that is to say, for not being abstract enough. He contends that the movement of multiple-use names toward a thorough depersonalization was complete by 1982, when "a group of anarcho-*art* punks from the London suburbs launched a 'movement' called the Generation Positive . . . with a call for all rock bands to use the name White Colours."[4] However, when Home initiated White Colours and, two years later, the multiple-use magazine *SMILE,* he was not yet aware that Monty Cantsin had been invented in Portland as early as 1977.

ORIGINS OF MONTY CANTSIN

At the time, Portland was a city with a vibrant punk scene and a hub of the international Mail Art network. Artists such as Al "Blaster" Ackerman and his friend David "Oz" Zack, Maris Kundzins, Tom Cassidy (aka Musicmaster), Kay Hocket (aka Rhoda Mappo), Steve Minor, John Shirley, Billy Haddock, and bands like the Neo Boys and Smegma frequently opened their bohemian homes and studios to traveling mail artists such as Lon Spiegelman, Cees Hacke, and Anna Banana as well as to performers and musicians like the British duo Genesis P-Orridge and Cosey Fanni Tutti. Some of these artists visited only for a few days or weeks. Others, attracted by the sparkling cultural milieu and the communal forms of living, stayed for longer periods.

This was the case with Istvan Kantor, a Hungarian-born Canadian performance artist who moved into David Zack's house in 1978.[5] The two had met in 1976 at the Young Artists' Club in Budapest, in one of the rare circumstances in which Zack had collected his mail art—mostly Xeroxed collages, drawings, and little booklets—for a solo exhibition. As Kantor recalls,

> [Zack] made collages from letters and photo documents, adding them with his own scribbles, typewritten notes, stickers, signs, drawings. He copied them and sent them to mail artists. He never kept originals either, making clear that the copy, including the process of copying, was the poem. Zack not only appropriated the works but he used the authors' name as well, crediting his own stuff to William Blake, Leonardo Da Vinci, dr Ackerman, Antonin Artaud, Istvan Kantor and others.[6]

Given his predisposition to appropriating other people's names, Zack came up with the idea of creating a pseudonym that anyone could borrow. As Zack recounts in a letter to Berlin Neoist Graf Haufen, the idea formed while he was using copy machines and tape recorders along with his Latvian friend, poet, and visual artist Maris Kundzins:

> Maris and I were in Portland. We'd been working with a Xerox 3107 that makes big copies and reductions. We were making giant folios; *monster folios* and *dinosaur folios* we called them. And one night Maris started fooling around with the tape recorder, singing songs in Latuvian [*sic*] about toilets and traffic. Well, we decided to make a pop star out of Maris. But it had to be an open pop star, that is, anyone who wanted could assume the personality of the pop star. . . . We were mouthing Maris Kundzins' name, and it came out Monty Cantsins. Then we got to saying *can't sin* and *can't sing* and quite a few other things to give the impression that this pop star could be a thief as well as a saint.[7]

If Zack's account is accurate, the name "Monty Cantsins" was generated by a certain playful alliteration on Kundzins's name. Besides being typical of sound poetry experiments—in which both Zack and Kundzins were well versed—it is significant that this game of repetition and variation on a name was performed before a recording device. In fact, tape recorders and Xerox machines were largely in use among mail artists and multiplied the exchanges of sound and paper collages within the Mail Art network.

As we shall see, the very emergence of the international Mail Art network in the early to mid-1970s would have not been possible without these technologies of automatic reproduction. While the wider accessibility of these technologies multiplied and "democratized" the production of collages, it also determined a transformation in the nature of the network. With less available time to respond to incoming mailings, each artist had to devise strategies to keep up with her correspondence. We have seen how Zack's elegant solution to this problem was simply to photocopy, cut up, and forward letters and postcards coming from different artists, sometimes simply adding a drawing or a ready-made signature.

Like Zack, since the beginning of his mail art activity, Al Ackerman had been relying on multiple pseudonyms—a practice he had borrowed from science fiction writers of the 1930s and 1940s such as Harry Bates and Clark Ashton Smith, who recurred to multiple pen names to differentiate their hyperprolific production.[8] As Ackerman himself recounts in a letter to Lloyd Dunn, in envisioning the Monty Cantsin concept, Zack simply reversed this practice:

> My custom in those days was to use a lot of different names when I did my mailings. I had about ten different pseudonyms or personas that I operated under. I'm sorry I can't reveal any of them here. Mainly my use of multiple names and aliases was a practical rather than a theoretical matter—a question of covering my tracks and throwing my enemies off the trail. Zack, who had matriculated at the University of Chicago and was strong on art theory, took this and reversed it. Instead of one person operating under a lot of different names, Zack came up with the concept that one name could be used by a lot of different persons. He proposed, at one of the meetings of The 14 Secret Masters of the World (a deeply secret organization that met in his front room) to bestow this general all-purpose "name" on Kantor. The name that Zack had come up with was "Monty Cantsin." The idea being that anybody could become "Monty Cantsin" and in this way

> achieve pop stardom. Thus, Kantor became "Monty Cantsin—Open Pop Star." It was a deeply historic moment. A Tuesday, as I recall.[9]

Even though Ackerman's account omits the role Kundzins played in the conception of the open pop star, it is only Kantor who kept using the nom de plume (dropping the final "s") consistently in the following years and decades.[10] As we shall see, Kantor's "overenthusiastic" appropriation of Monty Cantsin caused tension with other participants in the Neoist network, especially after Stewart Home and other European artists decided to join it.

In the beginning, Kantor's use of the name in Portland caused several amusing equivocations that were partly due, according to various reports, to the Hungarian's poor command of English. As Ackerman recalls with his characteristic sense of humor, Zack's friend Jerry Sims, who was supposed to become Kantor's "business manager," disliked his music so much that the unknowing Hungarian was never booked in a club. With Kundzins not much invested in the project, Zack's original plan to use the local music scene as a launch pad for the open pop star never took off. Thus the endemic lack of income forced Kantor and friends to choose a different, if rather unusual, theater of operations for Cantsin's early performances: the convenience stores of Portland:[11]

> These always took the same general form. Kantor, in the role of "Monty Cantsin," would enter a convenience store, go to the back and pretend to have a heart attack; he did this primarily in Hungarian which added a good deal to the confusion and uproar that would then ensue, and when the store manager and the other customers were being distracted sufficiently by "Monty Cantsin's" "heart attack" at the rear of the store, Zack would dart in at the front and carry out as many cases of beer or soda pop as he could manage to lift and exit with it. Then "Monty Cantsin" would pretend to recover from his attack, get up and beat it out of the store. This went on for many months, on an average of 4–5 times a week, at different convenience stores around town.[12]

Thus, in its early stages, the multiple-use name does not function much as an open reputation nor as a critique of the music industry's manufacturing of the pop star. Rather, Cantsin is associated here with day-to-day *survival tactics*—such as shoplifting or asking for change—that were also a distinctive mark of the late-1970s punk subculture. This means that a "disembodied" reading of Cantsin as a purely authorial strategy (à la Allen Smithee) would be reductive in that it would overlook the efforts of *being Monty Cantsin in the everyday* made by Kantor and friends. Conversely, it would be equally reductive to consider the open pop star as a random collection of tricks and make-dos that had nothing to do with cultural production.

As a matter of fact, in summer 1978, the Portland group evolved the Cantsin idea in a new direction. Through multiple appropriations, Cantsin was to become the front figure of a new art movement called ISM—a suffix that "stood for an incorporation of all the previous movements (-isms) of the avant-garde."[13] In late 1978, with Ackerman moving to Texas and Zack expatriating to Mexico, Kantor returned to Canada and settled in Montreal. In February 1979, Kantor organized the mail art exhibition *Brain in the Mail* at Véhicule Art, a local artist-run organization.[14] After this exhibition, Kantor evolved ISM (or No ISM) into Neoism, a pseudo-avant-garde whose very name paradoxically conflates the avant-garde's claim to originality (Neo-) with its standardization into a coherent body of aesthetic, philosophical, and political theories (-ism).

NEOISM NOW!

In Montreal, Kantor came into contact with a group of young artists, musicians, and philosophers who were heavily influenced by French existentialism and, according to Baltimore-based Neoist John Berndt, had "a very right-wing, crackpot brown-shirt fascist aesthetics."[15] This group—which included Tristan Stéphane Renaud (aka Zbigniew Brotgehirn), Jean-Luc Bonspiel (aka Kiki Bonbon), Pierre Zovile (aka Boris Wanowitch), Alan Sanchez (aka Alan Lord), R. U. Sevol, and Napoléon Moffat, among others—played a key role in developing the early phase of Neoism.[16]

The first action to publicly announce Neoism took place in Montreal on Election Day on May 22, 1979. It was called *Monty Cantsin Sits for a Portrait*. Passersby were invited to sit on a "Neoist chair" and have their picture taken, to be exhibited later as part of a series of Monty Cantsin portraits. "Because it was Election Day, people were curious if it was part of a political campaign," Kantor remembers. "They wanted to know what was Neoism. I tried not to say anything that could have sounded like a clear definition. That wasn't hard since I didn't have any."[17] In the following years, the action was repeated during Neoist gatherings and was simply meant to invite anyone to become a Neoist by sitting on a Neoist chair.[18]

According to Stewart Home, the group continued with a graffiti campaign on the walls of Montreal that reproduced and updated slogans of the French '68, such as "Liberate Imagination," "Never Work," "Seek Beauty Desire Passion," and "Everything before the 90's." In 1980, the Neoists "occupied" the Montreal art gallery Motivation 5, setting up a video link between the two floors of the gallery. Home contends that by then Neoism had replaced its original fascination for French Existentialism with a preference for Italian Futurism. In this sense, as the latest, edgiest technology for the production of art, "video was to the Neoists what the motor car was to Marinetti."[19]

Despite Home's attempt to portray the early Neoist poetics as a superficial exaltation of technology and of the new for its own sake, Futurism was probably not a major source of inspiration for early Neoists as the activities of the Montréal group were not reducible to a unified aesthetics.[20] As Home himself notes, more recent art movements, such as Fluxus and the New Wave subculture, played an important role. In particular, Kantor's *Blood Campaign*—a series of art performances launched in 1979 in which Kantor had his blood taken by a nurse—was originally inspired by the Fluxfeasts.[21] Whereas in the first few years Kantor planned to sell his blood "as an art object" to fund Neoism, in 1985 he began splashing vials of his own blood onto famous museums' gallery walls, including the Musée d'Art Contemporain in Montreal (1985), New York's MoMA (1988), the National Gallery of Canada in Ottawa (1991), and the Ludwig Museum in Koln, Germany (1998), to name a few. During these performances—which often resulted in the ban of the artist from the site and occasionally in arrest—Kantor–Cantsin traced a large "X" with his plasma between paintings or behind sculptures. The "donation" of these "gifts" was usually accompanied by other performative gestures such as singing Hungarian revolutionary songs or Neoist manifestos with electro-pop, New Wave, and industrial music backgrounds.[22]

On one hand, Kantor's interventions can be seen as a neo-avant-garde attack on the separation between art and daily life characteristic of modern art as well as a critique of exploitation in the art world.[23] (As Kantor puts it, "without of the blood of artists, there would be no museums."[24]) On the other hand, Kantor's punk haircuts, paramilitary uniforms, and grotesque singing style can be seen as a humorous travesty of body-art shock performances such as those of Chris Burden, Coum Transmission, Marina Abramovic, and the Viennese Actionists.[25]

Although Neoism has created multiple contradictory definitions of itself to defy categorization, it is probably not inaccurate to say that the Neoists only *performed* the resurgence of a modern avant-garde art movement. Such a resurgence was based on the emulation of typical avant-garde gestures such as the manifesto and the performance. But rather than expressing a coherent aesthetics or (revolutionary) program, Neoist texts seem to express irresolvable contradictions and disagreements among the Neoists. And their performances are often marked by farcical, nonsensical poses that are parodic in character. This ironic stance signals that Neoism exhibits an acute awareness of the impossibility of reviving the avant-garde, which is nevertheless evoked in several texts and actions.[26]

In this respect, repetition, citation, and irony are all features that set Neoism squarely in the postmodern camp. At the same time, "the Neoists wanted to avoid any single meaning imposed on their activities," as Home points out. "Thus Neoism was viewed simultaneously as modernist, postmodernist, an avant-garde transgression of modem and post-modem traditions, as underground, Neo-Dadaist and an outgrowth of Fluxus. It was also a rejection of all these things."[27] Furthermore, the personal commitment of some Neoists to experiencing these contradictions in their daily lives makes Neoism more similar to an experimental practical philosophy than an eclectic restaging of the modern avant-garde. In this sense, Neoism and Monty Cantsin cannot be understood outside of the Neoist experimentations, many of which took place in the context of bodily "gatherings and drills" known as the apartment festivals.

THE TRAVELING CIRCUS OF THE NEOIST APARTMENT FESTIVALS

Perhaps the most important contribution of the Montreal group to Neoism is the conception and organization of the International Neoists Apartment Festivals, weeklong semiprivate events held in the homes of "conspirators."

Also known as APTs, the apartment festivals kicked off in Montreal and continued on a yearly basis in various European and North American cities throughout the 1980s—becoming an opportunity for the Neoists to share live music, installations, performance art, screenings, conversations, confrontations, and friendship.

The first two APTs were organized in Montreal apartments in September 1980 and February 1981. The latter was attended by tENTATIVELY a CONVENIENCE—a self-styled "Mad Scientist / d-composer / Sound Thinker / Thought Collector"—and several members of the Krononauts, "a time-traveling society" based in Baltimore.[28] In a report of the event, tENTATIVELY describes apartment festivals as convivial gatherings, "neither 'performance-art' nor 'installation' festivals," but rather traveling parties *(fêtes mobiles)* of the emerging Neoist network:

> APT like Neoism as minus the superfluous middle which would disgustingly make it ART. APT as APT. APT as apartment: a space again skipping the ART intermediate of performance spaces as buffer between public & performer's private life, the Peking Poolroom as Kiki Bonbon's APT.[29]

In the following months, with tENTATIVELY becoming one of the main engines of the network, new APT festivals were held in Baltimore (APT 3, May–June 1981), simultaneously in Montreal and Toronto (APT 4, October 1981), and New York (APT 5, March 1982).

The New York APT showcased a wide range of Neoist activities, some of which took place indoors, at the artist loft Des Refusés, and others outdoors, in the streets of the West Village and the Lower East Side. Gordon W. Zealot, a former Hare Krishna and one of the publishers of Toronto's *END Paper,* set up a mobile kitchen on West Broadway and fed Neoists with greens and wind bread. Istvan Kantor (who later moved to New York as the "Self-Appointed Leader of the People of the Lower East Side") made a campfire at the corner of Houston and First Avenue. Napoléon Moffat distributed "Akademgorod keys" in Washington Square and read aloud a neo-Futurist text titled "The Legitimacy of Akademgorod":

> I'm in search of Akademgorod. I'm still searching for Akademgorod. Akademgorod is the city of scientists in Russia, in Siberia. It is a city

> built for destruction. It is also a city where all the brains of Russia think and create the *end*. Neoists should be in search of the city of scientists, in search of Akademgorod. The project is to find the city of Akademgorod and, by being there, justify the city. Neoists are living, are surviving by eating high technology. I'm ephemerally here, in this city, to ask you to join the crusade for Akademgorod. The goals of the crusade are to find the city and then establish the reality of Neoism into the reality of Akademgorod. *Be a part of Akademgorod.*[30]

Many Neoists took Moffat's call to search for Akademgorod seriously and began referring to the city as the "Promised Land of Neoism," making it a topos of the Neoist mythology. Whereas the real Akademgorod is a Siberian research town founded by the Soviet Academy of Sciences in the 1950s, the imaginary city of Neoism is the center of the "Great Confusion," where the measuring of time has been suspended (in Akademgorod "it's always six o' clock") and anything is possible.[31] Thus, in a typical Neoist inversion, a symbol of maximum order and control such as a scientific town in a totalitarian state is transformed into a symbol of total freedom and chaos.

In summer 1982, the Neoist network set its temporary headquarters in Würzburg, West Germany, for the "Neoist Network's First European Training Camp." The Neoists continued to perform public interventions, such as offering free haircuts to the passersby, and engaged in a series of Fluxus-inspired performances. In particular, Pete Horobin developed "Principle Player," an impersonal identity anyone could borrow to perform a set of scripts.[32] Even though the Würzburg training camp was attended by a small number of participants, its significance lies in the fact that Neoism was made available as an embodied practice to a number of European mail artists and networkers. As a consequence, between 1982 and 1985, a few artists and activists based in different European cities joined the Neoist ranks. Some of these Europeans—which included Pete Horobin and Stewart Home (London), Graf Haufen and Stiletto (Berlin), Arthur Berkhoff (Amsterdam / Almelo), and Vittore Baroni (Forte dei Marmi, Italy)—deepened the conceptual exploration of Neoism and Monty Cantsin.

For instance, Reinhardt U. Sevol—an early Montreal Neoist who had returned to Paris in the mid-1980s—started N. O. Cantsin and "Anti-Neoism," a schismatic fringe that claimed that Neoism never existed as such and was, in the words of Monty Cantsin, "simply a reaction to anti-Neoist aggressions."[33] Along those lines, the Dutch Arthur Berkhoff launched Neoism / Anti-Neoism / Pregroperativism, a one-man avant-garde that mailed and published a long series of cryptic texts and manifestos positing an impossible dialectical synthesis among different fractions of Neoism. Finally, Stewart Home engaged in a prolonged polemic campaign against Kantor, responsible, in his opinion, for having appropriated the Monty Cantsin identity for personal gain.[34]

Even though some of these interventions are so obscure as to appear almost meaningless to the outsider, they bespeak the internal proliferation of difference that characterized the Neoist network—an assemblage in which even the most idiosyncratic concerns were simultaneously affirmed and negated by individuals, splinter subgroups, and temporary alliances that constantly redefined the configuration of the network. And yet these diatribes—whether actual or simulated, interpersonal or simply part of the conceptual performance of Neoism—did not prevent the organization of new apartment festivals throughout the 1980s. After a couple of stops in Montreal (APT 6) and Baltimore (APT 7), the traveling circus of the APTs landed in London in May 1984.

APT 8 brought together for the first time a number of European and North American Neoists, including Horobin (the festival organizer), Home, Kantor, tENTATIVELY, Sevol, model and actress Eugenie Vincent, and mail artist Carlo Pittore, among others. In theory, with Home announcing the confluence of his anarco-punk "movement" Generation Positive into Neoism, the festival could have marked a qualitative leap for the network. But in practice, personal rivalries and a general inability or unwillingness to discuss a collective strategy did not render the event any different from previous APTs. The only intervention worthy of notice was the Neoist Guide Dog. Conceived and performed by tENTATIVELY and his girlfriend Gail Liftin, the action consisted in substituting a guide dog for the blind with a crawling human in public space. As tENTATIVELY recalls,

> my lover / travelling companion of the time, Gail Litfin, was diabetic. She'd had laser surgery on her left eye which had left that eye blind. . . . Since I was leading her around, we joked about me being her "seeing-eye dog." We bought a dog mask from a store specializing in animal masks (where Gail almost got caught shoplifting) & added a

> leash to my outfit for "completeness." The Festival's organizer, Monty Cantsin / Pete Horobin shot a film of Gail leaving our fest HQ with me on all fours as her "guide dog" (as they say in England), boarding a bus (where guide dogs ride for free, of course, & the driver didn't question the unusualness of this particular dog), & shopping in a mall (where we were kicked out of 1 store).[35]

After London, new APTs were held in the Italian village of Ponte Nossa (June 1985), Berlin (APT 64, December 1986), New York (the One Millionth APT, November 1988), and Paris (APT 63, December 1994 to January 1995).

It is clear, however, that participation in Neoism withered after the 1980s. There are several reasons for this, but the two main ones are the disintegration of the Montreal group and the harsh polemic between Home and Kantor over the "proper use" of Monty Cantsin. Even though a younger generation of Neoists, such as John Berndt and Florian Cramer, produced fresh actualizations and interpretations of Neoism in the late 1980s to early 1990s, the fissures caused by internal rivalries and diatribes were too many and ran too deep for the network to be repaired. As a matter of fact, while Neoists such as tENTATIVELY and Horobin spent time and energy on organizing APTs and strengthening the network, other Neoists were too focused on their own work to see Neoism as anything other than a promotional vehicle for their individual artistic practices.

Such a trend partly reflected the coming of age of a generation of artists who, in the late 1970s, were still too young to pursue individual art careers. But as time went by, Istvan Kantor became a prominent Canadian performance artist who was able to work professionally for a few years. Furthermore, it did not take long before Kantor's strong personality collided with those of other Neoists, such as R. U. Sevol, tENTATIVELY, and Home. The latter ended up joining Neoism for little over a year. Disgruntled by the antiactivist attitude and the lack of theoretical rigor of many Neoists, Home left the network before the Ponte Nossa festival, which he attended as an observer. Shortly thereafter, he began propagandizing a new movement called PRAXIS and Karen Eliot—a multiple-use name that was supposed to contrast the "male domination" of the Neoist scene and Kantor's overidentification with Monty Cantsin.[36]

In the following years, Home historicized and criticized the Neoist experience in three books: *The Assault on Culture* (1988, 2nd ed. 1991),

Neoist Manifestos (1991), and *Neoism, Plagiarism, and Praxis* (1995). The first enjoyed a certain editorial success on an international level, thereby affecting, if not creating for the first time, a public perception of Neoism. Even though the postmodern and anything-goes attitude of many Neoists led them to accept any criticism as well as any endorsement, many felt that Home's participation in the network had been too provisional (and polemical) to generate an account that was anything but very subjective.[37] Thus, beginning in the early 1990s, older and younger Neoists, such as Kantor, tENTATIVELY, and Cramer, began producing their own histories and archives. Cramer in particular recast Neoism as an epistemological experiment in speculation through Seven by Nine Squares, a website launched in 1995 that has grown to become the largest online repository of Neoist documents.[38]

RAY JOHNSON AND THE IMPOSSIBLE GIFT OF MAIL ART

The different interpretations of Neoism did not prevent some Neoists from finding some convergence points. For example, Cramer and Home coauthored an epistolary book in 1995 in which they agree that constructs such as "Monty Cantsin," "Akamdegorod," and "Neoism" are "self-contained signs and that everything that is done with them affects what they represent."[39] But whereas Home argues that the artificial character of Neoism makes it no less artificial than previous avant-gardes (which also sought to "create the illusion that a 'movement' that bore their name actually existed"), Cramer contends that the meaning of Neoism does not lie primarily in the tradition of the modern avant-garde. Rather, drawing from the kabbalistic tradition and the combinatorial experiments of authors such as Jorge Luis Borges, Bryon Gysin, and the OULIPO group, Cramer argues that the meaning of Neoism can always be created anew through potentially infinite semiotic permutations.[40] In this respect, Cramer's and other Neoists' interest in speculative thinking contributed to expanding the possible Neoist genealogies beyond the narrow confines of the European modern avant-garde.

To be sure, permutations and conceptual aporias were no stranger to the avant-garde. Cubist, Dadaist, and Surrealist collages/montages had shown the constructed nature of any representation by incorporating found objects and other nonartistic materials into the work of art. As Peter Bürger notes, "the insertion of reality fragments into the work of art fundamentally transforms that work. . . . [The parts] are no longer signs pointing to reality, they *are* reality."[41] To the artificial aesthetic of collage–montage, mail art added the possibility of incorporating the recipients of a mailed artwork directly into the artwork. In this sense, notes Craig Saper, the mail art "assemblings" from which Monty Cantsin and Neoism emerged are "social situations that function as part of an artwork or poem (that is, sociopoetic works)."[42] This sociopoetic dimension of mail art was already present in the 1960s' Correspondence Art, a network of mailings set in motion by conceptual pop artist Ray Johnson.

Johnson had started his career as an abstract expressionist painter who was close to the New York downtown scene of Robert Rauschenberg, Andy Warhol, Jasper Johns, and Cy Twombly. In the mid-1950s, he began exploring alternative systems of distribution for art by randomly pasting his works on train carriages ("moticos") and other public spaces or simply mailing them to friends. By the late 1950s, this mailing activity had become his central preoccupation. Every week, Johnson mailed out dozens of postcards, drawings, fragments of collages, found objects, and annotated newspaper clippings. In an effort to expand his network of correspondents, in 1958, Johnson began writing "Please send to . . ." on his mailings.[43] In other circumstances, he mailed incomplete drawings and collages along with instructions such as "Please add to and return."[44]

Aptly named the New York Correspondence School of Art (NYCS) by his friend and Fluxus artist Ed Plunkett, this network became the unofficial clearinghouse for a web of communications by mail that kept growing throughout the 1960s. To be sure, various avant-garde artists had experimented with the mail well before Ray Johnson. The Italian Futurists had mailed out tin postcards, Marcel Duchamp had invented a game of postal chess, and Berlin Dadaist Johannes Baader had pasted collages onto letters and postcards. None of these experiments, however, were meant to turn a network of postal exchanges into a work of art in its own right. For Johnson, instead, "correspondence" (or "corresponDance," as he used to call it) became both the subject and method of his art-making. His friend William S. Wilson notes how Johnson's correspondents were integral to his collages:

> Ray Johnson first notices something about a person, an image which might be central or marginal, and then he fills an envelope with scraps of images that comment on or add to or combine with that image. This process begins with a fondness for filing things, so he sends horses to Billy Linich, lobsters to Henry Martin, balloons to Karl Wirsum. He files a person under something in his mind, and then sends along through the mails whatever he feels belongs in the same file.[45]

In some circumstances, visual and textual correspondences are not limited to the collages contained in the envelope but overflow the wrapping to infect letterheads, stamps, cancellations, and names and addresses of recipients. As Ina Blom notes, once addresses and names begin floating as if disconnected from their original referents, "they take part in a complex and exhausting naming game that continually subjects them to pseudonymy, cryptonymy, paleonymy, metonymy, anonymity . . . in fact to all the accidents that can possibly happen to a name."[46]

Thus the dislocation and transformation of proper names emerge here from a game of visual, textual, and phonetic permutations. It is important to underscore that the mail artists who invented the name Monty Cantsin were all deeply involved in such game. (As we have seen, after generating "Monty Cantsins" through a sound poetry improvisation, Zack and Kundzins had immediately proceeded to disseminate the newfound name in the postal network.) In this sense, the multiple-use name strategy stems from a consolidated mail art practice of extracting names from addresses, newspapers, pictures, and sounds to put them in circulation and open them up to third-party uses. From this angle, a multiple-use name is nothing but the distributed use of a proper name, which by drifting through a web of permutations loses all reference to previous systems of signification. Deleuze and Guattari: "What counts is not parental designations, nor racial or divine designations, but merely the use made of them. No problem of meaning, but only of usage. Nothing original or derived, but a generalized drift."[47]

Likewise, by letting its collages drift through a network of senders–receivers, Ray Johnson let its compositions find their sense in their usage. In this way, Johnson's NYCS explored an aesthetics of postal communication whose core comprised the interactions among correspondents—an *aesthetics of networking* for which the mailed objects functioned as "pre-texts" to set in motion assemblages of enunciation whose addressees were integral to the assemblage. In this respect, Johnson's notations to forward, "add to and return" his mailings were essential to the production and reproduction of the network. And yet, not *every* mail art object had to be passed on, modified, or returned. Among the dozens of envelopes Johnson mailed out every week, many were simply *sent to,* with no expectation of further action on the recipient's side. As such, these physical artifacts simply forged and expressed an intimate relationship between sender and receiver.

This physical dimension of the mail art object reminds us that before the invention of the telegraph, communication was always attached to a material support. As John Durham Peters notes, "in Latin *communicatio* did not signify the general arts of human connection via symbols, nor did it suggest the hope for some kind of mutual recognition."[48] Rather, it was associated with the offering of tributes and gifts in public ceremonies, offers through which the communicant expressed the act of belonging to a community. From this angle, Blom is certainly right in describing mail art as "an act of ritual generosity" that relies on a medium, the postal system, which "provides the time delays necessary to make responses appear as spontaneous or 'unexpected' gifts."[49]

In *The Gift,* Marcel Mauss famously argued that barter and monetary exchange differ from the social ritual of the gift in that the latter implies a time interval that separates its reception from its restitution.[50] Blom also reminds us that in his reading of *The Gift,* Derrida developed a more radical theory of the *free give* as an impossible event, an excessive force that has the power to break the circle of meaningful exchanges, obligatory reciprocations, and expected returns embedded in an economic notion of the gift.[51] Against Mauss's anthropological reading of the gift as an offer that must be reciprocated, Derrida maintains that once we recognize that a true act of giving demands nothing in return, we can think of the gift as something that stands in a position of ineffable exteriority to the circle of economic exchanges. This exteriority does not mean that the gift is "transcendental and without relation."[52] On the contrary, "it is this exteriority that sets the circle going, it is this exteriority that puts the economy in motion."[53]

Thus the gift is not merely an object but *a force that gives and demands time,* a force that, by releasing time into a web of exchanges, has the capacity to initiate sociality anew. Opposite to the abstract, measurable time of modern economic exchange, this given time is an excessive, "mad," and invisible element that sets "the condition of presence of any present in general."[54] In fact, when the gift is recognized as such, it ceases to be a gift. Blom acutely links Derrida's effort to think the madness and impossibility of the gift to a fragment of a letter written by Ray Johnson to his friend Bill Wilson in 1958:

> Bill: There is that *moment* in giving. It has nothing to do with what or how, to whom or why. It is the same as any other *moment.* Since it does not exist, it escapes, and is not seen. We contain it by description, actions, realization. Ray.[55]

We know that Johnson was influenced by Zen Buddhism—a philosophy that he had studied at Black Mountain College in the 1940s. Thus Johnson's claim that the moment of giving "does not exist" shall be read here as a commitment not to categorize and isolate a specific action from the time-space continuum but rather, in Zen terms, to experience reality as nothingness *(Wu)* or emptiness *(sunyata).* From this angle, Johnson's artistic trajectory can be read as a flight from the categorizations of the art system. As we have seen, even though Johnson was introduced in the New York downtown scene, he chose not to become a painter and pop artist (legend has it that he burned most of his abstract paintings in Cy Twombly's fireplace in 1955). Beginning in 1961, he also organized "Nothings," informal gatherings in which, contrary to Allan Kaprov's renowned Happenings, very little, if anything, happened at all.[56] It was this strategy of invisibility and subtraction that earned Johnson the ironic title of "New York's most famous unknown artist" and that led him to leave the city in 1968 to conduct a reclusive life in Long Island, where he kept in contact with his friends mostly through the mail and the telephone.[57]

THE RADICAL INCLUSIVITY OF THE ETERNAL NETWORK

If we combine Derrida's notion of given time as an excessive force that has the power to set sociality in motion with Johnson's refusal to separate the moment of giving from any other moment, we can begin to analyze the ethos of mail art as emerging at the intersection of two elements: (1) the internal social contract that bound the mail art community and (2) the relationship between mail art and the art system. Both factors are historic in character inasmuch as correspondence art evolved from an intimate network involving a few dozen participants into the much larger Mail Art network, which generated a high volume of exchanges and thus a less personal relationship among correspondents. Despite this evolution, mail artists generally remained committed to a series of ethical and operational principles such as expanding the network to newcomers, sharing artifacts and ideas without claiming individual ownership, and exploring the (spiritual) nature of remote communication. Blom points out:

> To engage in the principles of the Mail Art system is to agree to a number of musts and must nots (do not judge, get rid of your vanity, try not to think about a work after you have sent it, do not expect returns, etc.). In the social contract of Mail Art participants, this ethics of ego-denial is rooted in the central principles that any object received through the mail should be received "guilt-free, with no reply expected"; that exhibitions of Mail Art will entail no fees, no juries and no rejection and, finally, that "all senders receive."[58]

This ethics of inclusiveness and commitment to the ideal of democratic participation in the arts informed not only mail art but also other art movements of the 1960s—most notably Fluxus. Because the movement was spread across North America, Europe, and Japan, Fluxus artists also used the postal system for exchanging ideas, event scores, and so forth. In some cases, they even experimented with the postal network's protocols and trappings.[59] Furthermore, fluxworkers such as Dick Higgins, Ken Friedman, George Brecht, and the poet–philosopher Robert Filliou became liaisons between Fluxus and mail art.[60] In particular, Brecht and Filliou conceptualized art-making as a *fête permanente* (permanent party) and an "eternal network" of ongoing exchanges across the globe. In an article published in the Canadian pioneering mail art publication *FILE* in 1973, Filliou, whose philosophy was also influenced by Zen Buddhism, poetically argued that art cannot be separated from the continuum of social life:

There is always someone asleep and someone awake,
someone dreaming asleep and someone dreaming awake,
someone eating, someone hungry
someone fighting, someone loving
someone making money, someone broke
someone traveling, someone staying put
someone helping, someone hindering
someone enjoying, someone suffering, someone indifferent
someone starting, someone stopping
The Network is Eternal (Everlasting).[61]

In the 1970s, the mail art's ethos of inclusiveness began to collide with the art system. As the Mail Art network had grown too large to be ignored, galleries, museums, and art magazines developed an interest in the new art form. Thus, in the more or less conscious effort to create artificial scarcities around the massive production of mailed artifacts, some critics and curators tried to discriminate between good (i.e., valuable) mail art and bad (i.e., unmarketable) mail art. In 1973, *FILE* magazine launched a scathing attack on the proliferation of "quikkopy crap" and "junk-mail" within the Mail Art network. And in 1984, Franklin Furnace's *Mail Art Then and Now International Show* broke the customary practice of previous mail art exhibitions to include and display all submissions.

Predictably, these provocations caused backlashes. *FILE*'s criticism of mail art prompted Anna Banana to become a mail artist and cofound with Bay Area artist Bill Gaglione the Dada-zine *VILE*.[62] And in response to the *Mail Art Then and Now* show, New York mail artist Carlo Pittore circulated an open letter in which he denounced the curator Ronny Cohen for breaking her original pledge to show all works entered. In a panel discussion organized at 22 Wooster St. Gallery in Soho, Pittore and John P. Jacob first symbolically "removed" Cohen from her position as moderator and then criticized her modus operandi. The transcript of the heated exchange that ensued, at the end of which Cohen abandoned the panel, is worth quoting at length:

DR. RONNY COHEN: We live in a real world. Mail artists, too, live in a real world. And in the real world there are no ideal conditions. You may like to have total control over your art, the display and exhibition of your art, but that in the real world, is almost impossible.

JOHN P. JACOB: I think that it's important to know, too, that Mail Art was not created for the real world, or the real world galleries. It was created by artists, for artists. And what we are here to say is that if a gallery wants to show Mail Art, and if you say "everything shown," then you show it. There was plenty of room on the walls. There was plenty of room for more books . . .

DR. COHEN: Well, you don't need to send in work if you feel that you must have total control.

JOHN JACOB: But we didn't know.

DR. COHEN: No, this is what I'm saying: you want total control so you have . . . what didn't you know? You were told that all works would be displayed, yes.

CARLO PITTORE: We've been down to the Franklin Furnace every day asking that the work be put up. We went to opening night and we said, "Where is the work?" And you said, "I wanted to display the 'Art' in Mail Art."[63]

The clash between the mail artists and the curator exemplifies the incompatibility of two distinct milieux—the amateur mail art and the professional art world. On one hand, professional art curators had to present mail art to a public that was often external to these networks and had little knowledge of their modus operandi. Overwhelmed by the high number of submissions and their uneven "aesthetic quality," some curators were thus tempted to exert their traditional power to select works they perceived as more appealing to the general public and possibly the collectors' market.

On the other hand, the Mail Art network had created a gift economy in which there was virtually no distinction between makers and receivers; it relied on a system of distribution that set no restrictions on the artworks that could be produced and circulated (other than those set by the protocols of the postal service); and it produced its own customary norms for organizing exhibitions. Such norms included the possibility for anyone to become a curator, no fees for the entered works, no returns after the exhibition, a free catalog for all participants, and the curator's pledge to include all artworks.[64] In other words, the Mail Art network had created *a sphere,* an autonomous system of art production and distribution that was governed by its own customary norms and its own notions of value.

THREE CONTRADICTIONS UNDERPINNING MULTIPLE-USE NAMES

My wager is that the inability or unwillingness of the Neoist network to openly acknowledge this set of customary norms is the main reason why Monty Cantsin never became an "open pop star." In other words, the failure to acknowledge the existence of a shared ethics, and to ground a politics of the multiple-use name in such ethics, may explain the decline of the Neoist network and Monty Cantsin's limited impact on its contemporaries. Even though such limitations do not diminish the significance of the Cantsin experiment in historic terms, I believe that the multiple-use name strategy was unable to address productively three different contradictions or paradoxes, which were already present in correspondence art and mail art:

1. the *contradiction of the gift*, or the contradiction between art as given time and art as exchange value
2. the *contradiction of art-making in a capitalist society*, or the contradiction between art as an activity that cannot be separated from the continuum of daily life and Art as something that is labeled, objectified, and extracted from such a continuum through commodification
3. the *contradiction of the multiple-use name*, or the contradiction between the distributed use of the alias in a network and its identification with specific individuals

In regard to the first contradiction, we have seen how Cantsin was originally created by David Zack and Maris Kundzins. In the last part of the letter to Graf Haufen cited at the beginning of this chapter, Zack explains that after evolving the name "Monty Cantsins" out of a certain playful repetition of Kundzins's name, he and his Latvian friend decided to contact Kantor:

> Maris and I sent a card to Kantor in Montreal, you are Monty Cantsin, the open pop star. Well Graf I have to assert what Kantor did with this simple postcard belongs in any history of art and also any history of the world. The idea that people can share their art power is a very good one I think. My own understanding of Neoism is that it is about

> sharing, about bash: cooperation between people, putting egos and tempers aside. Though not always seeming to.[65]

Thus Zack and Kundzins bestowed on Kantor the new name in the form of a gift-postcard. Kantor took this gift and turned it into a different kind of gift. As we have seen, Kantor's blood donations were meant to show that museums thrive off the blood of artists, so that Monty Cantsin's plasma would stand for the blood of every exploited and unrecognized artist. And yet, the paradoxical outcome of such provocations has been that Kantor has become a recognized performance artist in Canada, having received several grants from arts funding agencies, including the Telefilm Canada Award for Best Canadian Video (1998) and the Governor's General Award (2004)—the most prestigious Canadian award for achievement in the visual arts.

Thus, while the mail art gift had the power to set in motion an open web of exchanges and initiate a new kind of sociality, Kantor's gifts entered a direct relationship of exchange with the art world. In this exchange, the artist, the curators, the critics, and the institutions all contribute to determining the aesthetic significance (and the economic value) of such interventions. For example, in August 2005, Kantor announced his intention to mix his own blood into the concrete used by the Art Gallery of Ontario in Toronto to construct a new $200 million facility. Aptly named *Invisible Gift*, Kantor's project was met with the curiosity and mild skepticism of AGO curator David Moos. After asking Kantor to formalize a proposal and arranging a visit to his studio, Moos explained to the press, "What I have to figure out is whether this [Kantor] is a significant, interesting figure, or if this is someone who is a media star dilettante."[66]

Whether Kantor is an interesting artist or someone who just craves media attention by lending a face, a body, and even a blood group to Monty Cantsin, he inextricably tied the open pop star to himself. Perhaps this contradiction was already inscribed in Kundzins's and Zack's original gift ("*you* are Monty Cantsin, *you* are the open pop star," the card mailed to Kantor read). But once this association was made in the public mind, it was extremely difficult for anyone who was not cognizant of Cantsin's originating milieu not to identify the alias with a specific individual.

To be sure, some Neoist manifestos defined Monty Cantsin as a "null system," an "empty figure," a "copy," and so forth. But the very same texts also described him as a "Canadian-based artist who invented Neoism."[67] From a deconstructive standpoint, Cantsin appears here as something that cannot conform to either side of the polarity presence–absence. It is both a figure of disappearance similar to Ray Johnson's Zen philosophy of nothing and a name that is tied to a specific individual. But if the multiple-use name is a signifier of anonymity and yet something individuated—the mark of an absence that appears *in some form* in the field of representation—then an excessive personal identification with the alias occludes its capacity to function as an empty index.

This second contradiction between art as something that is invisible and indistinguishable from the continuum of social life and Art as a separate set of practices had already surfaced in correspondence art and mail art. Ray Johnson had tackled such contradiction by fleeing the art world, creating a network of correspondents, and exploring the gray zone where creativity merges with daily life. And mail artists had reclaimed the autonomy of the Mail Art network from the art system. The Neoists, instead, decided to adopt a strategy of semantic disorder by laying the emphasis on the Great Confusion and language's presumed inability adequately to describe the Neoist experience. Yet this refusal to speak an intelligible language ("Neoism applies itself to everything, and yet it is nothing," reads a typical Neoist statement plagiarized from Tzara) also ended up obfuscating the *actual power dynamics that existed within the network,* as well as the truism that not all Cantsin's interventions affected in the same way the public perception of the pseudonym.

Such obfuscation had a direct impact on the contradictory relationship between the distributed use of an alias and its appropriation by specific individuals. If Monty Cantsin is a name whose fixity only belies the shifting subjects to which it refers, some uses of Monty Cantsin—especially the ones that are valued by the art world and the culture industry—may hinder its capacity to function as a figure of distributed creativity. As we have seen, mail artists had developed a distinctive set of norms to protect the overabundant and noncommercial character of their art from selectivity and commodification. Although these norms were not legally binding, they entailed an inclusive and dynamic notion of authorship—one for which the (often pseudonymous) name of the author was more meant to mark a set of correspondences than the individual(s) behind them. By contrast, as previously noted, the culture industry often exploits the game of suppression and revelation, obfuscation and disclosure, set in motion by the pseudonym-effect as a marketing ploy. Yet for the culture industry, the author's legal signature, the contractually binding signature, is the stable anchoring point by which the rational entity we call "the author" is quilted onto a bodily subject.

If this is true, then the three contradictions that underpin the emergence of Monty Cantsin (art as given time vs. art as exchange value; art as life vs. Art as a reified set of practices; the pseudonym as improper name vs. the pseudonym as proper name) lead to a complete reversal of the three principles I employed to define the author-function as an apparatus for identifying and punishing, including or excluding, and attaching an exchange value to a proper name. First, the gift subverts the logic of exchange value by setting in motion an open system of exchanges. Second, when art merges into social life, it is no longer possible to draw a demarcating line between artists and nonartists. Third, when pseudonyms are not attached to specific individuals but keep passing from one user to another, they are no longer useful for identifying and punishing. It follows that the subversion of the author-function ceases to be effective every time an artist reclaims ownership of a shared given time, lets the art system label invisible art as Art, and tries to identify herself with a shared pseudonym. Hence, at its highest level of abstraction, the multiple-use name is a nonproprietary, invisible, and "condividual" process of subjectivation.

BEYOND CANTSIN: KAREN ELIOT, LT. MURNAU, AND MIND INVADERS

The irony is that though the concept of the multiple-use name emerged from the mail art ethos of selflessness and networking, a majority of Neoists could hardly refrain from impressing their individual mark on Neoism. In this respect, if Istvan Kantor overidentified with Monty Cantsin for his entire life, in several Neoist texts the alias appears related to proper names or other markers that make it traceable to different individuals.[68] Even Stewart Home—the most vocal advocate of a fully depersonalized use of the pseudonym—ended up authoring the collection *Neoist Manifestos* and other books with his birth name and continued to use Neoism as a self-promotional strategy long after abandoning the network.[69]

Such considerations call for a cynical reading of Neoism. Rather than a postmodern avant-garde deconstructing bourgeois notions of originality and novelty, Neoism could be read as a clever marketing strategy through which a handful of artists publicized their own work. On some level, the Neoists themselves encouraged, or at least did not discourage, such reading. But although self-promotion worked for some, it did not work for everyone, thus igniting interpersonal conflicts that contributed to the demise of the network. To be sure, avant-garde movements rarely span more than two decades. Thus it is possible that Neoism would have tapered off even without these tensions. And yet the question of whether Cantsin was meant to work as an abstract persona or to be identified with specific individuals had a specific weight for Neoism.

As we have seen, unlike Smithee, Cantsin was not a purely authorial strategy but an experimental process of subjectivation that was *experienced* directly by its participants. Thus Tatiana Bazzichelli pointedly notes that personal "over-identifications were unavoidable in a context where art practices and personal lives were so intertwined."[70] Bazzichelli also observes that these overidentifications brought to the foreground "the contradictory aspects of Neoism that were deeply rooted in the movement. If Neoism takes shape through speculations and paradoxes, it symbolises at one and the same time both the construction of a network and its deconstruction."[71] From this perspective, Cantsin may well be identified *both* with no one in particular *and* with specific individuals. And yet, as we have seen, these two positions did not exist side by side within the Neoist network but violently clashed, producing the kind of tension that lies at the core of the improper name. In this respect, Home's criticism of personal overidentifications with the pseudonym deserves further consideration—and this despite the fact that his own practice was not consistent with his theorization.

After abandoning the Neoist network in 1985, Home launched Karen Eliot, a shared signature for authoring a range of cultural interventions. In a text titled "Orientation for the Use of a Context and the Context for the Use of an Orientation," Home introduced some guidelines for the use of the multiple-use name:

> Anyone can become Karen Eliot simply by adopting the name, but they are only Karen Eliot for the period in which they adopt the name. Karen Eliot was materialised, rather than born, as an open

> context in the summer of 1985. . . . If one uses the context in personal life there is a danger that the name Karen Eliot will become over-identified with individual beings. . . . Previous experiments with multiple names, such as the Monty Cantsin fiasco, indicate that the failure to differentiate between the personal and the social and in particular over-identification by certain individuals with the context, is disastrous.[72]

In the following years, Karen Eliot was adopted by various Neoists, including Pete Horobin, John Berndt, Arthur Berkhoff, Graf Haufen, R. U. Sevol, and Drake Scott. The shared signature was widely used at the London Festival of Plagiarism, an anti-art event co-organized by Home, Graham Harwood, Ed Baxter, and others in January–February 1988.[73] Home also recounts that upon Eliot's launch, he had made a few textual installations for London art galleries, which he had signed using the new alias. "As a consequence," he writes,

> a number of individuals active in the London art world began to treat the name Karen Eliot as being synonymous with me. I counteracted this tendency by using a variety of different names, as well as my legal and birth names—and more or less abandoned using the Karen Eliot identity. Such strategies are essential if multiple names are to remain "open" and function for collective use.[74]

One may argue that the question is not how to disown a supposedly open pseudonym after being identified with it but rather *how not to be associated with it in the first place.*

It is significant that a few years earlier, another mail artist, Vittore Baroni, had faced exactly the same problem when he had created the multiple-use sound collage band Lt. Murnau. Launched in 1979, and based on the idea of making music by remixing preexisting recordings, Lt. Murnau was an imaginary cult band whose musicians had been replaced by audio samplers and mixers. Whereas these sampling techniques were later popularized by John Oswald's "plunderphonics" and the sound-collage band Negativland, Baroni used them within the so-called Tape Network, a network of musicians and collectors who exchanged audio cassettes through the postal system. In a letter to Stewart Home, Baroni recalls the early stages of the project and his attempts to publicize Lt. Murnau's recycled music through various ploys such as the anonymous dissemination of leaflets, the simultaneous release of cassettes and records in different countries, and the production of Lt. Murnau cardboard masks that anyone could wear. Yet his efforts to let the band take a life of its own were undercut by the original association of the project with himself:

> The main problem I found is that very few people were interested in working for a project that they felt belonged to myself, even if I tried to keep it mysterious in its origins. So in the end I always did 99% of the work, even if Jacques Juin did a lot of Murnau work in 1980–81 and a few others contributed nice work (Michael Vanherwegen, Roger Radio, among others). The whole project was focused on a very limited area, that of underground music, so it did not have the more varied overtones of the Monty Cantsin philosophy. Yet, I think the problems are the same. . . . The fact is that to participate you had to really work collectively, and this is something few in the art circles like to do without having their name in big letters.[75]

Two elements emerge from Baroni's account of the Lt. Murnau experience. The first is a movement toward depersonalization, which carries to the extreme—or perhaps to its logical consequences—the DIY ethics of the punk movement. If punk rock had shown that three chords was all a musician needed to know to form a band, Lt. Murnau did away even with this basic knowledge to suggest instead that musicians could forget about guitars and drums altogether and simply use old records and turntables to create collages of sound. The second element is that depersonalization could not be fully accomplished without liberating the band from its putative progenitor and primary caretaker.

Although Baroni found it difficult to dissociate himself from Lt. Murnau—a project he officially discontinued in 1984—he was more successful with other projects of the same period. After the launch Lt. Murnau, Baroni had met Piermario Ciani, who was a liaison between mail art and the creative fringes of the Italian punk and New Wave scene, most notably the Great Complotto, a coalition of bands that had founded the imaginary State of Naon in the town of Pordenone. Inspired by the Great Complotto's mythmaking, in 1980, Ciani had started Mind Invaders, a fictional rock band whose concerts, albums, reviews, and interviews (and subsequent disavowals) were entirely fabricated by a network of musicians and rock journalists.[76] A year later, Baroni, Ciani, and Massimo Giacon also launched TRAX—a "modular" art project "at unlimited variability," which actualized and democratized the concept of the Fluxkit first developed by George Maciunas in the 1960s. Participants in TRAX could in fact either act as Central Units (de facto becoming the Maciunases of their time) in charge of organizing a module—for example, a music event or the release of a TRAX collection—or alternatively as Peripheral Units contributing to one of the modules. From June 1981 to June 1987, ten Central Units of TRAX—"X ART" in reverse—collected the audiovisual contributions of five hundred Peripheral Units from thirty different nations. (Among those, *TRAX 1085 Neoist Ghosts,* printed and distributed in 150 copies, contained a copy of *SMILE* and an audiotape assembled by Baroni with various Neoist materials produced during the 1985 Ponte Nossa festival.)[77]

By and large, Lt. Murnau, Mind Invaders, and TRAX are projects that rely on concepts and practices that run parallel to other multiple-use names encountered in this chapter. As compared to the Neoists, however, these Italian artists seem to be truer to the selfless networking ethos that imbued mail art in the 1960s and 1970s. Rather than exploiting the network as a self-promotional vehicle, Baroni and Ciani tested its limits and potentiality in two critical areas. On one hand, the TRAX project demonstrated that the combined use of copy machines, samplers, and mixers with the postal system could provide a horizontal infrastructure for the production and circulation of cultural artifacts. On the other hand, this network of cultural workers was able to devise an elaborate mythmaking strategy to fabricate a fictional band like Mind Invaders through a plurality of accounts. Thus, whereas the Neoists never cared to understand how Monty Cantsin could have truly become a pop star, Ciani, Baroni, and friends explored how pop culture is manufactured by the media and the culture industry. As we shall see in the next chapter, these artists were ready to hand down this practical knowledge to a new generation of activists in the following decade.

4

LUTHER BLISSETT, THE MYTHMAKER

O mito é o nada que é tudo (The myth is the nothing that is everything).

—FERNANDO PESSOA

Luther Blissett is a secret agent that plays the Myth's game with the goal of undermining the authority of Myth (of Truth, Identity, Reason, etc.).

—PAUL K. FEYERABAND, AS PLAGIARIZED BY LUTHER BLISSETT

As any crime story, this story begins with a murder. It is the evening of February 15, 1990, when the local police station of Porec, a sleepy Croatian village in the Istrian Peninsula, receives an anonymous phone call. The informant says that a male body is lying on the railroad tracks a few miles away from the train station. When the cops arrive on the spot, all they can find is a hyperrealistic wax replica of a decapitated body. In 1991 and 1992, three other fake corpses are discovered in a parking lot in Umag, a public toilet in Rovinj, and a hotel room in Paklenika. As the Croatian press and the authorities begin to investigate, the disintegration of the Yugoslav Federation and the outbreak of the Bosnian War in March 1992 shift the public's attention from the simulated slaughters to the real ones. Yet, despite the war, the trail of simulated murders continues on the Montenegro coastline in 1993 and 1994.

In 1997, an Italian website publishes the harrowing pictures of the dismembered replicas, attributing them to an unknown Serbian artist named Darko Maver.[1] Managed by a "Free Art Campaign," the website claims that Maver has been arrested by the Serbian police in Kosovo, where the Serbian Army and the Kosovo Liberation Army are engaged in a quickly escalating conflict. The photographs would be the only remaining evidence of a performance in eight acts titled *Tanz der Spinne* (Dance of the spider).[2] Charged with antipatriotic propaganda, Maver is released after being detained without trial for four weeks, according to the Free Art Campaign. In August 1998, Kapelica Gallery, a contemporary art space in Lubljana, dedicates a retrospective to the artist. The photographic documentation of *Tanz der Spinne* is showcased along with Maver's early artworks, including photos of sculpted premature fetuses made of PVC. In January 1999, Maver is arrested a second time and detained in the prison of Podgorica, Kosovo.[3] On April 30, 1999, his body is found lifeless in a prison cell. A few days later, the Free Art Campaign issues a press release, along with a photograph of a seemingly dead man, doubting the official version given by the Serbian authorities, according to whom Maver would have committed suicide.[4]

The artist's premature death casts a new light on his work, which is read as an enigmatic interrogation of the hyperreality of (postmodern) warfare generated by media representations of suffering bodies in the Balkan Wars.[5] Inspired by this Baudrillardian reading of Maver's work, independent and mainstream art institutions—including the Venice Biennale of Arts—pay tribute to the artist with retrospectives and symposia. On February 6, 2000, a press release cosigned by Luther Blissett and 0100101110101101.ORG reveals that the entire Free Art Campaign has been orchestrated by a network of artists and activists based in the cities of Bologna, Ljubljana, and Rome. The life and death of Darko Maver are a pure invention, a myth designed to question the production of fame within the art system. The Dance of the Spider has been realized by downloading photographs of actual corpses from the shock website Rotten.com. The images of immature fetuses are also pictures of existing fetuses. And the photograph of Maver's corpse is that of "a long-time member of the Luther Blissett Project in Bologna."[6]

The self-styled "Great Art Swindle"—a pun on the Sex Pistols's *Great Rock 'n' Roll Swindle*—meticulously (and cynically) exploited two different elements: the first, strictly political, was the European Union's sense of impotence and guilt toward the Yugoslavian Civil War—a ferocious war that had escalated in the heart of Europe, triggering tragic memories and reopening old scars.[7] The second element, more specific to the art system, was the late 1990s body-art hype that had brought into the spotlight performance artists such as Stelarc, Orlan, and Ron Athey. By referencing the body-art imagery, with its repertoire of pierced, scarified, and bleeding bodies in the context of an actual war, Maver had produced an edgy if unsettling body of work that the European art world could hardly ignore. The Great Art Swindle was the last major prank by Luther Blissett and one of the first exploits of 0100101110101101.ORG, an offshoot of Luther Blissett and a net art group that constructed its elusive identity on the staging of fake events.

ORIGINS OF THE PROJECT

But who is Luther Blissett? And who are the real actors behind the Free Art Campaign? To answer these questions, we must rewind our story to summer 1994, when a number of individuals began using the name "Luther Blissett" to author various media stunts and interventions in public space. Inspired by the multiple-use names and bands of the previous decades, a group of artists and activists based in the Italian Northeast and Bologna launched a simple idea: anyone could become Luther Blissett simply by adopting the name.[8] In the following years, the nom de plume was shared by dozens of activists in Italy and other European countries to dupe the press into reporting nonevents, hijack popular TV programs, sell apocryphal manuscripts to publishers, conduct psychogeographic experiments, fabricate artists and artworks, denounce media witch hunts, and author best-selling novels.[9]

Until 1994, the only character known to the Italian public as Luther Blissett was a British soccer player of Jamaican origins who had played an unfortunate season in the Italian Serie A in the mid-1980s. Some journalists speculated that Blissett was chosen as a multiple-use name because the AC Milan scouts, who had acquired the player from Elton John's Watford in 1983, had mistaken him for the more talented John Barnes.[10] Others argued that Blissett was chosen because he was one of the first black soccer players to play in Italy.[11] Similar uncertainty surrounds the only circulating image of Luther Blissett: an artificial portrait of a yuppie-looking man created by superimposing three or four head shots.

But if the real Blissett was a well-known fiasco (at least to Italian soccer fans), he could hardly be associated with media activism and media pranks. The mystery surrounding the choice of Luther Blissett as a multiple-use name was not accidental. Rather, it was carefully cultivated as part of a mythmaking strategy aimed at turning Blissett into a folk hero of the information age. To decouple the birth of the condividual from any particular subject, the early participants in Luther Blissett linked the origins of the improper name to a web of fictional characters and imaginary progenitors, some of whom had participated in mail art and Neoism in the 1980s.

This mythmaking effort is apparent from the first ruse orchestrated by Luther Blissett. In January 1995, a troupe of *Chi l'ha Visto?*—an Italian prime-time TV show devoted to tracking down missing persons—was sent on the traces of Harry Kipper, a British conceptual artist who was allegedly touring several European cities on a mountain bike with the purpose of tracing the word "ART" on Europe's map.[12] The TV crew was first put in touch with radio journalist and mail artist Piermario Ciani, who claimed that the British artist had last been sighted in Bertiolo, a village in northeastern Italy. The TV journalists were then sent to London, where Stewart Home and Richard Essex of the London Psychogeographical Association showed them "Kipper's apartment." After announcing full coverage of Kipper's case, *Chi L'ha Visto?* decided not to air the reportage. At this point, Blissett issued a press release claiming that Kipper's imaginary performance was to be read as an allegory of the death of the artist, as a simulation to "free the Luther Blissett Project from any founder and origin," and as "an opportunity to test the networking abilities of people using the multiple name."[13]

The endeavor of obfuscating the origins of the multiple personality transpires also from *Mind Invaders*, the first book authored by and about Luther Blissett.[14] Named after Ciani's fictional band of the early 1980s, *Mind Invaders* traces the origins of the multiple-use name back to Ray Johnson. According to Baroni, the American mail artist "used to organize happenings and 'clubs' for groups of people with the same name randomly picked up from the phone books."[15] Although this anecdote is hardly proof of Johnson's involvement in Luther Blissett, the creators of Luther Blissett decided to attribute to him the inadvertent invention of the improper name—probably to pay homage to his untimely death, which had occurred under mysterious circumstances a few months before the publication of the book.[16]

Johnson was not the only credited artist. Being aware of the interpersonal conflicts over authorship and attribution that had bogged down the multiple personalities of the 1980s, the authors of *Mind Invaders* expanded the pantheon of Blissett's imaginary forefathers to include other legendary figures of the underground, such as Coleman Healy, Monty Cantsin, Harry Kipper, and Karen Eliot.[17] Like its predecessors, Blissett had a predilection for pranks, fabrications, and the undermining of the notion of individual identity and authorship. Unlike its predecessors, Blissett was adopted not only by underground performers and musicians but also by a new generation of students and activists who had played no role in the mail art and Neoist networks. These young activists organized themselves into three collectives—based in Bologna, Rome, and Viterbo—and in a number of smaller "cells" in other Italian cities, the United Kingdom, and Slovenia. As we shall see, under the banner of the Luther Blissett Project (LBP), the collectives made consistent and repeated use of the alias to author numerous interventions between 1994 and 1999. Even though the alias was borrowed by a wider range of individuals, this organized use of the alias was able to strategically channel the majority of Blissett's appearances and interventions.[18] Such an intense level of cooperation at a local level was coupled with a lack of personal interest in using the name. Unlike artists who could hardly renounce, in Baroni's words, "having their names in big letters," the LBP activists had no desire, at least initially, to associate their individual identities with the multiple personality.[19] This allowed them to invest most of their time and energy into targeting the media and the culture industry rather than into the endless diatribes that had splintered the Neoist network.[20]

BLISSETT'S COMING COMMUNITY: A MARXIST READING OF POP CULTURE

To be sure, the Neoist performances of the 1980s were infused with a goliardic and absurdist spirit that resurfaced, as we shall see, in the psychogeographic experiments of Radio Blissett, the three-sided soccer matches, and the urban performances of the Teatro Situazionautico "Luther Blissett." There were, however, at least two key differences between the open pop star Monty Cantsin and the multiple-use name Luther Blissett: the first is the aforementioned distinction between the artistic and activist milieux from which the two aliases originated; the second lies in the different strategic attitudes the two networks had toward pop culture and the media.

As we have seen, the Mail Art network and Neoism had for the most part a confrontational attitude toward the art world and the culture industry, which they sought to undermine by attacking bourgeois notions of identity, originality, and authorship. If Blissett shared with Cantsin this critique of authorship, unlike Cantsin, Blissett saw pop culture as a vast reservoir of narratives and imagery that could be tapped to expand the myth of the condividual. Whereas the punk generation had constituted its subjectivity in opposition to mass culture and the mainstream, Luther Blissett was mostly animated by a new generation very much imbibed with pop culture—or at least with its more utopian and transformative aspects.

For instance, the first pages of *Mind Invaders* drew inspiration from Hollywood movies such as *Spartacus* and *Slapshot,* cyberpunk novels, and the TV series *Star Trek.*[21] In "Darmok," an episode of *Star Trek: The Next Generation,*[22] the *Enterprise* crew comes into contact with the Tamarians, a race whose analogical language is rooted in a mythology that is too specific and remote to be accessible to the universal translators of the Federation. For the Tamarians, writes Blissett, "experiences, commonality, and emotional co-participation are one with being 'singularities' insofar as they escape the concept of in-dividual; the Tamarian Self is multiple and multiverse, their subjectivity is decentered."[23]

The Tamarians want to share their memory and culture with the *Enterprise* crew. Thus their commander, Dathon, teletransports himself, together with *Enterprise* commander Jean-Luc Picard, onto El-Adrel IV, an inhospitable and seemingly abandoned planet. Here the two captains have to confront a shimmering entity irradiating a deadly electromagnetic field. Dathon refers to this situation with the expression "Darmok and Jalad at Tanagra"—an episode from the Tamarian mythology in which two heroes had learned how to survive a ferocious beast by trusting each other. Likewise, in their common struggle for survival on El-Adrel IV, Picard and Dathon are able to communicate and understand each other for the first time, even though the Tamarian captain is eventually killed by the radiation. Dathon's sacrifice, however, is not in vain and serves as the foundation of a new myth to which both Tamarians and humans will henceforth refer through the common expression "Picard and Dathon at El-Adrel."[24]

Through this parable, the authors of *Mind Invaders* introduce the idea that the LBP's mission was to set off a "Tamarian Network of Events," a series of foundational and confrontational experiences whereby "a coming community" would be able to narrate itself into existence. Drawing from Giorgio Agamben's book on the coming community as an unrepresentable community of "whatever singularities" striving to find a common ground without claiming or establishing new identities, the founders of the LBP emphasized the importance of conflict as a twofold principle that could, on one hand, define the community from without, in opposition to capital and the state, and, on the other hand, keep it open to becoming on the inside.[25] Whether this antagonism was only theoretically postulated or actually came to inform the internal dialectic of the LBP is something I shall discuss at the very end of this chapter. As of now, it suffices to say that the potential antagonism among different components of the LBP was tempered by the common Marxist background of many participants.

In particular, some LBP activists were influenced by the writings of the young Marx on the cooperative nature of human beings and on capital's unstoppable tendency to replace the human community *(Gemeinwesen)* with the community of exchange value.[26] In "Comments on James Mill," Marx argued that exchange is a social process whereby humanity unveils its true essence:

> *Exchange,* both of human activity within production itself [i.e., the division of labor] and of *human products* against one another, is equivalent to *species-activity* and species-spirit, the real, conscious, and true mode of existence of which is *social* activity and *social* enjoyment. Since *human* nature is the true *community* [*Gemeinwesen*] of men, by manifesting their *nature* men create, produce, the *human community,* the social entity, which is no abstract universal power opposed to the single individual, but is the essential nature of each individual, his own activity, his own life, his own spirit, his own wealth.[27]

By creating Luther Blissett, the LBP activists aspired to lend a name to an exchange process that expressed the cooperative nature of human beings without sacrificing each dividual singularity. In this respect, the condividual was not meant to represent *Gemeinwesen* but *was itself Gemeinwesen* without ceasing to be a particular Luther Blissett at a specific moment in time. (In the conclusion, I will address the conceptual tension between an inessential notion of the community, expressed here by Agamben, and an essentialist position, expressed here by Marx, that endows the community with positive qualities of its own.)

Because of its historic nature, the singularity could not exist outside of the exchange processes enabled by the modern culture industries. In fact, according to the Bolognese LBP, pop culture constitutes a material "prerequisite for communism" insofar as the global exchange of local imageries allows different communities to expand and integrate their horizon with that of the species-being.[28] If Theodor Adorno and Guy Debord had read mass culture and the spectacle as industrial processes engineered from above to enforce and reinforce capitalist domination, the LBP preferred to tap into what Ernst Bloch had described as the "unfulfilled utopian potential" of mainstream narratives to turn them into open, rewritable, and participatory myths.[29]

To be sure, not all the LBP shared such a positive view of pop culture, as many Luther Blissetts retained a critical distance toward mainstream media and the culture industries. Yet the main demarcating line between Luther Blissett and previous multiple-use name projects such as Monty Cantsin and Karen Eliot lies in this new attitude toward popular culture. As we shall see in the next three sections of this chapter, such an attitude was also rooted in an emergent network of productive activities that tended to upset the traditional dichotomy of underground–mainstream.

THE RADICAL MILIEU OF THE LUTHER BLISSETT PROJECT

Even though mail artists such as Piermario Ciani, Alberto Rizzi, and Vittore Baroni had played a critical role in the early stages of Luther Blissett, the vast majority of the participants belonged to a new generation of activists. Mostly in their twenties, and educated in humanities and social science departments of Italian public universities, these activists gravitated by and large in the galaxy of groups and collectives that formed the Italian extraparliamentary Left in the mid-1990s.

These groups often coalesced in or around a network of squatted community centers known as Centri Sociali Occupati e Autogestiti (CSOA), which had begun spreading through the peninsula since the mid- to late

1980s. After the 1990 outbreak of La Pantera (The Panther)—a national student movement that had led to a three-month-long occupation of virtually every Italian university to protest the possible privatization of higher education—students, the unemployed, and precarious workers went on to occupy dismissed buildings and abandoned warehouses in city centers and metropolitan areas. With their unique mix of political cultures and subcultures, *centri sociali* such as Forte Prenestino, Villaggio Globale, and Corto Circuito in Rome; Livello 57 in Bologna; Pedro in Padua; Officina 99 in Naples; and Leonkavallo and Cox 18 in Milan; to name a few, organized a wide range of social and political activities, including demonstrations, festivals, seminars, workshops, day care and legal services, concerts, and rave parties. All together, these initiatives constituted, in the words of Naomi Klein, "a parallel political sphere" that was both self-organized and antagonistic to the state.[30]

The frequent recourse to direct action tactics such as street blockades and unauthorized street parties, the disruption of official events, and the occupation of buildings, as well as the emphasis on the self-management *(autogestione)* of these spaces and self-production *(autoproduzione)* of records, videos, magazines, and other cultural artifacts, were partly rooted in the practices of the 1970s social movements—namely, Autonomia and the feminist movement—and partly were a grassroots response to a new political situation that precluded access to resources and career opportunities for youths. The end of the Cold War had in fact set in motion a period of prolonged political instability in Italy, marked by the inability of the ruling groups to complete the political transition from the First Republic, which had emerged from the ashes of fascism, to the so-called Second Republic. Beginning in 1992, Mani Pulite (Clean Hands), a national investigation conducted by the Milanese magistracy into political corruption, led to the disclosure of Tangentopoli (Bribeville), a deep-running system of bribes whereby entrepreneurs won public contracts and political favors. The scandal set off the sudden disintegration of the Pentapartito—the five-parties coalition that had kept the country within the NATO alliance since the aftermath of World War II—preventing the Partito Comunista Italiano (PCI), the largest Communist party in Western Europe, ever from ascending to power. The collapse of the Pentapartito opened up a political gap that was quickly closed by the emergence of a new center-right coalition whose lynchpin was media mogul Silvio Berlusconi.

In a context in which a spiraling public debt required a discredited political class to make draconian cuts to social spending, the CSOA became a catalyst for a generation of young people who were given little opportunity to test their professional abilities within a stagnant job market and were completely disaffected with mainstream politics. In this respect, social centers and student collectives also functioned as incubators for grassroots media initiatives that innovated and challenged an otherwise conservative media environment. In the next two sections, we will see how this sparkling milieu incubated the early stages of the LBP in the cities of Bologna and Rome.

TRANSMANIACS, SITUAZIONAUTS, AND PSYCHIC NOMADS

In Bologna, a number of innovative media projects had sprung up in the aftermath of the Panther movement. These included the fanzines *Perle ai Porci* (Pearl to the pigs) and *River Phoenix,* the Transmaniaca collective, the radio programs *Il Puttanoroscopo* (which borrowed its title from Samuel Beckett's poem "Whoroscope") and *La Merenda Uruguaia,* the music groups Tribade Tecnica and Cavalla Cavalla, and the guerrilla-theater group Amorevole Compagnia Pneumatica.[31] These groups shared a desecrating attitude toward the mainstream, toward the rigidity of the PCI intelligentsia (which had been ruling the city since World War II), and also toward the stale, cyclic reemergence of alternative styles and subcultures. For instance, *River Phoenix,* "The Unofficial Fanzine of the NO Generation," focused on disinformation, the production of nonnews, and a playful use of the urban space loosely inspired by the Lettrist–Situationist *dérive.*[32] At the beginning of 1994, a column titled "Appointments with No One" had attracted the attention of Roberto Bui and Fabrizio Giuliani, at the time members of the Transmaniaca collective.

Named after John Shirley's cyberpunk novel *Transmaniacon,* the Transmaniacs explored a theory and practice of subversion for a generation that had grown up with a saturated media environment and in times of accelerated capitalist recuperation. As Roberto Bui writes in a youth pamphlet titled *Transmaniacalità e Situazionauti* (Transmaniacality and Situazionauts), the Transmaniacs seek to "liberate the language, use it to produce events, and use the events to create a new language" by quickly moving between liberated "interzones" before capital can recuperate them or shut them down.[33] Conversely, "a situazionaut, as the word says, is someone who navigates situations, crosses them and breaks them apart. I am speaking of the situations which are constructed by power, not of those constructed by us, who have a different value, of re-appropriation of life."[34]

In other words, the Transmaniacs formulated a nondialectical theory that maintained that the Spectacle had to be confronted not only from the outside—through a nomadic crossing of yet-to-be-colonized areas of social life—but also from within, through a systematic infiltration and sabotage of the media system.[35] This viral approach emerges also from some provoking statements made by members of the collective during their internal meetings, whose minutes were regularly posted on a local Bulletin Board System (BBS) and distributed via Fidonet nationwide.[36] Among those, there was the appropriation of a notorious phrase commonly attributed to Italian Communist leader Amedeo Bordiga: "Anti-fascism is the worst product of fascism." The slogan was meant to satirize, as Bui recalls in an interview with the author,

> a certain "automatic reflex," kind of Pavlov thing, which was very common in the movement, i.e. the propensity to go berserk each time there was a fleeting chance that a fascist was around. Most people came at demonstrations or meetings only when there was talk of a fascist presence, a vague threat of a fascist initiative, it was kind of a gang war mentality, a tribal thing, but there was no reasoning at all on what fascism was becoming, on the meaning of being a fascist or an antifascist in a radically transformed social, political and cultural landscape.[37]

This and other provocations surfaced also in the radio show *Transmaniacon* and in other happenings that various members of the collective staged, often in collaboration with other performance groups, in social centers and student squats. "The radio show was a manic display of speeches, weird sounds, absurdist theater, improvisational comedy and rants of any kind," says Bui. "We were in our early twenties and we were very provocative."[38]

In summer 1994, the "absurdist" performances of the Transmaniacs and the urban explorations of *River Phoenix* converged in the Agitazione

Orrorista (Horrorist Agitation), a series of guerrilla-theater interventions coordinated by Riccardo Paccosi's Amorevole Compagnia Pneumatica. On May 27, 1994, Paccosi simulates a self-gutting in a central street of Bologna by pretending to have spasmodic convulsions and extracting a long veil intestine from underneath his shirt. The performance, which is terminated by the police, is meant "to present capitalist society with an anguishing image of itself."[39] As one of the editors of *River Phoenix* points out, "Paccosi's self-gutting is probably the first action that sees the participation, in the guise of fake passersby or authors of outraged letters [to the press], of the core group that will later form the Bolognese cell of the LB Project."[40] The horrorist agitation continued with a campaign of fake letters to local newspapers supposedly written by disgruntled citizens to denounce the presence of animal entrails on public buses and in other venues, and then with the actual deployment of such entrails on a bus—an action that obtains some coverage in the local press.[41]

It is only in September, however, that the groups involved in the horrorist agitation decide to give birth to a new radio program called *Radio Blissett*. Broadcasted every Wednesday night from the frequencies of Radio Città del Capo, the live show featured a variable number of Luthers who "patrolled" the city by bike or foot and called the studio from phone booths. Listeners could also call in at any time and direct the patrols to various locations to join improvised social events such as street parties, three-sided soccer matches, and "psychic attacks" against public buildings and institutions. Beginning in February 1995, the Teatro Situazionautico "Luther Blissett," a new guerrilla-theater group founded by Riccardo Paccosi, began staging surreal and absurdist performances in the course of the radio show.[42]

The idea of drifting through the city in search of heightened emotional experiences was not new. The *dérive* had been first elaborated, as a theory and practice, by the Lettrists in the mid-1950s and was further refined by the Situationists in the late 1950s and through the 1960s. From the columns of *Potlatch*, the information bulletin of the Lettrist International, the Lettrists designed a series of "psychogeographical games" and experiments, which were meant to map out the emotive force fields and unities of atmosphere (ambiances) into which a city is subdivided. The data collected by the psychogeographers through multiple drifts would have contributed in turn to the design of a new kind of city based on the theory of unitary urbanism, defined by the Situationists as "the combined use of the arts and techniques for the integral construction of a milieu in dynamic relation with experiments in behaviour."[43]

It is worth noting that the Lettrist–Situationist theories did not arrive unfiltered to Italy. Because, during the 1980s, psychogeography had become fashionable within the academy, Stewart Home and the London Psychogeographical Association (LPA) had mixed it with mystic and occultist elements to make it less palatable to academic recuperation.[44] These mystic elements included the discovery and tracing of urban paths and intersections emanating a special psychic energy, respectively named "ley lines" and "omphali." (In archeology, the ley lines describe the alignment across the landscape of ancient monuments such as megaliths and pyramids.) The psychogeographers of the LPA claimed to have discovered numerous ley lines and omphali in London by tracing and aligning on a city map the psychic spots discovered in the course of various urban drifts.

Luther Blissett updated this occultist version of the *dérive* by adding a new layer: the real-time sharing of information among psychogeographers through the combined use of broadcast radio and the telephone system. Instead of mapping the psychological effects of the spatial organization of the city, the psychogeographers of *Radio Blissett* explored the temporary social relations that could be activated by remapping the urban layout with the radio and the telephone in that nonplace of the present we call "real-time communication."

The importance of real time became evident in Rome with the kickoff of a new *Radio Blissett* program, which aired on the frequencies of Radio Città Futura in May–June 1995. While in Bologna the patrols walked, biked, and called the studio from phone booths, in Rome the wider extension of the urban space was covered by a few car patrols, which were constantly reporting their drifts back to the studio via cell phone. "The function of the car patrols was to engage in aimless driving or connect listeners who were calling in from different parts of the city, occasionally pick them up, drive them to an improvised party or another social event, and finally converge all together on a predetermined target," says Andrea Natella, one of the founding members of the Roman LBP.[45]

The five episodes of the Roman *Radio Blissett* were thematic ("For the Abolition of the Proper Name," "For the Erotization of Everyday Life," "Against Copyright," "For Psychogeography," and "Against Wage Labor") and culminated in a series of psychic attacks against public buildings such as the Italian copyright office and the Roman Office of Employment. In comparison to the Bolognese *Radio Blissett,* which aired for a year and a half, the Roman program lasted only five weeks, but it involved a greater number of people. "While in Bologna listeners were calling the studio every now and then, and the rhythm of the show was quite slow," says Natella, "in Rome we always had at least two people calling in at the same time. Besides giving the program a very dynamic feel, this constant influx of phone calls allowed us to coordinate a great number of unexpected events and direct actions."[46]

That the Roman show had reached a critical mass became clear on the evening of June 15, 1995, when roughly fifty Luther Blissetts boarded the same night tram at several consecutive stops, carrying confetti, drinks, and portable radios blaring *Radio Blissett.* All claiming to bear the same name, the Luthers validated only one bus ticket and kept partying until two police cars stopped the tram. Requested to disembark, the psychogeographers declined to identify themselves except by the multiple-use name: "A cop fired shots into the air. The riot and shoot-out were broadcast live via a mobile phone."[47] Four Luthers were charged with disorderly conduct and participation in a seditious rally.

The media attention sparked by the tram riot had the effect of placing Blissett on the map. If up to that point seasoned activists saw Blissett with suspicion—that is, more as an intellectual gizmo for wannabe radicals than as serious activism—after the confrontation with the police, Blissett began to be perceived as an organic component of the movement, in particular of its anarchist–nomadic wing. This had been on the rise since 1994, when the sudden outbreak of the illegal rave scene in Rome and other Italian cities opened up a new phase in the squatting movement from a more traditional occupy-and-entrench strategy to temporary occupations of abandoned warehouses. The illegal rave movement, whose logistics was often provided by the techno music crews of the *centri sociali,* which frequently joined forces with British and French free-party sound systems traveling throughout Europe on modified RVs, appeared to many as the perfect instantiation of Hakim Bey's theory of the "Temporary Autonomous Zones."

In the book *T.A.Z.*, a bestseller and a must-read within the Italian radical subcultures of the time, the U.S. philosopher of ontological anarchism describes a TAZ as a sudden emergence of spaces of possibilities subtracted to the state's ability to control the territory:

> And—the map is closed, but the autonomous zone is open. . . . We are looking for "spaces" (geographic, social, cultural, imaginal) with potential to flower as autonomous zones—and we are looking for times in which these spaces are relatively open, either through neglect on the part of the State or because they have somehow escaped notice by the mapmakers, or for whatever reason.[48]

Drawing on Deleuze and Guattari's *Treatise on Nomadology*, Lyotard's *Driftworks*, and other philosophical works, Bey also introduced the concept of *psychic nomadism* to depict a rebellious, inquisitive, and explorative attitude toward the unknown common to artists, intellectuals, "reality hackers," "cyberpunk utopianists," and "migrant laborers, refugees, the 'homeless,' tourists, the RV and mobile-home culture."[49]

Even though the LBP eventually disowned Bey's influence by selling an apocryphal text by the anarchist philosopher to the Roman publisher Alberto Castelvecchi, Blissett's texts of the mid-1990s frequently employ terms such as "psychic nomadism" and "psychic warfare."[50] Sometimes these keywords appear in conjunction with "psychogeographic drift," adding a new layer of connotation to the term, which partially departs from the Lettrist–Situationist theorizations of the 1950s and 1960s. The Roman LBP clarifies this difference in a short essay, which draws a demarcating line between a modern understanding of the city as a static assemblage of different ambiances and a radical postmodern attitude that shifts the emphasis on subjective crossing of the urban space:

> Theories such as those of unitary urbanism (or similar ones) would be completely inadequate today for a project of radical deconstruction of the metropolis. As a matter of fact, the radical metropolis is no longer identifiable with actual territories, but it is composed of trajectories; with the crisis of citizenship and of the legally constituted

> territory, man [*l'uomo*] does not possess anything other than his own trajectories (always the same!), and his own right becomes a trajectorial [*traiettoriale*] right.[51]

The text continues by listing the tracing of ley lines, mural spray-painting and tagging (against the "Imposed Unique Identity"), the organization of illegal raves and bus parties among "the most radical forms of rupture in the networked apparatuses of urban control."[52] In other words, whereas the Lettrists saw the drift as the research branch of psychogeography—that is, a data-gathering procedure necessary to the conception of a new unitary urbanism—the LBP associated urban drifting with a variety of playful and subversive uses of the media that did not aim at recomposing a lost unity.

This recasting of the *dérive* as a tactical practice aimed at exploiting the gaps between the map and the territory suggests that Blissett was part of a larger movement of deterritorialization of grassroots activism. While the social centers exerted their "sovereignty" over occupied spaces, from which they entertained relationships with other, exterior subjects, the psychic nomads and urban drifters of the mid-1990s made what Michel De Certeau called a tactical use of the city—a use that "cannot count on a 'proper' (a spatial or institutional localization)" and "is always watching for opportunities that must be 'seized on the wing.'"[53] Through this tactical approach, the LBP combined the experimental practices of the modern avant-garde with a social and innovative use of the media to transform grassroots activism from within.

LOTS OF MONEY BECAUSE I AM MANY

Another key component in this emerging assemblage was the exploration of cyberspace, which had been imagined by the cyberpunk literature of the 1980s as a relatively uncharted territory where a number of illicit and convivial activities—such as data piracy and file sharing—could be pursued. Besides having a major influence on science fiction and popular culture at large, cyberpunk literature had a peculiar effect on the Italian subcultures and social movements of the late 1980s to early 1990s. This influence was largely mediated by the cultural work and publications of a Milan-based publishing house, the Shake Underground Edizioni.

Stemming from the early-1980s Milanese punk movement, the Shake editorial collective began publishing the magazine *Decoder* in 1988, moving along two main axes of inquiry: (1) the pursuit of nexuses and possible alliances among different urban subcultures such as mods, punks, and hip-hoppers and (2) a political reading of cyberpunk, revolving around the idea that information technologies could be used for grassroots organizing and a democratization of the media sphere.[54] This line of research found a first practical application in 1993, when, in collaboration with other groups, the Shake / Decoder collective was able to jump-start Cybernet, a national network of BBSs running on Fido software.

The Roman node of Cybernet was AvANa BBS, whose server was physically located and maintained in Forte Prenestino, the largest Roman social center, by a collective with strong ties to the Decoder group.[55] "Since 1994 I used to download [from AvANa BBS] these outrageous and super-funny messages posted by the Transmaniacs on Cybernet—transcripts of their internal meetings as well as accounts of the horrorist stunts going on in Bologna," says Andrea Natella, a cofounder of the Roman LBP. "The Bolognese were generally speaking more creative and less ideological than the Roman collectives which had occupied the university in 1990. So when they came up with Radio Blissett, I spread the idea in our department of producing a version of the show in Rome."[56] At the time, Natella was part of an activist "node" that held regular meetings in the Department of Sociology at the University "La Sapienza" of Rome. Along with the AvANa BBS collective and the more theory-oriented Rizoma Autogestione Metropoli, this group formed the main hub of the Roman LBP.[57] Other individuals coming from political and artistic experiences, such as the philosophy collective Prato Rosso, the network of self-managed seminars Réseau, and the radical sci-fi magazine *Codici Immaginari*, quickly joined ranks.

It is in this milieu, and in its online ramifications on the AvANa / Cybernet discussion groups, that a rich debate unfolded on the possible constitution of autonomous political enterprises *(imprese politiche autonome)*. The idea was to expand the market reach of the social centers' *autoproduzioni* by creating a network of self-sustaining bodies, such as cooperatives and collectively run businesses, that could simultaneously function as economic enterprises and activist projects. As previously noted, the social centers produced and distributed through their own network records, magazines, books, and T-shirts. Events such as concerts, parties, and festivals generated additional revenues through donations and the selling of food and beverages. Some social centers also provided day care services employing temporary workers through city-funded programs. Finally, the more popular bands coming out of the CSOA hip-hop scene showed a commercial potential that did not get lost on major music labels.

To retain this value within their communities, in 1993–94, a number of cultural producers gravitating in the social centers' galaxy began to discuss the possibility of constituting a set of autonomous political enterprises. Some activists called this process "going overground," or leaving behind the cultural ghetto of the underground to have a larger cultural and political impact on Italian society.[58] Others, warning of the risk of self-exploitation, argued that embracing the market could have weakened social struggles and saw this discussion as largely misleading.[59] Most members of the Roman LBP leaned toward the former position, convinced as they were that the rise of the networked society allowed the new "immaterial workers" of the late twentieth century to be increasingly autonomous of capitalist command and the large capital investments that had been employed in the culture industries until the 1980s.

Such a belief matured in the context of a larger conversation on the emergence of the new forms of labor under post-Fordism and on the universal right to an income for all human beings. Unfolding in the journal *Derive e Approdi* and countless books and publications, the Italian post-workerist *(post-operaista)* debate on immaterial labor and citizen income *(reddito di cittadinanza)* had its roots in the 1960s, when the Italian translation of Marx's *Grundrisse* (1857–61) ignited a long-lasting conversation on the relationship between the Marxian notions of dead labor (the labor objectified in machinery and technology) and living labor—the "form-giving fire" of human activity that Marx had identified with the entire potential of the worker's living body. This conversation can be roughly divided into three strands: workerist–autonomist, linguistic, and feminist.

If, in the early 1960s, Raniero Panzieri and the intellectuals revolving around the journal *Quaderni Rossi* (Red notes) had given a "Frankfurter" reading of the *Grundrisse*—that is, fixed capital and machinery were seen as a vehicle of oppression against living labor—by the end of the decade, Mario Tronti had suggested an almost opposite interpretation whereby the development of living labor anticipated and prefigured that of fixed capital.[60] Tronti's "Copernican Revolution" was grounded in an analysis of the new cycle of social struggles that had moved a significant part of the Italian working class into openly anticapitalist positions in the late 1960s.[61] By noting how the decentralization and reorganization of industrial production occurred right at the beginning of the 1970s—that is, in the aftermath of the 1968 student movement and the 1969 hot fall *(autunno caldo)*—the Italian autonomists interpreted the transition from Fordism to post-Fordism as a capitalist reaction to workers' struggles.[62] According to Antonio Negri, the workers' "mass refusal" of waged labor had the effect of pushing laboring processes outside the factory walls.[63] Such an exodus from the workplace set in motion new forms of subjectivity and multiplied the sites of contestation throughout society. For Negri and other autonomists, living labor is thus a creative force that, on one hand, struggles against work (and thus against itself) in the struggle against capital. On the other hand, a self-organized living labor generates a multiplicity of autonomous projects that point beyond capitalist relations. As Harry Cleaver points out, "the second, positive side to revolutionary struggle is the elaboration of the self-determined multiple projects of the working class in the time set free from work and in the transformation of work itself. This self-determined project Negri calls *self-valorization*."[64]

This point introduces us to the second analysis of immaterial labor, which is more strictly linguistic and whose main representative is Paolo Virno. A former member, like Negri, of Workers' Power, Virno also approaches Marx from the *Grundrisse.* In the notorious "Fragment on Machines," Marx notes how, to reproduce itself, capital has increasingly relied on socialized forms of labor, that is, "on the general state of science and on the progress of technology, or the application of this science to production."[65] As the "general social knowledge" or general intellect is channeled toward the development of more productive machines and the development of fixed capital, "a large part of the wealth already created can be withdrawn both from immediate consumption and from production for immediate consumption."[66] Thus, as increased productivity allows capitalists to "employ people upon something not directly or immediately productive," labor moves to the side of the productive process, turning more and more into "a supervisory and regulatory activity."[67]

Virno maintains that this kind of regulatory activity mobilizes the worker's communicative and linguistic faculties. In fact, contemporary immaterial workers are evaluated and rewarded not only for the fulfillment of specifics tasks but also for their ability to cooperate, modify, and "ameliorate the organization of labor"—that is, for their ability to increase productivity.[68] This leads Virno to argue that besides constituting the core of the media industry "in the post-Ford era, human communication is also an essential ingredient of productive cooperation in general; thus it is the reigning productive force, something that goes beyond the domain of its own sphere, pertaining instead to the industry as a whole, to poiesis in its totality."[69] Because politics entails a rhetorical ability to perform before an audience, Virno concludes that under post-Fordism, language and communication erode the boundaries between labor, political action, and intellectual life, making it increasingly difficult for politics to mediate among the economic and social forces from a position of exteriority.

But if communication and language are critical to both productivity and politics, they do not take place in a vacuum, attached as they are to the worker's living body. Since the early 1970s, scholars such as Mariarosa Dalla Costa, Silvia Federici, and Leopoldina Fortunati have analyzed the relationship between reproductive and productive labor and between unwaged and waged labor in relation to domestic labor, nurturing, and prostitution.[70] As Leopoldina Fortunati points out, "while Marx clearly saw the domestic sphere as an unproductive sphere, we saw the production of goods and services (prostitution included) as a crucial stage inside the whole process of production and reproduction."[71] Thus, if the workerists drew from the *Grundrisse* to underscore the less deterministic aspects of Marxian thought, the feminists pointed to other aspects of Marxian theory to demonstrate that Marx's definition of productive labor had to be revised to include those activities, such as care labor, housework, and sexual work, that were not strictly oriented toward the production of material goods but rather toward "producing and/or reproducing the commodity most precious for capital, the labor force."[72] In this way, the feminist movement questioned the Marxian definition of necessary labor as a rigid category that takes for granted what kind of labor is socially recognized as a value-creating practice. The importance of this line of inquiry has been subsequently acknowledged by part of the postworkerist school. For example, Hardt and Negri contend that "the very concept of labor is mobile and historically defined through contestation. In this sense the labor theory of value is equally a value theory of labor."[73]

But if labor and value are both independent variables in the structures of capital, then every social activity is potentially subject to such contestation. This means that immaterial labor, as an ensemble of affective, cognitive, and linguistic faculties, is not only limited to the economic but also becomes immediately a social, cultural, and political force. "Ultimately," write Hardt and Negri, "the production involved here is the *production of subjectivity,* the creation and reproduction of new subjectivities in society."[74] Since this production invests the entire social bios, the "biopolitical production [of immaterial labor] is on the one hand *immeasurable,* because it cannot be quantified in fixed units of time, and, on the other hand, always *excessive* with respect to the value that capital can extract from it because capital can never capture all life."[75] But if every social activity is potentially a value-generating practice, then "a social wage and a guaranteed income for all" is one of the fundamental demands of the multitude.[76] Likewise, autonomist economists such as Christian Marazzi, Andrea Fumagalli, and Sergio Bologna argue that because the high level of productivity incorporated in ICTs has the effect of breaking the link between economic growth and occupational growth, and between salaries and productivity, all citizens should be entitled to an income regardless of their condition of employment.[77]

The argument that links the excessive and immeasurable character of living labor to the request of a citizen income detached from productivity is clearly articulated in Luther Blissett's *Declaration of Rights,* a manifesto written by the Roman LBP in 1995:

> The industry of the integrated spectacle and immaterial command owes me money. I will not come to terms with it until I will have what is owed to me. For all the times I appeared on TV, films, and on the radio as a casual passerby or as an element of the landscape, and my image has not been compensated . . . for all the words or expressions of high communicative impact I have coined in peripheral cafes, squares, street corners, and social centers that became powerful advertising jingles . . . without seeing a dime; for all the times my name and my personal data have been put to work for free by statistics for

> adjusting the demand, refining marketing strategies, increasing the productivity of firms to which I could not be more indifferent; for all the advertising I continuously make by wearing branded T-shirts, backpacks, socks, jackets, bathing suits, towels, without my body being remunerated as a commercial billboard; for all of this and much more, the industry of the integrated spectacle owes me money!
>
> I understand it may be difficult to calculate how much they owe me as an individual. But this is not necessary at all, because I am Luther Blissett, the multiple [*multiplo*] and the manifold [*molteplice*]. And what the industry of the integrated spectacle owes me, it is owed to the many that I am, and is owed to me because I am many. From this viewpoint, we can agree on a generalized compensation. You will not have peace until I will have the money! LOTS OF MONEY BECAUSE I AM MANY: CITIZEN INCOME FOR LUTHER BLISSETT![78]

It is noticeable that Blissett does not reclaim an income from the government but identifies as counterpart "the industry of the integrated spectacle and immaterial command," that is, capital's ability to extract a profit from daily practices such as the wearing of branded clothes, the invention of slang terms, and the diffused creativity of urban subcultures. As value becomes increasingly social and the production of wealth is entangled with the production of new forms of subjectivity, Blissett reclaims the immeasurable and excessive nature of the condividual. If in the age of biopolitical production the locus of surplus value lies, as the autonomist Marxists contend, in the knowledge, language, and affects that society produces in common, then Luther Blissett is an expression of the immaterial workers' ability to cooperate and produce in common.

CULTURE JAMMING AS MYTHMAKING

As we have seen, the LBP had managed to cloud the origins of the multiple-use name by tracing it back to a Jamaican soccer player, a U.S. mail artist, and a dense web of fictional progenitors. This mythmaking strategy was especially pursued by the Bolognese LBP and one of its offshoots, the collective of historic novelists Wu Ming—a Chinese expression that translates as "no name" or "unknown."

In various articles and interviews, Wu Ming has compared Luther Blissett to other popular myths and folk heroes, such as Poor Konrad,

General Ludd, Captain Swing, and the Subcomandante Marcos.[79] This choice of inserting Blissett into a long genealogy of folk heroes serves the primary purpose of presenting the condividual as a positive mythic figure rather than a mere demystifier of power narratives. As Roberto Bui (aka Wu Ming 1) notes in an interview with Henry Jenkins,

> pranks, media stunts, and culture jamming were more the means to spread the myth than the ends of the project. *The most important aspect of our activities was not sabotage, but the way sabotage increased Blissett's mythical status*. . . . Fake news and media hoaxes served the purpose of making our very presence on the media landscape legendary, so that ever more people joined us and adopted the name. "Culture jamming" was just a subordinate part of the project: the practical exploration of a grassroots, interactive mythology was the most important thing.[80]

Thus, as a "Robin Hood of the information age," Blissett was supposed to embody the very process of "transmedia storytelling" (to use an expression coined by Jenkins) whereby cultural producers and immaterial workers could recognize themselves as part of a community.[81] This understanding of myth as an open social process is clearly articulated in the following definition of *mythopoesis* offered by Wu Ming 1:

> Mythopoesis is the social process of constructing myths, by which we do not mean "false stories," we mean stories that are told and shared, re-told and manipulated, by a vast and multifarious community, stories that may give shape to some kind of ritual, some sense of continuity between what we do and what other people did in the past. A tradition. In Latin the verb "tradere" simply meant "to hand down something," it did not entail any narrow-mindedness, conservatism or forced respect for the past. Revolutions and radical movements have always found and told their own myths.[82]

And yet Marx himself and twentieth-century Marxists such as Walter Benjamin, Theodor Adorno, and Roland Barthes had read myth as an instrument of class domination—a weapon employed by the bourgeoisie to cloud the real movement of history.[83] In *Mythologies*, Barthes famously defined myth as a type of speech that has the power to deprive each and every sign of its particular history with the threefold purpose of naturalizing culture, eternalizing history, and obfuscating the actual relations of production. Asked whether he believes myths are possible on the Left, Barthes argues that *myth always entails an ability to lie* and thus to afford a certain wealth to spare—a wealth that the "barren," "poverty-stricken," and realist language of the working class does not possess.[84]

On the contrary, for Wu Ming, myths can have a progressive and even revolutionary function, as long as their becoming is not arrested. As previously noted, such theory was predicated on a materialist reading of the new forms of labor in the information society. In particular, the LBP understood that since the very reproduction and expansion of the information economy requires a massive socialization of knowledge, a part of this social knowledge could be employed to celebrate its producers. In such context, Barthes's distinction between myth as the deceptive and nuanced language of the wealthy and realism as the honest, literal, if unsophisticated language of the working class did no longer hold. Unlike Barthes's poverty-stricken leftist myths of the 1950s (such as the myth of Stalin), Blissett's language was elaborate and nuanced and could afford to lie because it fed on the overabundance of the information age.

For example, the media hoaxes organized by the LBP required an ability to mimic the language and codes of mainstream media as well as to open up such codes to wider participatory assemblages. In this respect, Wu Ming 1's contention that hoaxes and pranks are instrumental and thus subordinate to mythmaking may underestimate the pragmatic knowledge that jammers acquire and share in the making of their stunts. In the case of the LBP, such knowledge was handed down as a set of narratives and theoretical statements that reflected critically on the multiple-use name strategy. In the next section, I will analyze some of the media hoaxes that served to cultivate Luther Blissett's myth and a critical body of texts that focused on the role played by the multiple personality in a mediascape dominated by moral panics and the power of the Roman Catholic Church.

MEDIA HOMEOPATHY

Founded in 1963, Comunità Incontro is an established network of more than two hundred Catholic community centers scattered all over Italy for the rehabilitation of drug addicts. Incontro's founding father, Don Pierino

Gelmini, is a well-known TV character who has been at the forefront of prohibitionist marches and antipedophile crusades for more than three decades. Thus, when, in December 1996, the Italian police arrest a middle-aged Cambodian man on his way to Belgium and charge him with child trading—a story widely covered by the Italian media—Luther Blissett decides to exploit the media attention. On January 4, 1997, a man identifying himself as Aldo Curiotto, the official spokesman of Comunità Incontro, phones Ansa, the main Italian newswire. Since Incontro has a branch office in Thailand, Blissett, posing as a distressed Curiotto, insinuates the doubt that there may be a Far East connection between Don Gelmini and the Cambodian man: "The Carabinieri did NOT arrest him, they are just interrogating him. Don Gelmini has NOT YET been charged with a traffic of child-abuse videos."[85] Predictably, Ansa diffuses the nonnews of the disavowal, and in the lapse of a few hours, TV newscasts and newspapers run interviews with an unknowing Gelmini.

The phone prank on Don Gelmini was not an isolated stunt but part of an elaborate strategy of "media homeopathy." The idea was to inject into the media bloodstream stories whose patent falsity would eventually induce the media immune system to a reaction of its own.[86] Such a strategy had already yielded significant results in 1996, when a new cell of the LBP operating in Viterbo—a medieval town fifty miles north of Rome—fabricated one of the more sophisticated and successful pranks of the entire LBP.

Founded in fall 1995, the Viterbese branch of the LBP was also mostly composed of college students and had a direct connection to the Bolognese LBP through Riccardo Paccosi, a Viterbese by birth.[87] Even though Paccosi had moved to Bologna, where he had founded the Teatro Situazionautico, he kept in touch with a circle of friends from his hometown who had participated in the occupation of the social center Valle Faul in 1993 and animated the Associazione Culturale "Cesare Dobici."

At the end of 1995, the local press reported the discovery of Satanic graffiti and animal sacrifices on the mountains surrounding the city. Inspired by the news, the LBP began spray-painting cryptic Satanic messages and swastikas on Viterbo city walls in January 1996. As the local press began investigating, the LBP flooded the local newspapers with numerous letters—purportedly written by indignant citizens—that insinuated a connection between the right-wing city government and fictional exoteric neo-Nazi groups. On a Saturday night of May 1996, having learned that the woods surrounding the city were to be cleaned up by an environmentalist group the following day, the LBP fabricates evidence of a black mass. The following day, *Il Corriere di Viterbo, Il Tempo,* and *Il Messaggero* provide extensive coverage of the environmentalists' "horrific discovery."[88]

As the media hysteria mounts, the LBP founds the ultra-Catholic Committee for the Safeguard of Morals (CoSaMo), a fanatical squad of vigilantes who claim to have started their own nocturnal patrols to hunt down the Satanists. In July, *Il Corriere di Viterbo* receives a videotape containing footage of a black mass in which "a screaming virgin" is supposedly sacrificed. (The video is murky and the woman is always off-camera.) Besides generating a new round of articles by the local press—which hardly questions the authenticity of the document—the video goes national on *Studio Aperto,* one of Berlusconi's newscasts, which broadcasts it in February 1997, presenting it as an "exceptional document." As the media hysteria reaches its peak, on March 2, 1997, the LBP mails extensive proof of the fabrication to the national public TV channel RAI 1. The extended version of the video featuring the gruesome "killing of the virgin" ends with a tarantella in which the Satanists and the virgin hold hands, dance, and sing along.[89] Visibly embarrassed by the national exposure, the Viterbo papers abandon the Satanic trail in the midst of polemics and reciprocal accusations of sensationalism.[90]

While the Viterbo hoax was still unfolding, the Bolognese branch of the LBP had decided to duplicate the experiment in Bologna. In June 1996, a human skull is left in the luggage lockers of the local train station with a message addressed to *Il Resto del Carlino,* the most popular Bolognese tabloid. The note is signed "Satan's Hunters" (Cacciatori di Satana), a mysterious group of Satanists who claim to have stolen the skull from the Satan's Children (Bambini di Satana), a notorious and real sect based in Bologna. *Il Carlino* runs an article, and a few days later, Luther Blissett uncovers the hoax by sending evidence of the fabrication to other local newspapers.

The Satan's Children owe their notoriety to the fact that, in 1996, *Il Carlino* led a moral crusade against Marco Dimitri and other members of the sect who had been arrested twice and charged first with sexual abuse of a sixteen-year-old girl and then for supposedly having employed a three-year-old child in a black mass. Although the national press is quick to spread the moral panic, amplifying the groundless charges pressed by prosecutor Lucia Musti, the defendants do not take long to demonstrate that Dimitri, who is notoriously gay, has never engaged in sex or child abuse and that the Satan's Children are in fact an adult consensual cult that has no connection whatsoever to pedophiles.[91]

In 1997, Blissett sends to press the book *Let the Children: Pedophilia as a Pretext for a Witch Hunt,* an independent investigation on the Satan's Children trial and its media coverage, which unveils how facts and witnesses have been manipulated in the service of an ultraconservative Catholic agenda. The book shows how the main witness of the trial, a sixteen-year-old girl whose fictional name is Simonetta, first tried to retract her accusations and contradicted herself several times; then was taken care of by the GRIS, an association investigating religious sects on behalf of the Catholic Curia of Bologna; and, finally, was never able to provide a single piece of evidence to back up her allegations.[92] Furthermore, the trial has shown how both Simonetta and Federico (the three-year-old child) have been "exorcised" by Catholic priests connected to the GRIS and pressured by the investigators and their ultra-Catholic mothers to call into cause Dimitri and friends.[93]

Besides undoing the prosecutor's evidence and accusations, *Let the Children* well illustrates the LBP's media-homeopathic strategy. The book juxtaposes in two separates chapters the Bolognese trial and the Viterbese witch hunt. Whereas the former had been mounted by an overzealous prosecutor with the uncritical support of the national media, the latter was a pure fabrication that the Viterbo press had managed to blow out of proportion. Blissett's homeopathic remedies have proved effective in that the Viterbese newspapers have accused each other of being unprofessional, to be eventually discredited by national TV. Furthermore, the Carlino hoax and the publication of *Let the Children* have prompted national newspapers such as *La Repubblica* to question Musti's investigation and the initial wave of sensationalism and moral panic.[94] Thus, by checking each other, the media have homeopathically activated the media's own immune system.

The publication of *Let the Children* does not go unnoticed. A few weeks after the book release, Lucia Musti files a libel suit against the publisher, the author(s), and two web servers that host electronic copies of the book.[95] Two years later, the prosecutor obtains a partial victory: the legal author of the book, Roberto Bui, is fined for defamation, whereas the publisher, Alberto Castelvecchi, is ordered to withdraw the remaining copies from the market and destroy them.[96] Meanwhile, the electronic version of the book is downloaded and mirrored by several websites as part of an international free speech campaign. In 2000, as a consequence of another wave of media hysteria instigated by the Sicilian priest Don Fortunato di Noto, three websites hosted by the Rete Civica Romana, a civic network managed by the City of Rome, are obscured for hosting materials "not apt to children." One of them, the Avana BBS website, hosts a copy of the book.[97]

As the publication and electronic reproduction of *Let the Children* snowballs into a national *affaire* involving publishers, sys-ads, priests, magistrates, and politicians, the Bolognese LBP develops a theoretical reflection on the historical and political function of national emergencies in Italy. In *Nemici dello Stato* (Enemies of the state), a book published in 1999, Blissett notes that the moral panic epitomizes "the fear of the great 'disintermediation' brought about by the Internet."[98] After the late-1970s emergency laws against terrorism, and the war on Mafia of the 1980s, Italian national emergencies were now shifting

> from the *molar* (the clash between masses, the battlepiece [*sic*], the confrontation on the stage of public life) to the *molecular* (the everyday micro-conflict, the control on individual differences by information technologies).... The new molecular emergencies serve to control and censor electronic communications, indeed, the behaviors of the new immaterial workers who are re-appropriating their know-how and tendency to innovation, becoming ever more *autonomous* from capital as direct command on the work-force.[99]

Thus the condividual embodies the immaterial workers' autonomy as well as their ability to organize and rebuff the attacks coming from those sectors of the state that threaten this autonomy through censorship and the threat of emergency laws. In this respect, *Let the Children* and *Nemici dello Stato* advance a lucid analysis of the political reconfiguration of the special legislation of the 1970s and suggest a set of ingenious tactics to face the new emergencies of the 1990s. In this way, the LBP demonstrated that media panics could be confronted with a twofold strategy that combined the traditional methods of the counterinquiry with innovative culture-jamming interventions.

To sum up, if early Luther Blissett books such as *Mind Invaders* and *Totò, Peppino e la Guerra Psichica* had exposed the principles of psychic warfare and guerrilla-communication through examples that were playful and occasionally confrontational, *Let the Children* and *Nemici dello Stato* showed that the same principles could be applied to serious and current political issues. Thus a comparative reading of these essays allows us to follow the LBP's arc from its early experimental and avant-garde practices to a more directly political brand of media activism. To be sure, such trajectory was not linear, as the late 1990s also see a return of more artistic interventions, such as Darko Maver. But it suddenly came to a close at the turn of the millennium, when several participants in Luther Blissett abruptly decided to disband the LBP.

INTERNAL CRITICISM AND SEPPUKU

Blissett's counteroffensive on the new emergencies was not without contradiction. Even if *Let the Children* had presented the media hoaxes of Viterbo and Bologna as part of a concerted and integrated strategy, the Viterbese ruse did not come to an end spontaneously. "I distinctly remember that at a certain point the Bolognese 'Central Committee' [of the LBP] exerted strong pressures on us to unveil the hoax," says Fango, a former member of the Viterbese LBP. "This was probably due to the fact that during the Dimitri trial the Bolognese were trying to demonstrate that the media coverage of the Satanic phenomenon was misleading. As long as our actions were confined to Viterbo, the Bolognese were fine with it, but when the case went national on Studio Aperto [a national newscast], they thought that the story could have had negative repercussions on the Dimitri trial. So they asked us to pull the plug."[100]

As soon as the Viterbese complied, albeit reluctantly, with the request, the Bolognese provided them with the opportunity of unveiling their hoax on RAI 1.[101] But if the outcome of this deal was positive for the Bolognese LBP—in that it functioned as a public reminder that the hysteria surrounding the Satanic sects was often baseless and engineered by the press—the Viterbese were not equally satisfied. "In actual fact, we had not set a deadline for our campaign," says Algernon. "We were fascinated with a Borges-like idea of deferring falsification to the infinite, without necessarily revealing the hoax. In this respect our group was a mad splinter [*scheggia impazzita*] of the LBP, which operated in complete autonomy, and eventually had to change its original plans because it came under pressure to do so."[102]

Even though Algernon and Fango's reference to the Bolognese "Central Committee" is undoubtedly tongue in cheek, their account hints at the existence of a hierarchy within the LBP. To be sure, if such a hierarchy existed, it was not formalized, as every participant in Luther Blissett was effectively free to use the name without prior authorization. Yet there existed an ongoing struggle internal to the LBP over the political desirability of some interventions and over their definition in the public sphere. "I remember that in 1995, along with two other women, I gave an interview to *Noi Donne*, a historic magazine of the Italian feminist movement," says Miriam Tola, a former member of the Roman LBP and of the Department of Sociology's Node:

> The interview touched on various issues including the fact that Blissett was a male name, and that this was in apparent contradiction with the supposedly transgender and post-identity stance of Luther Blissett. When the article was published some Bolognese Luthers criticized it for being confused, perhaps at risk of fostering a "weak" postmodern understanding of the Project. At the time I was only twenty-one, so it is possible that this criticism was appropriate, but this was not an isolated incident. Rather, I think it reflected a general tendency, internal to our group as well as the Bolognese, to argue over the political appropriateness of Blissett's interventions, that is, discussing what Blissett should do or not do, say or not say. For my girlfriends and I this debate was actually quite useful because it led us to discuss how identity and subjectivity are embodied in male or female bodies. Soon after the Roman LBP disbanded we decided to found, along with other women who had not participated in Luther Blissett, a cyberfeminist group called Orma Nomade.[103]

To sum up, Algernon and Fango's statements point to the existence of a conflict between two separate branches of the LBP over the kind of actions the condividual was supposed to undertake. While the Viterbese were exploring the multiple personality from a conceptual standpoint—the endless deferral of the media hoax was geared toward a permanent blending of facts and fiction—the Bolognese had a clear-cut political agenda and pushed to subordinate experimentation for its own sake to the actual outcome of the Dimitri trial. Tola's remarks, conversely, foreground the internal debate over the political and cultural significance of Blissett's interventions. Such a debate was ultimately oriented at a delimitation of the semantic field traced by the condividual's appearances in the public domain.

Perhaps, taken all together, these considerations cast a light on an irreducible contradiction. Whereas Blissett claimed to "play the Myth's game with the goal of undermining the authority of Myth (of Truth, Identity, Reason, etc.),"[104] in actual fact, the LBP struggled to project a meaningful, if not entirely coherent, image of Luther Blissett so as to avoid, in Tola's words, a "weak postmodern" reading of it. As we saw in the previous chapter, the Neoists emphasized that the "great confusion" and "radical play" were constitutive to Monty Cantsin, who had to fight against itself as much as against the culture industry. But because Luther Blissett was mostly a political project, and its large participatory base exposed it to the risk of being appropriated for contradictory purposes, some interventions were reframed within a unifying narrative—namely, Blissett as the folk hero of immaterial workers—which tamed the virtuality and schizo-tendency of the improper name.

This effort at containing the polysemy of Blissett through a unifying set of narratives clearly emerged on September 6, 1999, when several founding members of the Bolognese LBP agreed on sending out a press release that read,

> Seppuku!
>
> Many subjectivities of the Luther Blissett Project Italian columns have decided to greet the new millennium by committing seppuku, a ritual suicide. Suicide is the practical demonstration that Blissett gives up mere survival as a territorial, identitarian logic. Suicide is the ultimate and most extreme "take to the bush" of this folk hero. We are not advocating nihilism or relinquishment; rather, we are choosing life. Seppuku is not *the* course of action, Luther

> Blissett is a name that anybody can keep adopting also after next New Year's Day. There are countries where the fight has just begun, and we surely hope it goes on. . . . The Seppuku is not the end of Luther Blissett. It is the beginning of a new phase, a new way of using his face and name. For those who will commit it, Blissett's suicide will consist in giving up that signature and moving on to new conflicts. It is quite the contrary of what usually happens to suicides: they don't go anyplace, while their names are more oft-mentioned than before their death. . . . As Zhuangzi reminds us: "The perfect man has no ego, the inspired man has no works, the wise man has no name." And, as the matchless Cary Grant once put it: "It is better to leave a minute earlier, leaving people wanting more, rather than a minute too late, when people are getting bored."[105]

The seppuku served to draw a line between the LBP and the new experiences that were about to stem from it. Only six months before the announcement, four members of the Bolognese LBP had authored *Q*, a historic novel they had been quietly working on for four years.[106] Even though the novel is signed by Luther Blissett, the four decided to reveal their birth names to the press and launch the collective of writers Wu Ming the following year.[107] The younger generation of the Bolognese LBP, which had authored the Darko Maver's swindle, founded 0100101110101101.ORG, a net.art group initially focusing on questions of authorship, originality, and reproducibility in the online (art) world. Finally, several cofounders of the Roman LBP had already created the collective of "radical ufology" Men in Red (MIR), without formally announcing the disbandment of the LBP. Likewise, the Viterbese LBP had quietly ceased its operations in the aftermath of the Satanic stunt.

The seppuku and the choice of the four Blissetts to unveil their birth names—a choice that, according to the four, was dictated by the fact that some journalists had already discovered their legal identities—drew internal as well as public criticism. In a long essay published by the magazine *Invarianti,* Leonardo Lippolis accused the entire LBP of being nothing more than a launch pad for unscrupulous artists and writers who ended up occupying a golden seat in the Italian culture industry (Einaudi is one of the largest Italian publishers and is currently owned by Silvio Berlusconi) through the oedipal killing of a fatherlike figure like Guy Debord.[108]

Notwithstanding the criticism of the orthodox guardians of the Situationist heritage, the choice of discontinuing the name posed some serious questions, which were internally debated without necessarily resulting in public dissent.

Even though the ritual suicide was not prescriptive ("Seppuku is not the course of action," the announcement read), leaving other dividuals the freedom to continue to use the improper name, the choice of terminating the multiple personality remarked that the entire LBP had to be understood as a work of fiction—or, in the words of Wu Ming, a "Five-Year Plan" with a clear beginning and an end (1994–99).[109] In other words, the ritual suicide was a way for some of the initiators of the LBP to reclaim authorship over the condividual—whose parenthood they originally had denied, attributing it to other fictional figures—and to move forward to other endeavors. On one hand, such move was undoubtedly foresighted. After all, Luther Blissett was a coming-of-age experience whereby a new generation of cultural producers acquired advanced communication skills through social cooperation rather than regular professional training. Thus it is understandable that, at a certain point, some of these individuals felt the need to move toward more specialized forms of cultural production, such as writing or art making. And it is remarkable that some of them managed to keep doing it in a collective fashion, constituting in some cases some of the autonomous political enterprises that had been so intensely debated in the mid-1990s.[110]

On the other hand, Luther Blissett was and remains a construct that exceeds the ability of its creators to contain its deeds within a single narrative or set of narratives. This is evident, on a historical level, from the fact that the multiple-use name went international and has kept resurfacing in various contexts long after the seppuku.[111] On a more philosophical level, if the improper name Luther Blissett was meant to be an expression of the cooperative capacities of the multitude, then it is doubtful that such capacities can be reduced to a unifying narrative. In this respect, Wu Ming's definition of storytelling as a political activity ("To tell a story is to share, that is, to make a community")[112] is double edged in that if storytelling can be inclusive and participatory, it can also offer a representation of the community that does not reflect its internal differentiation and complexity. This is particularly true of mythic storytelling, which by definition provides an organic image of the community. (Thus—and I will expand on this point in the book's conclusion—Luther Blissett's artificial and reconstructed mythmaking may ultimately reveal the impossibility of myth in a society that is no longer founded and revealed to itself by mythic speech.)

In this respect, the tale that the LBP was a preordained five-year plan culminating in the publication of *Q* was rejected as preposterous by many of its members. It must be noted, however, that aside from generating some internal polemics, this dissent did not take public form, probably because most of the LBP members had already moved to new activities and projects. Two notable exceptions were the year 2000 *Luther Blissett—Open Pop Star,* an experimental music CD assembled by the Roman Psychogeographic Association and Aliens in Roma, and the 2005 DVD *Che fine ha fatto Luther Blissett?* (Where did Luther Blissett end?), which contained dozens of audiovisual tributes to the multiple singularity.[113] The Roman "posthumous release" offered a multifaceted acoustic portrait of the condividual by paying tribute to mythic forefathers, such as Monty Cantsin; featuring inspirational figures, such as Stewart Home and Jacques Camatte; touching on cult moments, such as the live radio recording of the tram shootout; and, finally, celebrating the death of the open pop star (the last track is titled "Seppuku"). The sleeve of the album, however, contained an important proviso on the ritual suicide:

> Announced since '97 the Seppuku effects only some experiences that have contributed to the diffusion of the multiple-use name Luther Blissett. . . . Nowadays, Luther Blissett is not identifiable with any individual, if not arbitrarily, it does not coincide in a definitive manner with any project, obviously not even the Luther Blissett Project. Luther Blissett is only the name of an OPEN POP STAR that anyone can impersonate, and whose mythology is entirely rewritable. Thus the multiple-use name Luther Blissett will keep being used even after the LBP's seppuku, probably along with innovative styles that will change its story and reputation.[114]

But if the posthumous compilation served as a healthy reminder that, as an open reputation, Luther Blissett would have survived the demise of the LBP—as well as any attempt to seal its destiny in a story with a defined ending—the impressive commercial success of *Q* pushed the notoriety of the multiple-use name well beyond its original authorizing context.

Q AS AN ALLEGORICAL MACHINE

As soon as it hit the bookstores, *Q* became an instant best seller, selling only in Italy more than two hundred thousand copies in fewer than three years. It was subsequently translated into twelve languages, including German, English, French, Russian, Spanish, Portuguese, and Korean. Spanning more than thirty years of European history, from the outbreak of the Reformation (1517) to the Peace of Augsburg (1555), *Q* tells the story of an Anabaptist who participates under different names in various insurrections and proto-communist conspiracies such as the Peasants' War (1524–25), led by Thomas Münzter against the German princes; the Münster uprising of the following decade; the radical Anabaptist sect of the Zwaardgeesten (sword-minded) or Batenburgers; and the Loyist community of Antwerp. After changing names several times and repeatedly risking his life, the hero finds refuge in Venice and Istanbul. In Venice, he takes the name of Tiziano, an Anabaptist who spreads misinformation with the goal of abducting and killing Q, the mysterious Papal emissary who persecutes Anabaptists and spiritualists on behalf of the cardinal Gian Pietro Carafa. Even though Tiziano succeeds in his plan (as Q is effectively killed), Carafa eventually ascends to the papacy, taking the name of Paul IV, in 1555—the same year in which the Peace of Augsburg puts an end to the religious wars in Europe. Carafa's victory, however, marks the beginning of the Counter-Reformation, with the institution of the *Index Librorum Prohibitorum,* the empowerment of the Roman Inquisition, the persecution of Protestants and Jews in the Catholic states, and the suppression of any space of theological pluralism within the Roman Catholic Church.

Because the hero partakes in radical sociopolitical experiments of all kinds, the novel has been interpreted as a political allegory for the late-twentieth-century subcultures and social movements, from the hippies and beatniks of the 1960s (represented by the Loyists of Antwerp) to the violent fringes of the Italian Autonomia (the Anabaptists leading the Peasants' Wars and the Münster uprising) to terrorist groups such as the Red Brigades and the Weathermen (the sword-minded Batenburgers).[115]

On a different level, the novel is an allegory for the impact that new media—the printing press at the time of the Reformation, the Internet in the 1990s—have on social and political change. In fact, Tiziano uses the illegal reproduction of an heretical book, *The Benefit of Christ Crucified*—

which Carafa is seeking to attribute to the spiritualists of Reginald Pole (the reformist cardinal who contends with him for the tiara)—as a bait to draw Q into his trap. As McKenzie Wark points out, this "book-within-the-book" is a typical postmodern device that allows the reader to shift the focus from the main story line (the novel's diegesis) to a formal, meta-reading of the book-as-artifact. But instead of using this postmodern approach to deepen the textual play within the book or in connection to other texts, *Q*, notes Wark, mobilizes "the book-within-the-book to ask questions about how to read the book-outside-the-book, the book in the world."[116] From this angle, *Q* can be divided into three parts: "In the first, a text is a tool for struggle; in the second, a form of subjective self-management; in the third, part of a network, a milieu that makes many different kinds of thing possible."[117]

Wark's allegorical reading of *Q* can also be extended to the manifold uses the LBP made of its own textual production. As we have seen, pamphlets, counterinvestigations, and theoretical texts such as *Mind Invaders, Let the Children,* and *Nemici dello Stato* functioned as "tools for struggle" in that they provided a sophisticated analysis of the evolution and mediatization of the state of exception, while suggesting a set of innovative tactics on how to resist it. Moreover, Blissett's defense of the Satanists against the Roman Catholic Church's secular arms and the analogy between *Let the Children* and *The Benefit of Christ Crucified* are almost literal in that both books ended up incinerated.[118] Second, a novel such as *Q* also had a self-reflexive function for activists insofar as it provided an understanding of how radical ideas and practices can metamorphose and resurface even after a powerful reactionary tide seems to have suppressed them once and for all. Third, along with the dissemination of false information and other media pranks, the LBP's textual production formed a network that made "many different kinds of thing possible" within the media sphere, the art world, the culture industry, and society at large.

Finally, another analogy between the book-within-the-book and the book-outside-the-book can be found in the specular destiny of *Q*'s author and main character. As we have seen, *Q*'s hero keeps changing names as he moves from one situation to another—a phoenixlike strategy that responds to the necessity to escape identification while symbolizing the ability of social movements to be reborn from their ashes. Likewise, the authors of the novel decided to discontinue the Luther Blissett signature in the aftermath of the book release, to be born again in the new millennium as Wu Ming, a signature used by Chinese dissidents that means both "no name" and "unknown."[119] This unexpected move generated a paradoxical situation as the condividual was withdrawn from the public sphere at the moment of its highest visibility. In "Seppuku," the last track of the *Open Pop Star* compilation mentioned earlier, a reciting voice calls this aikido-like movement "striking by subtraction" *(colpire per sottrazione)*:

> Let us begin the millennium with a seppuku / The ritual suicide is the ultimate extreme / Take to the bush of the folk hero / Striking by subtraction / Making room for new styles / Manifold rebirths / Starting the millennium with a seppuku / Is part of the art of war / Throwing your sword to the ground / Is part of the art of war / He who is swift in sword-less fighting / Will never be disarmed.[120]

Seen as a gesture for liberating the imaginal surplus and the virtuality of the alias, the seppuku proved to be in many ways a prophetic gesture. In the following years, the experience and modus operandi of the LBP affected a broad range of artistic and activist practices. On one hand, projects such as Wu Ming, 0100101110101101.ORG, MIR, and guerrigliamarketing.it were direct offshoots of the LBP.[121] On the other hand, the multiple-use name strategy was adopted, with various degrees of abstraction, by collectives and networks of the alter-globalization movement such as San Precario, Serpica Naro, Yo Mango!, and the Yes Men. And, as we shall see in the next chapter, it powerfully resurfaced, albeit under different guises and in a different context, with the hacktivist network Anonymous in the late 2000s.

5

ANONYMOUS, THE TRANSDUCER

> Identity. One of our most precious possessions. You believe we all have one, but you are sadly mistaken. Identity belongs only to those who are important. Those who have earned it by struggle and blood. Those who matter. You my friend, do not. Identity is a fragile and weak thing. It can be stolen or replaced. Even forgotten. Identity is a pointless thing for people like us. So why not let go of it and become Anonymous?
>
> —ANONYMOUS

The improper names discussed so far in this book have been introduced to fulfill specific aesthetic, political, and economic functions. Whether completely fictional or inspired by existing individuals, they are the offspring of human imagination, language, and communication. In this chapter, I am going to discuss the case of a shared pseudonym that displaces this exquisitely human ontology as it was originally descriptive of a software function. As the tag that marks the unsigned comments on the imageboard 4chan—an Internet forum that requires users to begin a discussion by posting an image—"Anonymous" was soon appropriated by those users to coordinate actions that require the participation of many. Thus, on one hand, Anonymous is a tag that designates an Internet user without attributes that may distinguish it from any other user. On the other hand, Anonymous functions as a collective assemblage of enunciation that entails coordination, collaboration, and intentionality.

My wager is that the problematic of Anonymous lies at the intersection of an impersonal, potentially deindividuating technology such as the imageboard and human subjectivity and will. In this chapter, I broaden this initial claim to suggest that Anonymous expresses the convergence of a technological drive toward indetermination with the human belief that open technologies are conducive to a freer society. More precisely, Anonymous emerges from the mutual constitution of these poles in a technosocial assemblage that is both techno-logically indifferent to the meaning and consequences of its actions and ethically committed to them.

I base this paradoxical claim on Gilbert Simondon's notion of transduction. Simondon introduces this concept to refer to an operation that progressively structures a physical, biological, technical, or social domain that is filled with potentials and in a state of "metastable equilibrium." The transductive operation, argues Simondon, coincides with a transition phase whereby the dimensions of such a domain emerge as correlated and in tension within a system that is unstable and incompatible with itself. Such instability (or metastability) implies that while some dimensions of the domain become individuated, others may remain in a potential state and give rise to further individuations.[1]

My claim is that Anonymous may be considered itself a metastable system that undergoes multiple individuations. In particular, I will show how Anonymous has undergone at least three transition phases since its inception around 2005. The first phase coincides with the transition from Anonymous as a default function of the imageboard 4chan to Anonymous as a collective assemblage of enunciation. Such individuation emerged from the confrontation of those who insisted on using personal identifiers in the imageboard and those who argued for complete anonymity as a more truly egalitarian mode of communication. Once Anonymous emerged as a "we," it further individuated between those who inscribed its actions within an ethical and political horizon and those who refused any moral justification for them. Finally, Anonymous underwent a third individuation as the name was contended between those who used it to denote secrecy and mastery of a superior technical knowledge and those who attached it to social movements whose politics is transparent, participatory, and nonelitist.

RAIDING *TIME* MAGAZINE

In March 2009, *Time* magazine launched its third online poll to determine the "100 Most Influential People" on the planet. If the list of candidates was filled with politicians, CEOs, spiritual leaders, scientists, and pop stars, one name stood out for its short, enigmatic quality: moot. The alias of the then twenty-one-year-old Christopher Poole, moot owed its notoriety to the Internet. More precisely, he had been catapulted to stardom by 4chan.org, an addictive Internet forum he had himself launched from his New York apartment in 2003. Thanks to a simple interface and the lack of registration, 4chan has attracted in a few years millions of users, who exchange images and short texts on subjects ranging from Japanese anime to fashion, weapons, animals, music, toys, porn, and video games. As the *god* of 4chan—as system administrators are referred to in Internet jargon—moot sits at the very top of the imageboard. Thus, when *Time* launched its poll, the 4chan users seized the opportunity to make their deity known to the rest of the world.

In selecting moot as a candidate, the editors at *Time* had overlooked an important element: 4chan users rarely play by the rules. Rather, they prefer to set their own rules for whatever game they decide to play. This is particularly true of the 4channers who hang out on /b/, the random board of 4chan.[2] Also known as /b/tards, the dwellers of this board launch calls to action and challenges that can mobilize thousands of users on a whim. In the case of the *Time* 100 poll, the /b/tards first decided that moot had to win the contest by any means necessary, and second, that that they would have inserted a secret message in the poll so as to prove that it had been manipulated. The message was to be created by ranking twenty-one selected candidates so that the initial of each first name would have spelled out the phrase "mARBLE CAKE ALSO THE GAME" (where *m* stood for "moot," *A* for "Anwar Ibrahim," *R* for "Rick Warren," and so forth).[3]

In the beginning, the challenge was made easy by the lack of any authentication software. Anyone could cast a vote simply by requesting the URL associated with a candidate. The 4channers seized this opportunity to craft automated voting software that could cast dozens and even hundreds of votes per minute. Some of these autovoters alternated votes for different candidates to avoid detection. Others cycled through different proxy servers so that the votes appeared to be coming from multiple IP addresses. Furthermore, the autovoters were often fired by unknowing Internet users through "spam URLs," which had been embedded by the /b/tards in various Internet forums.[4] If these tricks worked for a while, the *Time* staff eventually realized that something was wrong with the poll. Thus, after erasing millions of votes and restoring the poll to a previous (albeit not entirely untampered) count, they placed a reCAPTCHA authentication test on the poll.[5] As a result, although moot still maintained a comfortable lead over the other candidates, the secret message was compromised as too many votes had been cast by users who were not affiliated with 4chan.

The /b/tards first countered the staff's move by trying to break the reCAPTCHA system through ad hoc software. After several failed attempts, they realized that the only way to restore the message was to switch to manual voting.[6] In the final days of the poll, with the help of an interface that allowed them to speed up the manual input of CAPTCHAs, hundreds of volunteers were able to cast nearly two hundred thousand votes. This was still far fewer than the millions of votes produced by the autovoters in the first days of the poll but enough to restore the message. On April 27, 2009, the magazine closed the poll and announced the result. Although *Time* claimed that its staff had neutralized several attempts to hack the vote, the final ranking unequivocally showed that the contrary was true.

LULZ, TROLLS, AND THE RISE OF A-CULTURE

Even though it is very unlikely that moot would have ever earned such a prestigious title had 4chan users not hacked the vote, mARBLE CAKE ALSO THE GAME was a monument to the influence that 4chan exerted and continues to exert over Internet culture. Upon its launch in October 2003, users began flocking to the board, making it in few years the most popular U.S. Internet forum and one of the largest imageboards in the world.[7] Such popularity was due to a number of factors, including the lack of a registration process and the almost complete anonymity the forum ensures. Whereas the rise of social network sites such as MySpace, Facebook, and Twitter has produced a significant shift in online culture toward mostly known and mostly persistent online identities—that is, toward a reduction of the gap between real-life identities and online personae—4chan provides a safe haven for the experimental forms of subjectivity that had permeated the Internet cultures of the 1990s.

This is particularly true of /b/, the very first board of 4chan. If nowadays 4chan lists dozens of thematic forums, its first board was and remains dedicated to everything that does not fit into a category.[8] Because of its open and undefined nature, /b/ soon became an incubator for the experimentation of new forms of communication and subjectivity. Generating more than one-third of the entire 4chan traffic, /b/ is the source of sight gags, catchphrases, and popular Internet memes such as the LOLcats, the pedophile mascot Pedobear (a cartoon used, often ironically, to alert moderators to the presence of child pornographers), Anonymous (itself a meme), and crudely designed comics such as Rageguy and Trollface.

The latter is often associated with the presence of "trolls," an emerging class of online pranksters and troublemakers as old as the first Internet communities.[9] Whereas in the early 1990s, trolls mocked newcomers who lacked any sense of netiquette on Usenet newsgroups, in recent years, trolling has expanded to encompass a host of ethically questionable activities. These can be divided into two main families: making the life of individuals miserable and targeting online communities. In the first case, trolls' tricks range from finding the phone numbers and home addresses of specific persons to bombard them with unwanted deliveries and (threatening) phone calls to gaining unauthorized access to social media accounts to running fake blogs in the name of the target person. In the second case, trolls have been known for disrupting Listservs, multiplayer online games, blogging communities, classified boards, and even desecrating virtual memorials dedicated to missing persons.[10] By posting messages that are inflammatory, offensive, off-topic, and ultimately aimed at undermining trust among the members of an online community, trolls force the latter to introduce procedural rules that may reestablish "rational" and effective forms of cooperation and deliberation.

On /b/, however, trolling is so widespread that users—and especially new users—often wonder whether the community has any ethical foundation whatsoever. To a first-time visitor, /b/ presents itself as a barrage of shock-for-shock's sake images, flame wars, sexist and racist slurs, supposedly real "first-person accounts" of socially stigmatized behaviors, Internet drama, and other ostensibly futile message threads. David Auerbach notes that the main purpose of this "economy of offense" is to cultivate an elitist culture that reinforces the bonds among the /b/ dwellers while keeping at bay those who do not share the general libertarian mind-set.[11] To maintain and reinforce this line of demarcation, the /b/tards subject all contributions to an accelerated process of *détournement* and textual poaching.

The term that best describes the affective dimension of this semiotic composting is *lulz,* a corruption of the acronym *lol* (laugh out loud). Julien Dibbell writes that if in its strictest sense *lulz* means "laughs, jest, cheap amusement," in a broader sense it "encompasses both the furious creativity that generates /b/'s vast repertoire of memes and the rollicking subcultural intensity they inspire."[12] Gabriella Coleman adds that being a form of enjoyment and bliss that "celebrates its own raw power," the lulz is "divorced from any moral hinge."[13] The morally ambivalent character of the lulz may explain why /b/ can be simultaneously exhilarating and repulsive, illuminating and debasing, so that the user is constantly forced to ask herself whether a line should be drawn and where.

Yet every attempt to raise objections on an ethical ground is likely to attract even greater hostility. As this often cited post clarifies, /b/tards' actions and sentiments are—or should be—inspired only by the amoral force of the lulz:

> You COMPLETELY miss the point of /b/. /b/ is not Fark "oh hay guys i found a cute link ha ha." /b/ is not Slashdot's pseudo-intellectual discussion. /b/ is not LiveJournal, SuicideGirls, or HotOrNot. /b/ is a place for people to be monsters- the horrible, senseless, uncaring monsters that they really are.
>
> Tsunami owns the Asian continent and we laugh. Psychotic emo takes his sickness out on a cat and we laugh. A man rapes his granddaughter and we laugh, and ask for more. Suicide, homicide, genocide- we laugh. Racism, sexism, discrimination, xenophobia, rape, and baseless hate- we laugh. We are mindless "me-too"ism; we are irrational preference; we are pointless flamewars; we are the true face of the internet.[14]

It is worth noting that for being a "horrible, senseless, uncaring monster," the poster can properly articulate and reflect on phenomena that most truly sexist and racist individuals would probably be unable even to name. To be sure, Lisa Nakamura has pointedly noted that "the line between someone who is a racist and someone who behaves like a racist is pretty thin, especially in online discourse, where pretty much what you write is what you are."[15] And in his critique of cynical reason, Peter Sloterdijk has argued that self-awareness and cynicism often enable the kind of emotional detachment that allows individuals to engage in unethical behavior.[16] Perhaps, then, the lulz epitomizes what Franco "Bifo" Berardi has described as the lack of sensibility of a generation of digital natives that has lost "the ability to empathically understand the other and decode signs that are not codified in a binary system."[17]

In fact, the lulz is based on trolling, a technique or language game that requires unambiguous responses from other players to function. As infamous troll Andrew "Weev" Auernheimer points out, trolling "is a method, a style of rhetoric and action" that is based on the ruthless exploitation of Internet users' tendency to take themselves too seriously:[18]

> You look for someone who is full of it, a real blowhard. Then you exploit their insecurities to get an insane amount of drama, laughs and lulz. Rules would be simple: 1. Do whatever it takes to get lulz. 2. Make sure the lulz is widely distributed. This will allow for more lulz to be made. 3. The game is never over until all the lulz have been had.[19]

These rules suggest that trolling functions as positive feedback. Each action triggers a response that feeds back into the originating input, increasing the instability of a system. In this sense, the lulz is the exact opposite of a cybernetic system. If cybernetics is the ultimate science of control and negative entropy, lulz and trolling push systems toward turbulence and chaos. In this respect, the lulz is a "force which goes to the limit of what it can do, [a] force which affirms its difference, which makes its difference an object of enjoyment and affirmation."[20] At the same time, the coldly methodic character of trolling suggests that the lulz follows a *techno-logic*—a logic that embeds human as well as technical communication protocols.

We will return to the techno-logic of the lulz later in this chapter. For now, it is sufficient to note that once the lulz is understood as a destabilizing force and trolling as a noise-making technology, a purely semantic reading of offensive discourse leaves way for an analysis of its performative efficacy. Furthermore, to complicate things, in /b/, cynicism and cruelty often coexist with intimate discourse and care; /b/ can in fact host prurient revelations of dirty secrets and confessions of criminal acts, but also requests for help and advice. Yet because it is impossible to know whether these accounts are true, dramatized, or entirely fictional, belief is inextricably tied to the suspicion that self-disclosure might in fact conceal role-playing and trolling. In this sense, Auerbach is right to highlight the contiguity between 4chan and subcultures such as the sci-fi and anime fandoms, fantasy RPGs, cosplayers, and furries, which are all heavily invested in role-playing and masquerade. While the language game of these communities requires participants to leave reality behind according to specific rules, imageboards allow them to enact their fantasies in a social space that is not only removed from reality but also unpredictable and unscripted.

Auerbach sees 4chan's "economies of offense, suspicion, and unreality" as the engine of an emerging *A-culture,* which stands at odds with the reputation economy of the Web 2.0. A-culture, argues Auerbach, is offensive, cynical, and detached from reality because those who make it are not bound to any particular identity. At the same time,

> because the community is so autonomous from the real world, there is great opportunity to continually redefine one's role in it and even redefine the nature of the community itself. A-culture is a space for playing with unrestricted notions of identity and affiliation and for the establishment of a private set of in-jokes and references that come to constitute a collective memory.[21]

Such collective memory is not directly archived on 4chan. Because imageboards generate a high volume of traffic and are usually run by volunteers, they rely on a limited server capacity. This means that the older discussion threads are erased from the server to make room for the new ones. Hence the users who want to save old discussion threads have to recur to alternative archiving websites.[22] In other cases, /b/'s obsessions are duly annotated and turned into articles that are posted to satirical wikis such as Encyclopedia Dramatica (ED). Such transcription, however, is not without consequence, as ED stabilizes and therefore endows with an aura of legitimacy what would otherwise quickly fall into oblivion. While ED's layout and user-generated content resemble on a superficial level those of Wikipedia, the outcome is its polar opposite. In fact, ED has been aptly described as "Wikipedia's evil twin" for its "seemingly endless supply of twisted, shocking views on just about every major human tragedy in history."[23] Yet despite its seething satire and crude imagery, ED does not lack guidelines. But if Wikipedia contains the contributors' subjectivity by founding its editorial process on rationalist principles such as neutral point of view, verifiability, and no original research, ED's predilection for lulzy stories and Internet drama exalts on the contrary the contributors' quirkiness, irreverence, and cruelty—all qualities that besides being quintessentially subjective inevitably yield highly contested narratives.

In the previous chapter, we noted how the Luther Blissett Project (LBP) had theorized mythmaking as a cooperative and agonistic process whereby participants collaborate and sometimes clash over competing versions of a story. We have also seen how a faction of the LBP succeeded in stabilizing a version of the myth through narrative and performative closure. In the case of 4chan, ED, and other A-culture websites, such closure seems nearly impossible. This is partly due to the higher number and cultural heterogeneity of the participants and partly to the fact that trolling and the lulz subvert the community from within. To be sure, 4chan has created over time its own myths. But rather than relying on anthropomorphic storytellers, 4channers have entrusted their collective voice with a function of the software that runs the imageboard. This collective assemblage of enunciation emerged after a prolonged struggle among /b/tards over the meaning and function of anonymity in an online community.

ANONYMITY, EPHEMERALITY, CONDIVIDUALITY

Even though the *Time* 100 hack was organized by /b/ users, it was claimed and signed by Anonymous. The distinction between a /b/tard and someone who is affiliated with Anonymous can be thin, yet it is not insignificant. As previously noted, Anonymous is the tag that marks all the unidentified users who post on 4chan. Because /b/ users are not given the option to register—and are discouraged by the community to use other personal identifiers—each /b/ user *is* Anonymous as she posts on the board. To be sure, anonymous enunciation does not correspond to technical anonymity, as users can still be identified—and have been identified in a number of circumstances—through their IP numbers by the administrators of the website.[24] Yet /b/'s distinctive technoculture has emerged over time through a series of battles around the value and significance of anonymity in online discourse.

Even if anonymity is the default option, in the beginning it was not encouraged on /b/. On the contrary, moderators often nudged users to fill in the name field or identify their posts with a tripcode—a form of pseudo-registration that allows users to establish an identity without storing data on the server. As the number of 4chan users continued to climb, the ratio between anonymous users and those who relied on a pseudonym or tripcode increased. In 2005, the first flame wars erupted between the so-called namefags and tripfags on one side and the Anons on the opposite side.[25] While the former argued that only a recognizable user can take responsibility for her statements and actions, the latter believed that complete anonymity on the board ensures a more egalitarian form of communication, as posts are judged for their merit rather than a poster's reputation.

The Anons found an ally in Shii, a 4chan moderator who saw anonymity as an antidote to the vanity that characterizes pseudonymous forums. An admirer of 2chan, the largest Japanese Internet forum, Shii believed not only that registration kept away knowledgeable posters with little time on their hands but that complete anonymity enabled a more authentic social interaction.[26] As the founder of 2chan Hiroyuki Nishimura had pointed out in an interview with the *Japan Media Review* in 2003,

> if there is a user ID attached to a user, a discussion tends to become a criticizing game. On the other hand, under the anonymous system, even though your opinion / information is criticized, you don't know with whom to be upset. Also with a user ID, those who participate in the site for a long time tend to have authority, and it becomes difficult for a user to disagree with them. Under a perfectly anonymous system, you can say, "it's boring," if it is actually boring. All information is treated equally; only an accurate argument will work.[27]

In July 2005, Shii removed the name field and the possibility of using tripcodes from /b/. Forced anonymity was implemented until March 2007, then was removed and reinstated by moot several times. In the meantime, the culture of /b/ clearly shifted, with the vast majority of users now preferring complete anonymity.

It is worth noting that in the same years as the culture of anonymity became prevalent on /b/, Facebook went from a social network site accessible only to U.S. students to a service open to everyone with a valid e-mail address. Although there is no direct causal relationship between the rise of Facebook and that of 4chan, these two phenomena can be seen as interrelated. In contrast to Facebook's self-conscious reputation economy, 4chan has been described as a "place to be wrong" and "the id of the Internet."[28] These two opposite technocultures are enabled by specific software features. Facebook's functionalist interface revolves around individual profiles, counts and displays social connections, identifies the author of each action, and archives users' interactions. By contrast, imageboards do not store user credentials, let users contribute to a discussion thread without identifying themselves, and erase older messages as soon as the server capacity is reached.

This means that imageboards are characterized by the *anonymity, condividuality,* and *ephemerality* of social interaction. If anonymity constitutes the default option and the prevalent form of authorship in the imageboard, condividuality describes the process whereby discussion threads take on a life of their own. As technosemiotic assemblages, discussion threads are made of several dividual contributions that are not attributable to individuals or collectives who work on the basis of a shared vision. In fact, condividuality does not presuppose a community, only a concatenation of parts. This is precisely what enables the more generative threads to transmute into memes, which are sampled and remixed in virtue of their open and modular structures. Furthermore, the ephemeral nature of discussion threads sets in motion distinctive forms of cooperation for the production of relevance.

While Facebook measures status and influence by quantifying social relationships and social sentiment, 4chan users determine what matters for the community by replying to specific message threads. Replies can in fact refresh a thread and "bump" it to the front page, whereas the less popular threads sink to the back pages until they are erased from the server.[29] Bernstein et al. suggest that the high volume of posts combined with deletion set in motion a "powerful selection mechanic," which would explain "the site's influence on internet culture and memes."[30] In other words, /b/'s production of memes can be expressed as the ratio between the attention time spent by the community on a single thread and the competition among multiple threads to capture and retain that attention: the higher the ratio, the more likely a thread is to morph into a meme.

Bernstein et al.'s reliance on the notion of selectivity is clearly indebted to Richard Dawkins's theory of memes. In *The Selfish Gene,* the British ethologist proposes the institution of a new scientific discipline for the study of cultural evolution, which he calls *memetics.* Borrowing from evolutionary biology, Dawkins argues that in the same way as a gene is responsible for the transmission of hereditary traits in living organisms, a meme—be it an idea, a skill, or a fashion—is a "unit of imitation" whose replication and diffusion can explain cultural evolution.[31] The role of memetics would be to analyze how the intrinsic features of a meme make it more or less responsive to the selective pressures of the cultural environment. Yet memetics is not without shortcomings and has never achieved the scientific status Dawkins had hoped for it. In particular, it has been noted that by defining memes (as well as genes) as "replicators," Dawkins endows them with a virtual agency that is independent of context. "This tacitly suggests that the system in which a replicator is embedded can be treated like a passive vessel," notes Terrence Deacon.[32]

Imageboard culture shows that the opposite is true, as Internet memes emerge organically from discussion threads that are condividual modulations of an image-concept. Furthermore, Internet memes are a cultural form that is improper in character. Although to be identified as such, a meme must have recognizable features, its referents keep shifting as the meme is copied, forwarded, and remixed in different contexts. Even more, memes' dividual and punctual iterations often acquire meaning only in relation to one another. Thus, even though memeticists describe memes as discrete and bounded units, such units are never fully individuated and identical to themselves. Following Simondon, we might say that (Internet) memes are filled with potentials that become individuated at each iteration of the meme. Because the meme is more than one and not fully coincident with itself, it does not simply adapt to the selective pressures of the environment. Rather, the meme is in a coadaptive relation with the information environment; that is, it affects the environment as much as it is affected by it. In some cases, Internet memes may even stand in a *transductive* relation to the information environment; that is, they bring about the reciprocal individuation of dimensions that did not exist before.

For example, Anonymous allows for the experience of anonymity online to be named as *a shared experience.* Once anonymity becomes Anonymous, it also becomes pseudonymous. That is, it is no longer an undifferentiated or anomic social phenomenon, but something that can be mobilized and contended by different parties towards a specific goal. Thus, by providing a *minimum threshold of subjectivation,* Anonymous makes it possible to articulate a double differentiation. On the outside, it denaturalizes the reputation economy of the Web 2.0 as individuality and persistent identity appear now as related and in tension with collective individuation and ephemeral subjectivation. On the inside, the shared pseudonym enables the emergence of further individuations—or its contention among subjects who attach opposing and irreconcilable meanings to it.

ONLINE RAIDS AS A FORM OF MACHINIC PLAY

The shift from Anonymous as a simple tag to Anonymous as a collective force was not only evident from the fact that 4chan users adopting a tripcode were chastised as egomaniacs. As soon as Anonymous became a "we," it began to be used in conjunction with sudden attacks against specific individuals and organizations. Especially in the period 2005–8, these online "raids" do not seem to be inspired by anything but the personal enjoyment of their perpetrators. Beginning in 2008, however, a political wing of Anonymous emerges. First through a series of coordinated actions against the Church of Scientology, and then against governments and corporations that censor and restrict access to information and information technology, Anonymous becomes an increasingly organized and global political movement. As we shall see, this led to a schism within 4chan between those who continued to plead allegiance only to the lulz—the so-called lulzfags—and the new moralfags, who attached an ethical and political commitment to their actions.

Among the lulzy interventions of the early period, it is worth mentioning the raiding of the Habbo Hotel, a social network site for teenagers whose main hub is designed as a virtual hotel. Since 2005, rumors had spread on 4chan that the moderators of Habbo used their power to ban black avatars from the game.[33] In response, 4channers flooded the site several times, creating scores of identical black avatars sporting large afros and wearing gray business suits. In these purportedly antiracist protests, avatars formed swastika-like patterns that prevented other avatars from accessing the pool, which was declared "closed due to AIDS." As the game moderators banned the black avatars from Habbo for their disruptive behavior, they were accused of being racist. The "Pool's Closed" raid even led to the organization of a street rally in front of the headquarters of Sulake, the Finnish corporation that runs the game.

In other circumstances, raids target specific individuals, using a whole arsenal of tricks such as coordinated phone pranks, sending unwanted pizza deliveries, and publishing personal addresses, phone numbers, or credit card and social security numbers—a practice known as doxing. Among these attacks, the raid on white supremacist Hal Turner's radio show, the arrest of alleged Internet pedophile Chris Forcand, the trolling of a virtual memorial dedicated to a seventh-grader suicide named Mitchell Henderson, and the hack of the Epilepsy Foundation website provide an array of case studies that well illustrate the moral ambivalence of the lulz.

In December 2006, Anonymous began flooding with prank phone calls the radio show of white supremacist and Holocaust denier Hal Turner and took his website offline with a distributed-denial-of-service attack (DDoS), a network attack that consists in jamming a server with an excessive number of bogus requests.[34] Turner reacted by suing 4chan and four other websites for copyright infringement and financial losses presumably derived from the outage of his server but was unable to obtain a court injunction, and the case was dismissed in late 2007.[35] In the Chris Forcand case, some Anons chatted with this alleged Canadian pedophile, posing as underage girls under the pseudonym "serious"—a practice known on 4chan as pedobaiting. After Anonymous published the chat logs on the Web and forwarded them to Forcand's church, the Toronto Police Department got interested in the case and eventually arrested Forcand.[36] This episode led the press to refer to Anonymous as a group of "Internet vigilantes."

If the Habbo Hotel raids, the Hal Turner raid, and the Forcand case seemed motivated—at least superficially—by political and ethical concerns, the cases of Mitchell Henderson's suicide and the raid on the Epilepsy Foundation website left many baffled for their lurid moral implications.

Upon Henderson's tragic death in April 2006, his classmates created a virtual memorial on the social network site MySpace. The web page came to the attention of /b/ through MyDeathSpace.com, a website that collects virtual obituaries. For reasons that remain unknown, some /b/tards decided that Henderson had killed himself over a lost iPod and began trolling the memorial. In the following months, Henderson's parents were harassed by anonymous phone calls. Young callers claimed to be "Mitchell's ghost," to be calling from the cemetery and to have found his iPod, and so forth.[37]

The attack on the Epilepsy Foundation website in March 2008 also seemed characterized by a basic lack of empathy for human suffering. In this case, hackers purportedly associated with Anonymous inserted flashing animations in a support message board for people affected by epilepsy. At least one forum visitor later claimed to have experienced a seizure.[38]

Although the identity of the perpetrators of the Epilepsy Foundation raid is uncertain, some claim that the raid was organized by the amoral faction of Anonymous in response to the hacktivists who had launched a global campaign against the Church of Scientology few weeks earlier.[39] Thus, in early 2008, Anonymous no longer designates a collective assemblage of enunciation but two opposing assemblages—the so-called moralfags and the lulzfags. Given that neither of these two factions could prevent the other from identifying itself as Anonymous, the raids of this period can be seen as agonistic challenges over the mode of disposition and usage of the improper name. Even though the moralfags were also capable of lulzy actions,[40] my wager is that these challenges are a form of play whereby the community of Anonymous users began to draw internal boundaries that did not exist before.

I use the term "play" here in an ambivalent way, to indicate a creative activity that can have both constructive and destructive outcomes. Forefathers of contemporary game studies, such as Johan Huizinga and Roger Caillois, define play as a free and voluntary activity that creates a separate order from reality. Caillois acutely observes that players form a magic circle either by playing according to rules that create fictional worlds or by imitating real life in games such as children's make-believe.[41] Whether governed by rules or make-believe, for Caillois, play's creative power can have a "civilizing quality" only if it is embedded in purpose-oriented activities. In particular, the exuberant and turbulent nature of children's play tends to take a more structured form over time, as players set up conventions through the mastery of techniques and utensils, and pure expression leaves way to the pleasure of solving increasingly complicated problems.[42]

Caillois's insights are useful in thinking of 4chan raids as a unique mix of unruly forms of play and purpose-oriented activities. In fact, raids such as those on Hal Turner, Habbo, and *Time* magazine all have clearly defined objectives. This means that while trolling and role-playing permeate 4chan's economy of unreality at every level, they do not prevent

4channers from designing games of their own. Such games are rule bound as conventions emerge over time through the exchange of tips and know-how among /b/ users—a pragmatic knowledge that is occasionally archived on websites such as ED, chanarchive, and *Know Your Meme.* Paradoxically, however, the ephemeral and antagonistic nature of raids makes them playable only within and against other (language) games. They are played within another game as raiders mimic the behavior of avatars, radio listeners, or poll respondents to gain access to a regulated environment. And they are played against such spaces as they aim at subverting their internal norms and dynamic.

Perhaps, then, 4chan raids can be described as a form of *machinic play*—a concept that encapsulates both the ability to subvert the rules of technosocial machines that have been engineered to do something else and the acquisition of pragmatic skills that enable the development of new machines and new language games. Bringing together some of the concepts developed so far in this chapter, we may define online raids as a form of play predicated upon five distinctive features:

1. *Antagonism.* As sudden assaults on a website, forum, game, show, or individual, raids aim at dismantling a structured space. Likewise, in its "pure form," play is an unruly and confrontational activity that bubbles up from common concerns about freedom to move.
2. *Anonymity.* The primary function of an online raid is to mobilize communities that have a strong anti-individualistic ethos and forcefully deny the reputation economy of the Web 2.0. Play knows nothing of names and reputations, as it is only concerned with the production of its own becoming.
3. *Transitivity.* In an online raid, players act as uninvited guests or spoilers in other "magic circles." This means that machinic play is not only self-referential and internal to an assemblage but is the line of flight that opens up the assemblage to other assemblages.
4. *Ephemerality.* Raids are characterized by their unpredictable and nomadic quality. As both Huizinga and Caillois point out, play cannot structure itself in a game with fixed rules without ceasing to be play.
5. *Pragmaticity.* Ephemerality does not mean that a technical, aesthetic,

> and political knowledge cannot be handed down. Through repetition and the mastery of techniques, play calls forth a practical knowledge that invokes its own rules. Yet such knowledge remains productive only insofar as it keeps privileging the virtual over the actual, difference over repetition, invention over normativity.

As we shall see in the next section, the emergence of a political wing of Anonymous was bound to accentuate this tendency toward the creation of organized forms of play by incorporating the raid into structured operations and long-term campaigns. Such operations were going to be informed by broad ethical principles that were shared by most Anons. These included the renunciation of personal publicity (a practice shamed as "namefagging"), a refusal to attack the media, and an unyielding commitment to exposing the secrets of those in positions of authority.

FROM THE LULZ TO SERIOUS BUSINESS

On January 15, 2008, the news website Gawker published an internal promotional video of the Church of Scientology titled "The Cruise Indoctrination Video Scientology Tried to Suppress."[43] In it, a wide-eyed Tom Cruise professes his faith in the futuristic religion created by science-fiction writer L. Ron Hubbard in the 1950s. Mixing omnipotent statements ("We are the authorities in getting people off drugs. We are the authorities on the mind. . . . We are the way to happiness, we can bring peace and unite cultures") with an absolute belief in the technology, writings, and policies of the founder, Cruise's strange monologue became an immediate sensation.[44] Contributing to its popularity was not only the actor's celebrity status but the knowledge that the whistleblowers who had leaked the video—many of whom were former Scientologists—had encountered difficulties releasing it. Since Scientology is known for aggressively pursuing anyone who makes an unauthorized use of its materials, several news organizations that had received the video had backed down, until Nick Denton, the founder of Gawker, decided to publish it.

By the evening of the same day, /b/tards were discussing the possibility of organizing a raid against Scientology. The original post that launched the discussion thread read,

> I think it's time for /b/ to do something big.
> People need to understand not to fuck with /b/, and talk about nothing for ten minutes, and expect people to give their money to an organization that makes absolutely no fucking sense.
> I'm talking about "hacking" or "taking down" the official Scientology website.
> It's time to use our resources to do something we believe is right.
> It's time to do something big again, /b/.[45]

Even though many initially doubted that 4chan had the capacity to take on a well-funded organization such as Scientology, it soon became clear that the support and enthusiasm for taking action exceeded by far any prior raid. In the matter of few days, Project Chanology—a pormanteau of "4chan" and "Scientology"—was born and quickly spread to other boards, such as 711chan, eBaum, and YTMND.

The first actions unfolded along rehearsed patterns, such as a series of DDoS attacks against the Scientology servers, prank phone calls at the Dianetics hotline, and the transmission of black faxes to dry up print cartridges. More interestingly, the participation of thousands of users required a whole new level of coordination that could not be sustained only through imageboards. Since 2007, some Anons had begun setting up Partyvan, a network of Internet Relay Chats that had precisely the function of connecting users of different imageboards. Because of its flexibility, the IRC protocol enables the creation of multiple text-based chats that users can easily join by creating a handle. The Project Chanology IRC channels included #xenu and #target for general discussion, #press for announcements and press releases, and #raids for the coordination of specific actions.

On January 21, the Anons in #press uploaded a short video clip to YouTube. One of the better known documents produced by Anonymous ever since, "Message to Scientology," showed footage of ominous clouds brushing a desolated industrial landscape. After threatening to destroy and expel the Church from the Internet ("for the good of your followers, the good of mankind—for the laughs"), a robotic, computer-generated voice continues:

> We cannot die; we are forever. We're getting bigger every day—and solely by the force of our ideas, malicious and hostile as they often

> are. If you want another name for your opponent, then call us Legion, for we are many.[46]

Appropriating a passage from the New Testament in which Jesus encounters and exorcises a man possessed by the evil spirit Legion ("My name is Legion: for we are many"), Anonymous links its own "immortality" to the numeric force of its army—a rhetorical strategy that had also been adopted by the Luddites. But rather than threatening the physical destruction of machinery, Anonymous claims to draw its power from its ability to become a signifier for every form of revolt. In the last passage of the message, Anonymous identifies with the so-called SPs, an acronym that in Scientology's jargon stands for "suppressive persons"—that is, antisocial individuals and former insiders who turn against the Church:

> We are your SPs. Gradually as we merge our pulse with that of your "Church," the suppression of your followers will become increasingly difficult to maintain. Believers will wake, and see that salvation has no price. . . . Yes, we are SPs. But the sum of suppression we could ever muster is eclipsed by that of the RTC. Knowledge is free. We are Anonymous. We are Legion. We do not forgive. We do not forget. Expect us.[47]

Thus Anonymous embodies both a Christian demon that is multiple and the plurality of the enemies of Scientology (the SPs). At the same time, Anonymous claims to be a collective entity, a "we" that unifies or at least brings in relation with one another these multiple constituencies. In the introduction to this book, I used Deleuze and Guattari's concept of the collective assemblage of enunciation to describe a nonreferential and noncausal mode of connecting signs and actions, language and praxis. I have also argued that the Luddite movement was an assemblage in which threatening discourse (language) was linked to yet relatively independent from the destruction of machinery (praxis).

Likewise, "A Message to Scientology" inaugurated Anonymous's praxis of announcing operations by means of YouTube videos. Whether such announcements are actually followed by concrete actions is less relevant than their performative ability to engender reality effects. For example, the immediate popularity of the video drove thousands of users to Partyvan, which collapsed for the excessive traffic immediately after. As soon as the network was restored by the Partyvan administrators, the Anons in #press created the channel #marblecake, which became an organizational hub for the entire project. In this restricted IRC channel, the decision was made to take the protest from the Internet to the streets.[48] By dividing up the network into city-based channels, the organizers were able to both unclog the main Partyvan channels and facilitate the formation of affinity groups based on physical contiguity (something that contradicted A-culture's supposed autonomy from real-life relationships).

On February 10, 2008, an estimated seven thousand demonstrators staged simultaneous protests against the Church in more than one hundred cities across the globe. The protesters sported masks resembling Guy Fawkes, a seventeenth-century British revolutionary turned into a pop culture icon by the 2006 Hollywood movie *V for Vendetta* and then transformed into a 4chan meme associated with epic failure.[49] Holding up signs that read "Religion Is Free $cientology Is Neither," "Scientology=Epic Fail," and "Don't Worry We Are From the Internet," the protesters denounced the Church's manipulative practices and the intimidation of former affiliates. A second wave of street protests took place on March 15, with participation matching or exceeding that of the previous month. As the Anons forged bonds with older generations of anti-Scientology activists, international days of protest continued to be held in the following months, tapering off only in the summer. What had begun as an online protest organized by a largely apolitical and recreational social network had morphed into a full-fledged global activist campaign.

Although there are many reasons for such a rapid twist of events, it is worth noting that the conflict between Scientology and Anonymous was not entirely new. Project Chanology was in fact the latest iteration of a long-running war between the Church and the Internet, which had begun in the mid-1990s when dissenters had leaked some of Scientology's most secret texts onto the Usenet newsgroup alt.religion.scientology. If Scientology had failed at suppressing the circulation of those texts at the time, it was not more successful with the Tom Cruise video. In both cases, the Church's attempt to enforce its IP rights had clashed with the cyberlibertarian ethos that is prevalent among geeks and hackers. As Coleman points out, the conflict between Anonymous and Scientology is rooted in the antipodal cultural relationship between the hacker ethics—with its emphasis on producing open, accessible, and workable technologies—and a secretive religion such as Scientology, which releases proprietary technologies that do not work and cannot be improved by its affiliates.[50]

Above all, Project Chanology marked a new transition phase in Anonymous. If, until 2008, raids and pranks were mostly driven by the lulz, with Project Chanology, Anonymous began to resemble an organized political movement. This is clear from the advanced usage of IRC for organizational purposes and the emergence of a self-appointed group of organizers who took on multiple tasks, such as dividing up the network into regional chat rooms, distributing guidelines for the street protests, setting up discussion forums, writing press releases, holding regular meetings, and coordinating the work of many others. Predictably, it did not take long before some Anons accused the organizers of #marblecake of being "leaderfags," that is to say, of violating Anonymous's anticelebrity ethos for their self-serving political agendas. Yet the emergence of an informal leadership within Anonymous was less a by-product of personal ambition than of the exponential growth of a network that now mobilized thousands of participants. In fact, the simple need to set up an infrastructure to facilitate the remote interaction of such a large group of hacktivists entailed the emergence of hierarchies based on technical competence.

To begin with, as Coleman notes, in IRC, a great deal of power is concentrated in the hands of the administrators who "install, configure, and maintain the server."[51] Identified by symbols such as "@" and "+o," IRC administrators and operators own various privileges that allow them to invite users to, kick users off, and ban users from a channel (or a network); give users enhanced status; and even read users' private messages.[52] Second, the continuing presence of certain monikers in an IRC channel allows users to tell the regular hangers-on from the occasional visitors. Such presence is particularly relevant during and after a DDoS attack or other operations that entail legal risks, as it tells participants who is willing to run such risks and who is not. Third, in IRC, moderators can easily create private and invite-only channels wherein actions are planned behind closed doors by a selected few. In contrast to imageboards—where message threads are visible to everyone—this feature of IRC is conducive to the formation of affinity groups that can act autonomously within a larger operation or assume a leading organizational role (as in the case of #marblecake). As we shall see, this technoelite played a crucial role in operations such as Operation Payback, Operation Avenge Assange, Operation Tunisia, and Operation HBGary Federal, among others.

To sum up, if in 4chan the characterization of Anonymous as a leaderless "swarm," "horde," or "hive mind" is supported by software that enforces almost complete anonymity, in IRC, pseudonymous personae acquire a distinctive status within the network. This means that imageboards and IRC function as two distinct authorizing contexts and machines of subjectivation. Although it is true that anyone is formally free to borrow the moniker Anonymous, when the improper name is mobilized in conjunction with impromptu actions such as the 2006–8 raids, it comes to designate a *swarm* whose complex behavior emerges from the distributed coordination of relatively simple tasks, such as operating an autovoter, posting a link, launching a DDoS tool, sending a fax, or making a phone call.[53] By contrast, when Anonymous is associated with prolonged and sophisticated campaigns, such as Project Chanology, it designates a *network* whose organization requires a more advanced specialization of tasks and functions. In such a context, individuals with strong technical, cooperative, affective, and linguistic skills tend to emerge for their ability to program, hack, and configure software; share technical expertise; think strategically; coordinate and motivate others, and so forth.

Before moving forward, allow me to clarify an important point: I am not trying to set up a simple dichotomy between the emergent behavior of the swarm and a supposedly hierarchical configuration of (hacktivist) networks. As Alexander Galloway and Eugene Thacker point out, networks can accommodate both centralized and decentralized topologies, control and emergence, regulation and the free flow of information. Yet, whereas swarms exist only in time—that is, as dynamic assemblages that are constantly evolving and self-adjusting—we are used to map networks as topologies that are synchronically apprehended. Galloway and Thacker note that the spatialization of networks is more the result of a modeling effect of graph theory—which attributes a place and an agency to each node—than an immanent property of networks.[54] Nonetheless, my argument here is that the technocultural features of IRC enable a form of organization that, though not static, is certainly more structured than the one enabled by an imageboard.

In *A Thousand Plateaus,* Deleuze and Guattari juxtapose the smooth and the striated to describe two different typologies of space: smooth spaces, such as seas and deserts, lack stable markers, are constantly changing, and as such can only be navigated and crossed by sailors and nomads; by contrast, striated spaces are the segmented and measurable spaces over which the modern state exerts its sovereignty.[55] Extending this metaphor to network-based subjectivity, we might say that the imageboard is a *smooth machine of subjectivation* in which each post contributes to and is an expression of Anonymous. Conversely, the IRC network functions as a *striated machine of subjectivation* in which pseudonymous users contribute to Anonymous as an open reputation but also grow a personal reputation through their individual contributions.[56] Lacking an archive and the name of an author, the imageboard is always resetting itself—its message threads are like waves and dunes that can only be interpreted and crossed, not owned. With its multiple entry points, local and global servers, public and private channels, IRC's topology resembles instead an urban space whose dynamic evolution is facilitated by administrators and operators with varying degrees of authority.

It is opportune, however, to consider the smooth and the striated as abstract categories, as in reality the two often overlap. As a feature of the imageboard software, Anonymous functions as a collective and impersonal assemblage of enunciation whereby message threads materialize and go out of existence. Yet if, on one level, Anonymous is the name of an unpredictable and radically forgetful discursive space, temporary patterns and refrains—such as catchphrases, memes, and raids—do emerge and leave traces over time. In this respect, Anonymous is always *a* particular Anonymous or an assemblage of dividuals whose interventions are individuated, traceable, and memorable.

Thus Anonymous swings between two poles. At one end of the transductive operation, there is the pole of smooth discourse and pure anonymity. As a function of the imageboard software, Anonymous is the line of flight that opens up discourse to its own timelessness and ambiguity, making it impossible to order it and archive it through discrete publications and individual attributions—what Michel Foucault called the modern "author-function."[57] At the other end, there is the pole of striated discourse and (shared) pseudonymity. As an improper name that is borrowed by a network of users to organize specific actions and operations, Anonymous traces recognizable patterns that cut through the chaos of the imageboard as a subjectless assemblage of enunciation.

The coexistence and hybridization of these two poles—a smooth, anonymous, discursive space and a striated, pseudonymous discourse—may explain why seemingly incongruous definitions of Anonymous as swarm, collective, hive mind, meme, movement, and network are not necessarily incompatible. The fact that these two regimes infuse the same improper name may also explain why Anonymous is simultaneously constituent power and permanent subversion, culture hero and amoral force, a collective "united as one and divided by zero."

BOTNETS WITHOUT BORDERS

On September 5, 2010, Girish Kumar, managing director of the Indian firm Aiplex Software, declared to the online news agency DNA that his company had been conducting DDoS attacks against Torrent websites that did not comply with copyright notices for newly released Bollywood films.[58] Few days later, Kumar repeated the story to the *Sydney Morning Herald,* adding that Aiplex had also been hired by Hollywood film companies and was ready to provide its services to the Australian film industry.[59]

Although the film industry had long been suspected of resorting to extralegal measures to take down large Torrent sites, such as the Pirate Bay and Demonoid, Kumar's unusually candid statements provided the first piece of evidence that this was the case. Given the popularity of the Pirate Bay—the self-styled "world's most resilient Torrent website"—among 4channers, the idea of retaliating against Aiplex quickly gained traction on /b/. From there, it bounced on various IRC networks, where Anonymous begun discussing how to coordinate a DDoS attack against the Indian firm. Since late August, some Anons meeting on the IRC server OccultusTerra had been planning a DDoS against the Office of the U.S. Trade Representative (ustr.gov) to protest against ACTA, the Anti-Counterfeiting Trade Agreement, which had caused an international uproar for the sweeping regulations it would have enforced if approved. The IRC operators had immediately shut down the channel dedicated to the coordination of the DDoS for planning an illegal action.[60] This was not atypical for IRC servers, and the planning of the DDoS against Aiplex faced the same obstacles.

To circumvent these obstacles, "the Anons jumped from IRC network to IRC network, pasting links to the new rooms on 4chan and Twitter each time they moved so others could follow."[61] This constant drifting did not prevent them from setting up the initial targets and logistics of what came to be known as Operation: Payback Is a Bitch in a few days. Although the initial participation in this operation was not comparable to that in the early phases of Chanology, Anonymous could count on an infantry of a few hundred LOIC users recruited mostly through 4chan and an artillery of a few botnets. The LOIC, an acronym for Low Orbit Ion Cannon, is an open source application that enables users to flood a target website with junk packet requests to make it unreachable.[62] While the effectiveness of LOIC is provisional on the synchronic participation of hundreds or even thousands of users, depending on the robustness of the target host, a botnet is a network of tens of thousands (sometimes even hundreds of thousands) of infected computers that is controlled by a single operator. As we shall see, the coexistence of these two kinds of weaponry—one distributed and requiring the participation of many, the other centralized and controlled by few—was bound to spark numerous tensions within Anonymous.

In the beginning, however, most Anons seemed more excited with the availability of botnets than concerned with the differential levels of power generated by the limited availability and secretive use of these tools. On September 17, 2010, the first target of Operation Payback, the Aiplex Software website, was knocked offline—supposedly by a single Anon with a botnet.[63] Unsatisfied, Anonymous invited all LOIC users to target the websites of antipiracy lobbies such as the Motion Picture Association of America, the Recording Industry Association of America, and the International Federation of the Phonographic Industry, giving them an initial combined downtime of more than thirty hours in two days.[64]

On September 21, Anonymous expanded its operations to ACS:Law and Davenport Lyons, two law firms known to the British public for pursuing thousands of file sharers. As ACS:Law struggled to put its website back online after several hours of downtime, it accidentally made available a large backup file. The file contained company e-mail that showed how the methods used by the firm to demand out-of-court settlements from presumed copyright infringers overstepped legal boundaries and amounted to a form of blackmail. Furthermore, it exposed unencrypted Excel spreadsheets with the personal information of thousands of Internet users that ACS:Law had accused of illegally downloading music or adult material.[65] This alleged breach of the U.K. Data Protection Act prompted an investigation by the Information Commissioner's Office into ACS:Law. As a result, in February 2011, the company CEO, Andrew Crossley, decided to shut down the firm.[66] A year later, the Solicitors Disciplinary Tribunal ordered Crossley to pay a hefty fine and suspended his license for two years.[67]

Galvanized by the success and publicity, Anonymous extended Operation Payback to any country where Anons could identify appropriate targets. In October and November, several antipiracy lobbies and copyright authorities were DDoSed and knocked offline, including the British BPI, the Australian AFACT, the Spanish SGAE, the Italian FIMI, the French HADOPI, the Portuguese ACAPOR, the U.S. Copyright Office, and the Dutch BREIN.[68] By coordinating in IRC and using social network sites and imageboards to publicize their actions, organizers undertook a variety of tasks, which ranged from selecting targets to recruiting activists to deploying a robust communication infrastructure. In other words, Operation Payback showed that Internet users were able to organize and confront the organized interests of copyright holders at a global level without recurring to any institutional mediation.

Such organizational effort was by no means linear, as the Anons had to confront several technical and political hurdles. On a technical level, in the very first days of Payback, the #SAVETPB public IRC channel had itself been disrupted by a DDoS attack and flooded with hundreds of fake usernames controlled by a botnet.[69] Evicted, once again, by the IRC hosts that received takedown notices, a group of IRC administrators affiliated with Anonymous decided to create an independent chat network by pooling different servers to which they had access.

On November 3, 2010, AnonOps, the first IRC network entirely affiliated with and controlled by Anonymous, was launched. The importance of this event cannot be overstated, as it brought to an end, at least momentarily, the nomadic phase of Anonymous. Rather than constantly hopping from one network to another, the Anons could now rely on their own infrastructure—an infrastructure that had to be managed, maintained, and defended by possible counterattacks. This means that IRC operators and administrators not only wielded power over communication among IRC users but also retained exclusive access to strategic resources such as domain names and servers. In this way, the needs of cyberwarfare created a technoelite whose power sharply contrasted with Anonymous's horizontal structure and democratic decision-making processes.

Throughout the course of Operation Payback, this technoelite met in a secret IRC channel called #command. Even though some organizers would occasionally be recruited from the public #SAVETBP, this invite-only channel functioned as an organizational hub that remained invisible to most Anons. It is in this channel that key decisions on what to target and for how long were made, often by taking a formal vote among the organizers.[70] And it is here that elaborate discussions on Payback's strategic direction inevitably unfolded. While in the beginning the organizers had declared that the operation had "no time frame" and would have continued indefinitely, in early November some of them begun to wonder whether Payback could have yielded tangible political results.[71] As a result, the Anons meeting in #command decided to issue a list of demands to governments worldwide, which called for an immediate cessation of the piracy lawsuits and for a progressive reduction of the copyright life-span rather than its abolition.[72] This unexpected move was supported by a joint letter of the British and U.S. Pirate Parties that urged Anonymous to cease all DDoS attacks immediately and to remain "within the bounds of the law" in the common fight for copyright reform.[73]

Unsurprisingly, Payback's "reformist turn" was met with skepticism and even outrage by the Anons who had been mostly relying on the public AnonOps channels to coordinate the attacks. Not only had the organizers refused to consult the other Anons, but the very existence of a #command channel clashed, once again, with the notion that Anonymous was an entirely horizontal and self-organizing swarm. Furthermore, the list of demands went almost completely unnoticed by the press. While DDoS attacks and website defacements provided fodder for sensationalist headlines, the notion that Anonymous had formulated rational if not reasonable demands did not really fit the story line of the shadowy hacker network all intent on spreading havoc online.

Yet Anonymous's demands were rational—so rational that, by November 2010, the lulzy, Dionysian drives that had infused the first phase of Anonymous seemed to have evaporated. The fact that Anonymous was increasingly acting as an organized political actor became clear as soon as its path intersected that of whistleblowing website WikiLeaks.[74] On November 28, 2010, the organization led by Julian Assange released a first batch of 220 U.S. State Department classified diplomatic cables as a preview of the world's largest leak of classified material in history. The so-called Cablegate immediately attracted the ire of the U.S. government, and in early December, EveryDNS and Amazon cut their web hosting services to WikiLeaks. Shortly thereafter, citing presumed violations of their terms of service, PayPal, Visa, and MasterCard also cut their finance services to WikiLeaks. To some activists, these concerted actions appeared to satisfy specific government requests in retaliation for the violation of state secrets. For many others, the very fact that PayPal continued to process donations to organizations such as the Ku Klux Klan while cutting them to an organization that had not even been formally indicted was morally unacceptable and outrageous.

In late November, the organizers in #command were already debating how to proceed after their leading role had been contested by the vast majority of Anonymous and participation in Payback was dwindling. It did not take them long to realize that the uproar caused by WikiLeaks was a golden opportunity to take the operation in a new direction. On December 4, the day after PayPal had cut its funding to WikiLeaks, Anonymous DDoSed and took down *The PayPal Blog*. In the following days, AnonOps targeted postfinance.ch—a Swiss bank that had cut access to the WikiLeaks defense fund—the registrar EveryDNS, and the official website of Senator Joe Liebermann, who had encouraged Amazon to cut its hosting to WikiLeaks. On December 7, the AnonOps servers came themselves under a massive DDoS counterattack that knocked them offline for several hours. The same day, complying with a European arrest warrant issued by the Swedish authorities for sexual misconduct, Assange turned himself in to a police station in England.

The news of Assange's arrest made a sensation on a global level. As AnonOps set its target on the websites of Visa, MasterCard, and PayPal for the newly christened Operation Avenge Assange, thousands of users joined the #operationpayback channel on AnonOps. The salience of this moment is captured by an Anon in a IRC conversation with Gabriella Coleman:

> A: and within a few hrs
> A: it went viral
> A: we sat and watched numbers [of IRC channel population] rise
> A: from around 70
> A: which was about the lowest we had ever been
> A: we were saying wow it's gonna be 500 soon
> A: (our previous high was ~700)
> A: then we passed that
> A: then we hit 1000
> A: then the madness broke
> A: and we got to >7000
> A: we had to suddenly increase server numbers
> A: and it was a crazy crazy time
> A: we were stunned and a little frightened tbh [to be honest][75]

As the network administrators scrambled to increase the server capacity to avoid AnonOps crashing from excessive traffic, they were quietly joined in #command by two botnet operators, Civil and Switch. Each botmaster controlled a network of thousands of infected computers, which were operated directly through private IRC channels.[76] Furthermore, many LOIC users had set their clients in the HiveMind mode, a feature of the software that allowed the operators of the #loic channel to set all clients on the same target and operate them remotely at once.[77] Thus the AnonOps operators could now rely on the combined power of a few hundred synchronized LOIC clients and roughly thirty thousand zombie machines controlled by the two botmasters.[78]

Such firepower was badly needed to take down PayPal, a portal that, unlike Visa.com and Mastercard.com, is used by millions of users worldwide for all sorts of financial transactions. It is to be noted, however, that with the exception of a dozen organizers meeting in #command, the LOIC users were completely unaware that the botnets operated by Civil and Switch contributed about 95 percent of the total firepower of the DDoS attack. Parmy Olson notes that this lack of transparency was not considered problematic by the core organizers:

> The upper tier of operators and botnet masters . . . did not see themselves as being manipulative. This is partly because they did not distinguish the hive of real people using LOIC from the hive of infected computers in a botnet. In the end they were all just numbers to them, the source added. If there weren't enough computers overall, the organizers just added more, and it didn't matter if they were zombies computers or real volunteers.[79]

Such lack of transparency not only affected the ability of LOIC users to make informed decisions about their participation in the DDoS but also exposed some of them to the risk of legal prosecution.[80] Because LOIC does not obfuscate the users' IP numbers, only those Anons who knew how to cloak their IPs participated in the attack without fear of reprisal. The others were simply advised to respond to a possible investigation by denying any knowledge of the software and blaming it on a "botnet virus."[81]

Yet while the opacity of AnonOps's decision-making process and the existence of hierarchies based on technical expertise were not unproblematic, the notion that thousands of Anons who participated in the operation were simply "manipulated" is not accurate either. In fact, many decisions made in #command were based on ideas that were discussed in the public channels. Furthermore, many Anons took on tasks whose coordination was not centralized. These included writing press releases, making propaganda videos and digital flyers, recruiting other hacktivists through social network sites, talking to reporters, and so forth. And yet, AnonOps's choice of recurring to DDoS attacks to redress grievances turned the #command channel into a necessary hub for the coordination of attacks that mobilized a range of technical competences and resources.

As previously noted, the botmasters Civil and Switch controlled their networks of zombie computers through regular IRC channels. In the same way as BillOReilly, the main operator of the #loic channel, could visualize a list of all the LOIC clients that were set in HiveMind mode, so Civil and Switch could visualize a list of all the active infected computers in their botnets and operate them through private channels. Hence, from a technical standpoint, whether the machines were voluntarily connected to the LOIC botnet or involuntarily connected to a malicious botnet did not make any difference.

From a political standpoint, however, the fact that thousands of users were actively involved in the operation did make a difference. In fact, it was the LOIC users' motivation and purpose to turn the DDoS on PayPal into a political event. As we have seen, a company like Aiplex Software also rented and operated botnets in the service of the copyright industry, yet its motivation was financial rather than political. Furthermore, botnets are used not only for DDoS attacks but also and foremost to relay large volumes of e-mail spam. From this point of view, networks of infected machines appear to be neutral resources whose political or economic function is ultimately determined by their mode of employment.

This instrumental reading, however, tells only one part of the story. Botnets have in fact a political economy of their own. For example, the market value of a botnet depends not only on the number of zombie computers but also on their geographical location. Loads of infected machines in the United States and Europe are significantly more valuable and expensive than those in Asia because they rely on more stable connections and are available for longer periods of time.[82] Furthermore, because bots are neutralized by antispam filters, owners have to frequently replenish their load supplies as well as ensure that the botnet command-and-control servers are properly obfuscated and can quickly migrate when detected. Hence botnets are dynamic assemblages whose composition, value, and performance depend on numerous factors—including their fast-evolving topology, their owners' purchasing power, the demand for DDoS and spam services, the market price of payloads, and the technolegal power accorded to antispam firms within a given jurisdiction.

From this angle, botnets are not merely tools. Rather, these nonhuman operators exhibit an autonomy that poses an ongoing threat both to Internet security and the network economy. To grasp the nature of this autonomy, we have to consider that infected computers are never just infected by accident. Although computer literacy certainly decreases the chances of malware penetration, Internet users often *seek* and *enjoy* free access to resources—be they proprietary software, music and video files, e-books, or live streaming events—that are distributed through inherently insecure platforms.[83] And even when they do not enjoy such exchanges, the users still play an active role in turning their computers over to the botnet. The fact that not all users are equally aware of these security risks is less significant than that a large portion of Internet transactions occur outside of sanitized commercial platforms. From this point of view, the botnet seems to capture and organize libidinal flows that exceed and bypass the logic of exchange value.

Matteo Pasquinelli has introduced the expression *libidinal parasite* to describe symbiotic organisms—such as porn videos, Second Life avatars, and other popular Internet phenomena—that drive the network economy by accumulating "libidinal surplus-value."[84] Drawing from the work of Michel Serres on the tertiary logic of parasitism, Pasquinelli argues that these immaterial parasites channel libidinal surplus toward an expansion of the technological and material infrastructure that makes up the Internet. In this respect, their function is ultimately productive in that it increases the demand for new hard drives, servers, PCs, routers, media players, and so forth. Yet not all digital parasites transfer energy from the immaterial to the material in a productive way. Botnets, for example, parasite the bandwidth and processing power of millions of machines that inflict economic losses to companies and end users on a daily basis. In fact, it is estimated that the e-mail spam handled by botnets is a negative externality that costs the net economy a hundred times as much as what it generates for the spam industry.[85]

Neither just a tool nor simply a productive machine, the botnet is thus both productive and antiproductive. It is productive in that, to survive and grow, it has to be profitably rented, maintained, disguised, and expanded. And it is antiproductive in that it forces software engineers, network security experts, firms, and users to spend considerable resources on containing its ability to jam and take over the network. From a cybernetic standpoint, the botnet is thus a *noise-making machine* that threatens the successful transmission of coded signals. Whether delivering spam or causing server outages and network freezes, the botnet is the noisy background against which functional communication occurs. At the same time, without noise, signal could not be defined as such in the first place. As Michel Serres notes, "systems work because they do not work. Nonfunctioning remains essential to functioning."[86]

As we have seen, the botnet's noise is nothing but a by-product of a libidinal economy whereby Internet users seek access to resources that are free and readily available yet unsafe and potentially dangerous. At the same time, the botnet stands in a transductive relationship to the liquid economy of desire, that is, it organizes and synchronizes libidinal flows that would otherwise remain separate. To be sure, the botnet does not directly control users' desire—only the processing power of machines that have been infected because of their users' desires. The botnet quietly brings this residual machinic libido under control and employs it for its own ends. It does so according to a logic that Serres would describe as inherently parasitical—a logic of "abuse value" that takes without giving and yet makes communication among otherwise incommensurable orderings possible.

From this point of view, the instrumental use of botnets (by or against the copyright industry, for or against WikiLeaks) is less significant than the fact that thousands of machines are connected to one another to open up a margin of indetermination within the system. In fact, it is entirely possible for the same infected computer to participate in DDoS attacks executed by opposing parties who can rent and operate the same botnet at different times. As we have seen, this undecidability also characterizes Anonymous and the improper name. Yet while authorizing contexts and communities of practice can circumscribe the mode of disposition and usage of an improper name, as nonhuman operators, botnets resist any ethical and social determination. In this sense, botnets share something with the amoral nature of the lulz, whose self-propelling logic makes it akin to a positive feedback that pushes a system toward instability.

If this is true, then Anonymous's more or less overt use of botnets complicates and risks to derail the ethical and political turn that began with Project Chanology. And this is not only because a single botmaster wields more technical (and therefore political) power than hundreds of Anons combined, but also because as a form of machinic libido that is out of control, the botnet injects noise into the very authorizing contexts (IRC for the most part) that are meant to contain the radical openness and ambiguity of the improper name. Whether such disruptions come from without, in the form of DDoS attacks conducted by sworn enemies of Anonymous, or from within, in the form of DDoS attacks conducted by former allies,[87] the use of botnets threatens the patient compositional work that subtends every form of activism. Thus access to a superior technical power can undermine the constitutive protocols of grassroots democracy and subject the community to the permanent subversion that is a hallmark of trolling and the lulz. In this respect, the botnet is nothing but a *machinization of the lulz.*

Herein lies the entire problematic of hacktivism. As a metastable system, hacktivism is in tension between the power of mastering technology proper to hacking and the cooperative competences required by activism. My wager is that, while in the period 2008–10, the transductive relation between these two poles expresses itself as a tension between the ethical nature of hacktivism and the amoral character of the lulz, beginning in 2011, this tension transmutes into a tension between the embodied, slow-paced, and democratic politics of social movements and the disembodied, fast-paced, and elitist politics of computer hacking. As we shall see in the next section, the more strictly political wing of Anonymous encountered and merged with grassroots social movements that occupied streets and squares in the Middle East, Southern Europe, and the United States. At the same time, the more technically skilled wing of Anonymous went on hacking sprees that were increasingly disconnected from political ideals and objectives.

FROM THE ARAB UPRISINGS TO OCCUPY

On December 17, 2010, twenty-six-year-old street vendor Mohammed Bouazizi set himself ablaze in front of the governor's office of the rural Tunisian town of Sidi Bouzid. Motivated by the local police's confiscation of his produce and wares, Bouazizi's extreme gesture sparked a wave of street protests.[88] The vendor's self-immolation was not the first of its kind, nor was this the first time Tunisians took to the streets to protest police abuses. What turned Bouazizi's sacrifice into a highly political gesture—a gesture that eventually came to signify the resistance of an entire people to political oppression—was that this time protesters took to the streets with "a rock in one hand, a cell phone in the other," as Bouazizi's brother later recalled.[89] Knowing that Tunisian media routinely ignored street protests, locals decided to film their own actions and post videos to Facebook, which, unlike most video-sharing sites, escaped censorship. From Facebook the videos were picked up by Al-Jazeera Mubasher, a satellite TV channel that specializes in airing raw, unedited footage. The sudden visibility of Sidi Bouzid's uprising allowed the protest to spread to other

Tunisian cities and snowball in what came down in history as the Jasmine Revolution.

Some Anons had already set their eyes on Tunisia in early December, after the dissident Tunisian blog Nawaat.org had published seventeen U.S. State Department cables released by WikiLeaks on a dedicated website called TuniLeaks.[90] The cables showed that between 2008 and 2010, the U.S. diplomacy expressed concern for the Tunisian government's violations of human rights and the growing unpopularity of the Ben Ali regime, which had ruled the country with an iron fist since 1987. Consistent with its record of aggressive Internet censorship, the Tunisian government swiftly blocked access to TuniLeaks and the Lebanese newspaper *Al Akhbar*, which had published the cables on its website.[91] It took a few days for the news to be reported by Western media. Furthermore, in early December, all AnonOps's efforts were still directed against the financial firms that had cut their services to WikiLeaks.

Yet as the revolt begun spreading from Sidi Bouzid to other cities, some Anons set up an #OpTunisia channel on AnonOps. Here they were joined by a few hacktivists based in Tunisia. It soon became clear that the government's acts of censorship went well beyond the obfuscation of WikiLeaks-related websites. In fact, the Tunisian government specialized in sophisticated phishing operations that consisted in stealing Internet activists' usernames and passwords by filtering their Facebook and e-mail accounts at the ISP level.[92] Anonymous responded to the censorship with a two-pronged approach. On one hand, two small hacking teams meeting in the invite-only #opdeface and #internetfeds channels attacked, took down, and defaced several government websites, including those of the president, the prime minister, the ministry of foreign affairs, and the stock exchange.[93] On the other hand, the hacktivists developed a plug-in for the Firefox browser that allowed users to disable the phishing scripts used by the government.[94]

The plug-in was both posted online and distributed via IRC as part of a "care package" for Tunisian protestors containing First Aid guides, anticensorship tools, and propaganda materials. Assembled with the collaboration of Tunisian Anons and partly translated into Arabic, the package was distributed by Anonymous and Telecomix—a hacktivist cluster many of whose affiliates had ties to the Pirate Bay. The set of PDFs contained in the package blended activist expertise on how to organize street protests and avoid arrest with hacktivist knowledge of how to anonymize online activities. For example, the eighty-one-page-long *Anonymous Security Starter Handbook* divides personal safety into "Physical Safety and Internet Safety. It is important to remember that these two spheres overlap: a lapse of internet safety could lead to physical identification. However, by keeping in mind a few important rules you can drastically reduce the chance of being singled out and identified."[95] Consequentially, the document provides sensible tips on how to anonymize Internet activities and avoid identification offline.

It is worth noting that the "Do Not List" for physical safety ("do not trust anyone to be who they say they are; do not give any personal information that could be used to identify you to anyone; do not mention anything about relationships, family, or relatives; do not mention ties to activist groups") shares the same paranoid logic of the "Do Not List" for Internet safety ("do not use any or all of your actual name in account and usernames; do not mention anything that could be personally identifying; do not mention time zones; do not mention physical characteristics or abilities; do not mention relationships, family, or relatives").[96] It is as if the economy of suspicion that characterizes the hacker underground has been generalized and extended to the entire social fabric. To be sure, in the context of the Jasmine Revolution, paranoia was not an invention of Anonymous but a widespread psychological condition that was amplified by the government's all-too-real arrests of bloggers (some of whom were related to OpTunisia) and political opponents.[97] Nonetheless, it is significant that Anonymous's contribution to the Tunisian revolution consists in sharing a knowledge that is not merely technical but infused by a cyberlibertarian ethos one of whose core principles is, in the words of Steven Levy, "mistrust authority, promote decentralization."[98]

The care package combines, in fact, a negative notion of freedom—as individual freedom from governmental control and coercion—with the more positive freedom to share ideas and know-how. Gabriella Coleman and Alex Golub point out that these two notions of liberty are embodied in specific hacker practices. On one hand, the ethics of "cryptofreedom" (as freedom from government control) can be traced back to the early 1990s cypherpunks, a libertarian network of programmers and civil rights advocates who aimed at achieving privacy through the proactive use of cryptographic technologies such as PGP software.[99] On the other hand, the ethics of sharing is most notably associated with the F/OSS community, or with the freedom to access, change, and distribute software by making its source code available to everyone.[100] Coleman and Golub add that these two strands of hacking sit, somehow uneasily, next to a third strand whose protagonists enjoy "the thrill of breaking rules and gaining access to forbidden knowledge not necessarily to make the world a better place or secure civil liberties, but for its own pleasurable sake."[101] This transgressive strand encompasses a host of practices such as phone phreaking, software cracking, social engineering, and trolling.[102]

It should be noted that although, on a practical level, these brands of hacking differ widely, their underlying ethos provides a common ground for their coexistence and hybridization. In fact, the ethics of cryptofreedom is functional to both the legal practice of sharing know-how and resources and the illegal practice of hacking into password-protected databases and private intranets. This Janus-faced politics is a distinctive trait of Anonymous and is clearly at work in OpTunisia. Indeed, both the antifishing Firefox plug-in and the defacement of the Tunisian government websites had been developed and carried out by the #internetfeds hacking team, which had first coalesced during Operation Payback. As we shall see, shortly after Operation Tunisia, the group revived Anonymous's lulzy origins by executing a series of spectacular hacks that received worldwide media attention. Meanwhile, other Anons continued building connections with Middle Eastern activists as the Jasmine Revolution sparked a cycle of uprisings in North Africa, the Middle East, and around the world.

Not only was the care package updated and distributed in several countries touched by the Arab Spring—including Egypt, Libya, Bahrain, Gaza, and Syria—but at the launch of each operation, new Anons from the Arab and Muslim world joined the AnonOps IRC network. During the Egyptian revolution, Anonymous and Telecomix worked together to provide alternative means of communication to protestors on the ground. After the Egyptian government blocked access to Facebook and Twitter in the initial days of the uprising, Telecomix set up proxy servers for publishing videos of the protests and made its IRC available for retweeting messages on behalf of Egyptian activists. On January 28, 2011, the Egyptian government made the historical move of shutting down Internet access for almost the entire country. In response, the hacktivists convinced two European ISPs to restore their old modem banks and faxed information into the country on how to access them. Land telephone lines were also used to fax medical information on how to treat tear gas, scramble communications, and set up local wireless networks that relied on cell phones and other available hardware. (The latter proved particularly useful in the overcrowded Tahrir Square.)[103]

The politics of facilitating access and providing secure communications to dissenters continued through summer 2011 as a growing number of Syrian activists joined Telecomix and Anonymous's IRC networks. In this case, hacktivists associated with Telecomix were able to hack into five thousand unsecured home routers and post messages on how to encrypt communications and safely browse the Internet. Furthermore, they published fifty-four gigabytes of Syrian Internet users logs that showed how the Syrian government was spying on its citizens using surveillance technologies produced by Californian firm Blue Coat.[104]

The Arab Spring changed not only the demographics of Anonymous but also the perception of what Anonymous was becoming and could become in the eyes of many European and U.S. hacktivists. The Egyptian revolution in particular forged bonds among hacktivists based in Europe and North America and Egyptian revolutionaries on the ground. In a video interview, longtime hacktivist and Anonymous affiliate Commander X recounts the significance of this encounter:

> Some of this shit is personal. And one of the things about the movement as a whole, when Egypt rolled around, is that Egypt broke us emotionally. Watching in real time, [on] the live feeds that we helped set up, Egyptians getting *massacred* with machine guns . . . it was different. And I have never in cyber-activism wept before. It has never *bothered me* like that, it has never been able to touch me the way Egypt touched me.[105]

The sudden realization that aliases and words flickering on a computer screen are linked to living bodies that are at risk of being arrested, tortured, and killed—bodies that often exposed themselves to such risks *because* of their online activities—helped Anonymous mature a new ethical consciousness. It was as if for the first time Anonymous was able to perceive the vulnerability of others, to see their faces through the moving images they had helped distribute to make state violence visible.

The term *face* does not refer here only to a part of the human body. Drawing from the work of Emmanuel Levinas on the face-to-face encounter and the nonreciprocal relation of responsibility, Judith Butler argues that the face designates a nonnarcissistic and ethical relationship to the other:

> Levinas tells us, in fact, that "humanity is a rupture of being." . . . To respond to the face, to understand its meaning, means to be awake to what is precarious in another life or, rather, the precariousness of life itself. This cannot be an awakeness, to use his word, to my own life, and then an extrapolation from an understanding of my own precariousness to an understanding of another's precarious life. It has to be an understanding of the precariousness of the Other.[106]

From this angle we can gauge the evolution of Anonymous's contribution to the Arab Spring from a solidarity based on the extrapolation of a preexisting knowledge (the pro-WikiLeaks anticensorship campaign) to an emotional understanding of what it means to live under an oppressive rule. It is significant that this rupture and "awakeness" are prompted by the visualization of images that Anonymous initially helps distribute, that is, that are meant for everyone to see. In this sense, Anonymous's media activism upsets the normative schemas of intelligibility that were imposed by government-controlled media over the uprising. If, as Butler argues, normative media power effaces the other to prevent symbolic identification with it, then by returning a face to protestors, Anonymous facilitated "our apprehension of the human in the scene."[107]

It is certainly not without irony that an elusive organization such as Anonymous—an organization whose name is improper, whose most recognizable image is a mask, and whose affiliates rarely, if ever, meet in real life—would put a "human face" on the Egyptian revolution. Nonetheless, this recognition of the other's vulnerability did have consequences for Anonymous's modus operandi and ethos. On a practical level, it became immediately apparent that the disclosure of personal information could expose protestors and cyberactivists to retaliatory actions by their government. This required caution and a new sensibility about the way potentially identifying information was handled—a sensibility that Anonymous had lacked when it encouraged the use of unsafe tools such as the LOIC software. It also meant that Anonymous would increasingly try to support and meet the needs of social movements on the ground rather than pushing its own agenda.[108]

On an ethical level, the Arab revolutions helped Anonymous understand that the cyberlibertarian dictum "information wants to be free" is neither a moral imperative nor a universal law. Rather, the hacker struggle for keeping information free and in common—a necessary condition for hacking—undergoes itself a mutation when it intersects with a fully embodied politics. And this is not only because the human body is vulnerable in a way that codes and machines are not but also because bodily signification implies an ability "to interpret signs that are not verbal nor can be made so, the ability to understand what cannot be expressed in forms that have a finite syntax."[109] If networked systems exchange information in a functional way—that is, either by ignoring the content of the data they exchange or by "understanding it" exactly in the same way—bodily communication calls forth a sensibility to the nuances of an utterance, the unstated and the unsaid.

It is by searching for this experiential knowledge that many Anons from Europe and North America decided to join social movements against austerity measures and for "real democracy" such as the Spanish 15-M and Occupy in 2011. In the encampments and general assemblies that mushroomed in hundreds of Greek, Spanish, and U.S. cities, Anonymous discovered a different kind of politics—a politics based on the art of listening, taking care of others, deliberating, arguing, camping, marching, and facing arrest. This was still a media politics, but a politics rooted in quite a different medium—the social body, with its visible stratifications and power relations, its spatial constraints and bodily affects. It was also a prefigurative politics that was less concerned with attaining specific objectives than with announcing a world-to-come in its daily deeds. In this respect, Anonymous's contribution to Occupy was more positively oriented at setting up communication infrastructures, sharing skills, and publicizing the protests than at DDoSing websites or breaking into computer systems.[110] Such slow-paced, transparent, and constructive politics stood in many ways at odds with the frantic, secretive, and spectacular politics that was emerging simultaneously from a different wing of Anonymous.

THE POLITICS OF INSECURITY

The year 2011 was thus a critical one for Anonymous. As Anonymous conjoined to social movements around the world, it began to undertake a politics that was deictic in character, that is, a politics that heavily relied on local conditions and contextual information. This was a politics that did not tackle global issues through localized interventions (as in the case of Project Chanology and Operation Payback) but that was inextricably tied to public spaces charged with a high symbolic power. I would like to call this pole of Anonymous's third transduction the *deictic pole* to refer to a form of hacktivism that is anchored to real-world referents and rooted in local contexts. At the opposite end of the transductive operation (as previously noted, transduction implies the mutual constitution of two poles) exists an *abstract pole* according to which hacktivism should be concerned only with its own advancement. This pole is abstract in that it is deterritorialized and more strictly technical. Indeed, 2011 marks also the year in which Anonymous begins breaking into protected systems with more regularity. If, until 2010, Anonymous had privileged forms of intervention that did not require advanced technical skills, beginning in 2011, more sophisticated hacking techniques, such as SQL injections and smurf attacks, were employed to jam servers and break into protected networks and databases.[111]

As previously noted, the hacking team that conducted most of these attacks coalesced during OpTunisia.[112] After hacking and defacing several websites of the Tunisian government, the group focused on what appeared to be an impending threat to Anonymous. In early February 2011, Aaron Barr, an executive at HBGary Federal, a U.S. private security firm, declared to the *Financial Times* to have identified the real names of the "core leaders" of Anonymous.[113] A few days later, the team compromised the HBGary Inc. (the parent company of HBGary Federal) website and e-mail server. After defacing the website with a pro-Anonymous message, the

Anons published more than seventy thousand internal company e-mails, hijacked Barr's Twitter account, and even claimed to have remotely wiped his iPad. The e-mails showed how HBGary Federal had been conspiring with other data intelligence firms to design a smearing campaign against WikiLeaks and its supporters.[114] The campaign was traceable to Booz Allen Hamilton, a government contractor and consulting firm working on behalf of Bank America to respond to WikiLeaks's announced release of two banks' internal documents.[115]

The HBGary Federal hack was significant in the short history of Anonymous for three distinct reasons. First, it marked a clear shift away from tactics of electronic civil disobedience to hacking. Although most Anons enthusiastically approved of the hack, the action was planned and executed by a handful of individuals coordinating via secret IRC channels on AnonOps. As rumors spread about the identity of the authors, the IRC pseudonymous reputation economy granted them celebrity status within the network—an apparent contradiction with Anonymous's anticelebrity ethos. Second, the hack brought together political engagement and entertainment, hacktivism and the lulz, reconciling the ethical and amoral sides of Anonymous. In particular, the hijacking of Barr's Twitter account and a series of amusing anecdotes—such as HBGary's CEO's and president's failed attempts at convincing (via IRC) Anonymous to return stolen internal documents—made the hack both newsworthy and highly entertaining.[116] Third, the internal praise and media attention galvanized the group, pushing it toward more endearing challenges. Capitalizing on their celebrity status, and feeling restricted by the broad ethical principles underlying Anonymous, the six members who had originally met in #internetfeds decided to break off from the network and create a new hacking crew, the LulzSec.

Shorthand for "Lulz Security" (deriding cybersecurity), LulzSec changed in many ways the history of computer hacking—not so much for its technical skills but for the way it meticulously exploited media attention. Between May and July 2011, the group amassed a large "fan base" on Twitter as it publicly announced attacks on government, corporate, and news organizations, taking down or defacing their websites, dumping users' credentials, and leaking internal documents. Government targets included Infragard (a nonprofit organization affiliated with the FBI), the

CIA, the Serious Organised Crime Agency (a British law enforcement agency), the U.S. Senate, and the Arizona Department of Public Safety. Among the news organizations, LulzSec hacked the website of the British tabloid the *Sun*, publishing a fake article on the untimely death of media mogul Rupert Murdoch and defaced the PBS website to criticize a sensationalistic documentary on Chelsea Manning. Corporate targets included Bethesda Game Studios, the porn website pron.com, and Sony, whose subsidiary Sony Pictures Entertainment was hacked by LulzSec after the PlayStation Network had been DDoSed by Anonymous in retaliation for Sony's choice to prosecute hacker George Hotz. Accepting requests from fans via Twitter, LulzSec also took down the websites of multiplayer games such as Minecraft, EVE Online, League of Legends, and The Escapist as part of their "Titanic take-down Tuesday." Finally, teaming up with Anonymous and other hacking crews, the group spearheaded Operation AntiSecurity (AntiSec), a hacking movement that targeted law enforcement agencies and white hat security companies around the world.[117] Besides the aforementioned government targets, AntiSec hacked the defense contractor Booz Allen Hamilton, FBI contractor ManTech International, NATO, and intelligence company Stratfor, among others.

At first sight, it is difficult to make sense of LulzSec's hacking fury, as most of its actions seem disconnected from one another. With exception of the Arizona Department of Public Safety, which was hacked by a politically motivated hacker, Jeremy Hammond, in response to Arizona's racist immigration policy, the LulzSec core members' motivations for picking specific targets ranged from the purely entertaining to the vaguely political. Yet, as previously noted, trying to inscribe the lulz within a moral and discursive horizon may not be the most productive way of approaching a force that goes to the limit and seeks no justification outside of itself. Perhaps, then, LulzSec's hacking spree should simply be described for what it was: the selective exploitation of security vulnerabilities from a list of hundreds of vulnerabilities provided by automated scanning tools. To be sure, selection implies ethical judgment, and there is evidence of the fact that LulzSec's members occasionally decided not to deface or steal information from targets they had penetrated. Nonetheless, selectivity and self-restraint were only second-order postures, which derived from the power to hack anything that could be hacked.

Following McKenzie Wark, I use the term *hack* in its etymological sense, to refer to a cut that opens up information to its virtual dimension. "To hack is to release the virtual into the actual, to express the difference of the real," writes Wark.[118] The LulzSec crew expressed such difference by combining technical skills and PR skills, the elitism of the self-selected few and a crave for media attention. As we have seen, this dual politics was also present in Anonymous. But the LulzSec crew perfected it by wrapping their own exploits in a coherent narrative and aesthetics that turned hacking into a fashionable, sexy, and entertaining business. As the Sex Pistols of the Web 2.0 generation, the LulzSec reached stardom by disseminating mayhem, leaving the scene at the peak of its fame. When the group announced its disbandment at the end of June 2011, the notion that nothing on the Internet could be considered safe anymore had been propagated by thousands of media reports around the world.

The politics of insecurity promoted by LulzSec is thus a politics that privileges difference over repetition—the search for unknown vulnerabilities (zero-day exploits) over the repetitive patching of what is known to be vulnerable. The illegality of such politics makes it necessarily secretive and detached from wider assemblages. The individuals who populate the hacker underground grow, in fact, a reputation on the basis of the exploits they are able to claim and receive tips, tools, and offers of collaboration accordingly. In this respect, the reputation economy of the hacker underground necessarily revolves around proper (pseudonymous) names. At the same time, movements such as Anonymous and AntiSec allow for the circulation and exchange of know-how within wider reputational milieux. Anonymous in particular has made it possible to link the secretive, exoteric politics of hacking to a variety of social movements. To be sure, such links are often tenuous and purely symbolic. Yet the Middle Eastern uprisings have shown how Anonymous was able to bring electronic civil disobedience, network exploits, and a democratic politics of access within a common discursive space. Furthermore, as an improper name, Anonymous has suggested a common thread among struggles against oppressive governments, media censorship, intellectual property laws, restrictions on access to information technologies, and the network security industry.

ANONYMOUS AND THE VANGUARD-FUNCTION

To sum up, in this chapter, I have argued that the elusive entity we call Anonymous can be described, following Simondon, as a metastable system that keeps individuating itself as it passes through three distinct transition phases. On a first level, Anonymous expresses a tension between the potentially deindividuating power of information technology—as Anonymous designates a whatever Internet user—and the conscious use of the improper name for affirming a collective form of individuation. Such tension initially expresses itself as a conflict between the Anons and the so-called tripfags (users who recur to an identifier) on the imageboard 4chan. Once the Anons prevail, it continues through the coexistence and hybridization of an entirely anonymous discursive space in the imageboard and a pseudonymous reputation economy in IRC. The imageboard and IRC function as two distinct authorizing contexts and machines of subjectivation. With its anonymous, condividual, and ephemeral discussion threads, the imageboard is a smooth discursive space where each post contributes to and is an expression of Anonymous. Conversely, the IRC network functions as a striated machine of subjectivation where pseudonymous users contribute to Anonymous as an open reputation but also grow a personal reputation through their individual contributions.

Anonymous's use of IRC as an organizational platform corresponds to the need to coordinate operations that require a more advanced specialization of tasks than is required by raids, which coordinate relatively simple tasks. Such operations emerged in 2008 as Project Chanology also set in motion a political wing of Anonymous. In the second transductive operation, Anonymous was contended between those who attached an ethical and political commitment to the improper name and those who claimed that Anonymous should be concerned only with its own enjoyment, the lulz. In Deleuzian terms, the lulz is like desire—a force that affirms its difference by going to the limit of what it can do. In this sense, the lulz is not simply a depoliticized alternative to hacktivism. Rather, it is an élan vital that, by relying on different techniques and technologies—be they trolling, automated botnets, or hacking for its own sake—drives hacktivism as it destabilizes it from within.

The third transduction of the improper name is set in motion by the increasingly global reach of Anonymous. With Operation Payback and Operation Avenge Assange, Anonymous organizes Internet users at a global level against the organized interests of copyright holders and the governments that restrict the free flow of information. As the global struggle for liberating information from the fetters of private property and state control morphed into political support of the popular uprisings that began shaking the Middle East in early 2011, Anonymous underwent a new individuation. On one hand, the Anons who helped protesters circumvent censorship, surveillance, and Internet shutdowns matured an ethical consciousness rooted in a recognition of the vulnerability of the other. On the other hand, the hacking teams that came together around the same time went on hacking sprees that were deterritorialized and detached from a shared political strategy. Thus, with the third transduction, Anonymous swings between an embodied politics that is slow paced, participatory, and deictic—a politics that cannot be detached from local conditions without losing its referent—and an abstract politics that is fast paced, secretive, and deterritorialized.

It is important to underscore that this oscillation between situational experience and abstract knowledge is not simply ambivalent or undecidable. On the contrary, because transduction is the *common operation* of two heterogeneous realities, it denotes the emergence of a new form of individuation. In his book *Tweets and the Streets,* Paolo Gerbaudo describes the 2011 occupations of Tahrir Square in Cairo, Syntagma Square in Athens, Puerta del Sol in Madrid, and Zuccotti Park in New York City as the production of a new kind of space. Denominated by hashtags such as #sol and #tahrir, these occupied "trending places" are for Gerbaudo "fixed points that *transfix,* points that capture and attract internet publics from a distance."[119] Likewise, in the Guy Fawkes masks punctuating the streets of Cairo, Rio, Montreal, Istanbul, and Ferguson, Missouri, and in their associated operations, we can glimpse the emergence of an assemblage of enunciation whose embodied and informational dimensions are increasingly inseparable.

This does not mean that Anonymous's global operations, such as Project Chanology, Operation Payback, Avenge Assange, and AntiSec, have exhausted their trust. In fact, Anonymous may well be, as Wark suggests, the vanguard of the hacker class—a class that asks "the property question" as it struggles to keep information in common.[120] Yet it is undeniable that after 2011, Anonymous seems to add an informational layer to preexisting social movements rather than playing a leading or strategic role. Perhaps, as Berardi suggests, it is the very notion of the modern vanguard to have become obsolete altogether as it entails "an exaggerated notion of political will over the complexity of contemporary society."[121] Or perhaps the contrary is true. As Rodrigo Nunes points out, the current "twilight of vanguardism" only overshadows the proliferation of groups that are capable of taking on a "vanguard-function" within a networked politics that makes (temporary forms of) leadership potentially accessible to anyone.[122] In this sense, Anonymous is not expected to lead a revolution but only to provide leadership in certain areas, such as setting up secure communication infrastructures, unveiling the identity of police officers who are accused of wrongdoing, and gaining access to restricted information.

The shift from the modern Leninist vanguard to the postmodern networked vanguards, however, re-presents the problem of the political direction of a movement at a higher level, namely, how to organize the different groups that take on different vanguard-functions. This is fundamentally a problem of mediation, which, given the increasing centrality of networked technologies, is also a problem of mediation between human and nonhuman actors. Perhaps, then, the best way to conceptualize Anonymous is to think of it as a transducer, a converter of libidinal flows that run through human and nonhuman operators. We have seen how, as a machinic accumulation of libidinal surplus, the botnet organizes libidinal flows that would otherwise remain separate. This transduction occurs through the common operation of two heterogeneous realities, namely, Internet users' desire to access information and the technical power of distributed computing. These two poles converge in a metastable entity that evolves by responding to the changing circumstances on the basis of its own drive for self-preservation—a drive that feeds on a machinic, libidinal economy.

Likewise, as a metastable system that keeps individuating itself, Anonymous seems to possess an interior milieu, a memory of its prior individuations that functions as a medium and source of information for future individuations. Such memory is neither only technical nor only human, but expresses the mutual constitution of human and technical ensembles with a high degree of indetermination. According to Simondon, the machine with a superior technicality embeds "a certain margin of indetermination . . . that allows for the machine to be sensitive to outside information."[123] More than any specialization or automation, it is this margin of indetermination that allows machines to communicate with each other and with other beings. In this respect, at the most general level, Anonymous may be the name of an emerging *koiné,* a new lingua franca whereby machines' openness to the surrounding milieu meets the human belief that defending such openness works in the service of a freer society.

Such an encounter, however, is fraught with risks, at least for us humans. First, as we have seen, humans are behaving increasingly like machines—that is, as cruel, "lulzy" beings devoid of empathy. Second, the machinization of desire expressed by botnets disrupts the very authorizing contexts that are meant to trace an ethical horizon for the movement toward an open society. Third, the frantic search for the vulnerabilities in the machine may prevent us from recognizing other vulnerabilities—vulnerabilities that require a sensibility for that which cannot be encoded in a finite syntax. In this respect, Anonymous's ability to mediate between the technical and the human may also be seen as a potential for transducting different notions of otherness, technological and corporeal velocities, finite codes and sensuous languages. Such power may ultimately project the improper name beyond a properly human language and ethics—in a domain where humans and machines may be able to search for and affirm their freedoms only in relation to one another.

CONCLUSION

THE IMPROPER NAME AS MEDIUM AND GAP

At the end of the previous chapter, I advanced the hypothesis that Anonymous may have an interior milieu, a memory of its previous individuations that functions as a source of information for future individuations. Following Gilbert Simondon, I also suggested that such a milieu is co-constituted by human and technical ensembles with a high degree of indetermination. In this conclusion, Simondon's ontogenetic model will help us refine our initial analysis of the improper name as a singular process of subjectivation. First, I show how Simondon's theory of the subject as something that is "dephased" and does not properly coincide with itself can be mobilized to think the relation between singularity and the common as the actualization of a potential. Then I free the notions of the common and the community from any essentialism to revisit the theory of the improper along deconstructive lines. Finally, I argue that improper names can bridge the gap between immanence and deconstruction by advancing a theory of mediation that returns to the etymological root of the term *medium*.

Simondon's theory of the subject rests on the notion that, far from exhausting the process of individuation at birth, human beings, as all living beings, keep individuating themselves throughout the course of their lives. Such individuation consists in the reciprocal articulation of two heterogeneous realities: the interior, psychic life of the individual and the external world, which includes social and collective life. The former is strictly connected to an individual's "preindividual nature"—an indeterminate state, filled with potentials, which is a source for future metastable states. Simondon's profound insight is that individuals experience themselves as subjects, not when they are interpellated by the authorities, but by encountering other individuals—each of whom carries her own charge of preindividual reality. "It is truly not as individuals that beings are united with one another in a collective, but as subjects, that is to say, as beings that contain the preindividual," he writes.[1] From this angle, subjectivation is for Simondon a process of *transindividuation* whereby the individual activates her charges of preindividual reality as she shares her own problematic with other individuals. Because all individuals are internally open to the preindividual, they are already "group individuals" as they enter social and collective life. Thus transindividuation is nothing but a transversal concatenation whereby group individuals—what I have referred to as the condividual—activate their possible other selves, their possible other individuations.

It is worth noting that Simondon does not conceive transindividuation as a return to an original state of nature wherein the subject may dissolve its own problematic. On the contrary, as Paolo Virno notes, the common is actively produced by group individuals through dynamic, unresolved, even conflictual relations. "In the 'between,' the Common shows its second face: besides being pre-individual, it is *trans-individual*; it is not only the undifferentiated backdrop, but also the public sphere of the multitude."[2] Put differently, the production of the common is a mode of actualization of what preindividual nature contains only *in potentia*. Thus the differentiation proper to the process of individuation is not only a *subtraction* from the common-as-potentiality but also a positive *contribution* to the common—what Virno calls the mode of being of "ultimate actuality."[3]

From this angle, individual instantiations of the improper name, such as Ned Ludd, Allen Smithee, Monty Cantsin, Karen Eliot, Luther Blissett, and Anonymous, are simultaneously more and less than the complex of possible expressions of the name. They are more insofar as by actualizing the name, they add something to its potential mode of being. And they are less insofar as each determination can never exhaust the common-as-potentiality. If this is true of every actualization of a potential, the notion of the improper entertains a particular relationship with the common in that it allows us to think relationality *as such,* that is, without relying on a primary ontological ground such as preindividual nature (Simondon) or the linguistic capacities of the species-being (Virno). A threaded philosophical debate that begins with a dialogue between Jean-Luc Nancy and Maurice Blanchot on the "inoperative" and "unavowable" community in the 1980s and continues in the 1990s with the contributions of Roberto Esposito, Giorgio Agamben, and Alphonso Lingis, among others, can help us advance in this direction.[4]

In works such as *The Inoperative Community* and *Being Singular Plural,* Nancy contends that although existence is always relational, exposed, and in common, there is nothing in this "being-in-common" that presupposes a common substance, identity, or essence. Rather, the *cum* of the community simultaneously joins and sets apart beings that can access the proper of their own existences only insofar as they are ex-posed ("posed in exteriority") and offered to one another.[5] To Nancy's theorization of the *cum* as internally divided and spaced, Esposito adds that the common and the community are also etymologically defined by the mutual obligation of the *munus*—the gift that demands to be returned. "In all neo-Latin languages (though not only), 'common' *(commun, comun, kommun)* is what is *not* proper [*proprio*], that begins where what is proper ends," writes Esposito.[6] But if the members of a community are bound together by reciprocal donations, obligations, and debts *(muni),* then the community cannot provide any positive sense of identification and belonging.

A community that does not allow its members to recognize each other can paradoxically know itself only by forgetting and "ignoring itself," as Blanchot puts it:[7]

> Can there ever be any community that fulfils these conditions? And if there is any such community, how could we recognize it, how could we even speak about it, if it should be "unavowable"? The conditions for community seem to be as aporetic as the conditions that Derrida (1991) describes for the "gift": at the moment when something is recognized as a gift, it ceases to be a gift; at the moment when something is recognized as a community, it ceases to be a community.[8]

As I have shown in chapter 3, Derrida advances a notion of the gift as a given time that sets a circle of exchanges in motion. If time cannot be apprehended as such, because "time is nothing" and "does not properly belong to anyone,"[9] the postal gifts that circulate within the Mail Art network point to a time whose "eternal" and continuous dimension makes the measurable time of modern society thinkable. Likewise, the exteriority and quasi-transcendence of the *donum* (the gift that demands nothing in return) to the *munus* (the gift that must be reciprocated) is precisely what makes the latter possible. Thus, in disassociating pure giving from reciprocation—and hence from recognition of the other's deed—Derrida posits a nonrelation between giver and receiver and hence the impossibility for the community to recognize itself.

This deconstructive notion of the community as something that assumes the impossibility of being transparent to itself emerges at different turns of this book. In chapter 2, I have shown how the last heirs of the guild system and the first heralds of the industrial age shared the symbolic power of Ned Ludd despite their disparate demands, objectives, and cultures. If Luddism can be thought as a collective assemblage of enunciation, it is because contingent historic conditions (the Napoleonic Wars, the end of the paternalist economy of the guilds, a repressive government, and so forth) force a temporary alliance between these two social strata. In this respect, Ernesto Laclau's notion of the empty signifier is useful, not so much because it revives the Gramscian question of class alliance, but because it addresses such a question *from without,* as a by-product of contingent historic conditions. It is here that the (Lacanian) notion that political identities are always incomplete and ultimately defined by a radical otherness that both threatens and constitutes the political space meets the Derridean postulate that the conditions of possibility of a system coincide with its conditions of impossibility.

At the same time, this big Other (the Industrial Revolution) is never quite able to *fix* the Luddite identity, which keeps shifting between an antimodern rejection of industrial capitalism (embodied by machine-breaking) and a proto-modern critique of the political economy that underpins such a shift (expressed by the requests of higher wages and political reform). In this sense, the Luddite assemblage combines a horizontal, metonymic movement that conjuncts without synthesizing with a vertical, metaphoric movement toward universality and revolution that Laclau and Mouffe identify with the hegemonic relation. If Hayden White's definition of synecdoche allows us to bring these two movements together, the latter remains unfulfilled because the changing conditions of possibility of the system (the end of the war and the subsequent rise of the Eight-Hour Movement and Chartism) foreclose the solidification of the extemporary alliance between craftsmen and industrial workers in a hegemonic bloc.

The difficulty of thinking the improper name as purely immanent is also evident in chapters 2 and 5. In the case of Allen Smithee, it is the post-Fordist restructuring of the film industry that explains why the Smithee of 1969 functions as a lubricant for labor relations while the Smithee of

1999 becomes an impediment to their smooth administration. In the thick of the crisis of the studio system, Smithee is an efficient solution to labor disputes within a changing production process that begins to invest the film director with new powers (and new responsibilities) to extract value from its creative vision. Once this power is consolidated, however, Smithee's negative reputation turns the alias into a threat to the capital investments it was originally meant to safeguard. Likewise, besides a generic commitment to communicative equality, there is nothing in the original constitution of Anonymous that links it to struggles against censorship, intellectual property, autocracy, or social and economic injustice. Yet contingent historic circumstances such as corporate and government censorship, the eruption of the Arab Spring, and other social movements prompt this ambiguous signifier to empty itself out of its attachment to a specific technoculture to bridge a wide set of practices and struggles.

The fact that improper names express communities that do not share an essence does not mean that they cannot be thought as autonomous processes of subjectivation. While Ludd, Smithee, and Anonymous emerge to fulfill immediate and practical needs, Monty Cantsin and Luther Blissett show how the multiple-use name can be devised as an artificial mythmaking strategy. This awareness is apparent in the explicit connection between these two experiences and in particular in the transmission of a pragmatic ethos from one generation of activists and artists to the next. Significantly, the guidelines regarding the introduction of the multiple-use name are meant to *prevent* identification between specific individuals and the alias, that is, to preserve its communal and improper character. This privative, antiessentialist stance is evident in Monty Cantsin, whose users prefer not to trace any ethical horizon for the open pop star that may overdetermine singular uses. It is less apparent in Luther Blissett, where the emphasis on mythmaking and the choice of "suiciding" the folk hero signal an attempt at containing the ambiguity of the multiple-use name through narrative closure.

And yet Blissett's mythmaking remains necessarily artificial and self-reflexive—a narration that reflects on its condition of possibility in a society that is no longer enchanted by mythic speech. Because myth, argues Nancy, essentially communicates itself and nothing else, at the very moment it is named and identified as such, it ceases to be myth. "The unavowable community, the withdrawal of communion or communitarian ecstasy, are revealed in the interruption of myth," writes Nancy.[10] In this sense, the Luther Blissett Project, as well as previous avant-garde attempts at engineering modern myths, are significant precisely because they reveal the impossibility of community as a self-transparent totality. Such revelation does not limit itself to interrupt mythic speech but has a voice of its own that moves beyond negation. Nancy: "It is the voice of community, which in its way perhaps avows, without saying it, the unavowable . . . or more precisely presents, without enunciating it, the mythless truth of endless being-in-common, of this being *in* common that is not a 'common being.'"[11]

In this sense, the singular voice of the improper name projects the community beyond itself, to offer it to other nonhuman, or more-than-human, domains. It is through this route that we can return to Simondon's philosophy of individuation. In thinking being as infinite and indeterminate, Simondon seeks the principle that can set individuation in motion without exhausting its potentiality. In the transductive operation, he identifies the movement that not only structures a domain filled with potentials but also constitutes heterogeneous domains such as the living and the nonliving, the psychic and the collective, the technical and the human, in relation to one another. It is by reflecting on the risks and possibilities embedded in the technical–human transduction that this study ends with an exhortation to think the improper name beyond a properly human politics and epistemology. If Martin Heidegger has warned of the risks that the *ordering* of modern technology poses to mankind's proper relationship to Being, Simondon's emphasis on *indetermination* as the driving principle of the becoming of all beings points to a singular and therefore improper relationship between the technical and the human.[12]

In this respect, Anonymous marks a point of departure from previous improper names in that it embeds a logic that is no longer properly human. Trolling, raids, botnets, and illegal hacking have in fact the capacity to disrupt the very authorizing contexts (imageboards, IRC) wherein Anonymous can determine how the name is to be used and for what purposes. Whereas sharing a human name often entailed a form of belonging to a social (Blissett), cultural (Cantsin), or professional milieu (Ludd, Smithee), the Anonymous tag also encompasses the autonomy of nonhuman operators who are partly resistant to ethical and social determinations. From this angle, Anonymous allows us to gauge the impact of this techno-logic on a properly human politics, and vice versa.

To sum up, the notion of the improper can be situated at the intersection of two distinct philosophical trajectories. The first trajectory, immanent and materialist, and embodied here by Simondon's ontogenetic model, allows us to think the improper name as the transductive actualization of a potential through the *common operation* of two heterogeneous realities. From this angle, Ned Ludd articulates, if only for a short time, craftsmanship and industrial labor, the destruction of industrial machinery, and the demand for higher wages; Allen Smithee shows how the modern conflation of property and propriety, ownership and reputation, in the name of the author is suspended and reversed by the accumulation of negative symbolic capital; Monty Cantsin captures the tension between an invisible, continuous, and gratuitous art that merges with daily life and an art that enters the circuit of exchange; Luther Blissett expresses a contradictory attempt to forge a positive mythmaking strategy through the demystification of media narratives; and Anonymous transduces social and technical milieux characterized by a high degree of indetermination.

The second trajectory of the improper is inscribed in the deconstructive tradition, which claims that the community and the common are not transparent to themselves and can only be thought from without. Such a perspective emphasizes the irreducible opposition as well as the mutual constitution of the polarities outlined previously. From this point of view, Ludd ultimately expresses the impossibility of recomposing the paternalist economy of the guild system with the political economy of industrial capitalism; the accumulation of negative reputation in the Smithee signature shows that the regimes of property and propriety cannot be decoupled for too long within the modern culture industry; the Cantsin experience demonstrates that the inclusive ethos of mail art cannot be reconciled with the selectivity of the art system; Blissett's artificial mythmaking reveals the impossibility of myth, or the inessential being-in-common of condividuals who no longer live in a world founded by mythic speech; and Anonymous shows how the amoral and self-propelling logic of the lulz is ultimately incompatible with a notion of politics aimed at pursuing "rational objectives" and with a solidarity based on the recognition of the vulnerability of the other.

On one hand, these two connotations of the improper are a by-product of the philosophical frameworks that have been employed to analyze them. On the other hand, improper names allow us to bring these two philosophical traditions in conversation with one another. In a certain sense, the productive tension between immanence and deconstruction is already inscribed in the two attributes or polarities of the improper name, the collective pseudonym and the multiple-use name. The initial baptism of a collective pseudonym is in fact an immanent transductive operation as it is nothing but the actualization of a potential within a metastable system. And the dissemination of the alias in the public sphere entails a loss of identity and a crossing over into domains that may threaten from without the alias's original function. In this respect, improper names are both the *name of the medium* that allows for a shuttling the we and the I, potentiality and act, and *the name of the gap* that appears as soon as the transductive operation dissipates.

Thus, as a mode of mediation between incommensurable orderings, the improper allows us to return to the etymological roots of media. In Latin, the term *medium* simply meant "middle," as shown by expressions such as *in medium conferre* (putting something in common), "*rem in medio ponere* (publicly presenting an issue) or *in medium quaerere* (demanding something for all, as a common good)."[13] In these formulations medium is associated with the public and the common and stands for a mode of mediation that is independent of technological support. Because this medium is impermanent and does not store information, it needs to be constantly reinvented and re-produced to function. Thus, on a first level, the improper cannot be told apart from the signifying and asignifying operations that make up the common. Second, this middle increases or decreases its power depending on participation and usage. And third, this middle does not mediate between preexisting subjects but *is itself* the process of transindividuation that opens up the subject to its constitutive incompleteness and virtuality.

Although this book has been researched over the course of many years, beginning in 2011 my thinking and writing have been heavily influenced by historic events such as the Tunisian and Egyptian revolutions and the formation of anticapitalist social movements such as the Spanish 15-M, the North American Occupy, and the Turkish Gezi Park. I believe that the theories and practices analyzed in this book are relevant to the internal dynamic of these movements in many ways. For example, an understanding of the improper name as a collective assemblage of enunciation can be easily extended to the relation between action and signification within these movements. Rather than being based on representation and correspondence, the language and actions of these movements are connected by spontaneous initiatives that are rarely approved or even known by the totality of participants. Rather, as Rodrigo Nunes points out, it is a group's ability to catalyze collective action around an objective that determines the emergence of leadership-positions, or a "diffuse vanguardism," within the movement.[14]

This kind of perspective is quite different from the one adopted by a number of activist theorists who have described these movements as inherently horizontal, democratic, and consensus driven.[15] Because in a collective assemblage actions enjoy a relative autonomy from signification, they can generate internal tensions among activists who are concerned with the overall direction of a movement.[16] As I have shown throughout this book, this tension between collectivism and autonomy, centralization and decentralization, lies at the core of the politics of improper names. If the relationship between Tahrir, 15-M, Occupy, Gezi, BlackLivesMatter, Anonymous, and their referents is fundamentally improper, it is because these names function as signifiers for "a post-consensual practice that is dissociated from integrated modes of decision-making, and that prepares the ground for productive internal struggle."[17] In other words, while the search for consensus expresses the ideal of a self-transparent community, the politics of improper names exhorts us to think these movements as internally divided yet committed to sharing a common name. To be sure, authorizing contexts such as assemblies and collectives will always try to manage and contain the radical ambiguity of the name. But ultimately it is the circulation and use of this signifier *beyond* these authorizing contexts that determine its capacity to draw unexpected connections among a wide set of initiatives.

The paradox is that the more this circulation increases, the more the name's indexical function—its ability to circumscribe a discrete referent—is undermined. In this sense, the politics of improper names always points to a double gap. The first gap is external and is broadly determined by the historic conditions that set the perimeter for the circulation of the name and for its shuttling between ambiguous and hegemonic denotation. The second gap is internal and coincides with the voice of the unavowable community, a voice that, by revealing the impossibility of community as a self-transparent totality, projects it beyond itself. The challenge for contemporary social movements is how to develop connections among a plurality of actors and agents who, by acknowledging those gaps, are driven by a healthy agonism over the mode of disposition and usage of a shared symbolic power. Rather than a mythic search for consensus or an ideological commitment to horizontalism, it is the awareness that such power stems from the tension between irreducible practices and organizational forms that will be driving the transformative social movements of the twenty-first century. The improper name is only one medium through which such tension can be productively articulated and put to work.

NOTES

INTRODUCTION

1 From now on, I will use the third person neutral to refer to the complex of actions attributable to a condividual like Luther Blissett. As I will argue in the final chapter and the conclusion, shared pseudonyms can also encompass nonhuman actors and as such are not necessarily gendered. I will instead use the gendered third person to refer to actions and utterances conducted and pronounced by specific individuals under a shared pseudonym, even though such individuals my not always be identifiable as a he or a she.

2 The notion of *dividual* is borrowed from Gilles Deleuze. In "Postscript on the Societies of Control," Deleuze argues that the emergence of the network society transforms individuals into dividuals, that is to say, into entities whose behavior is monitored and modulated by coded accesses to databanks. If in Michel Foucault's disciplinary societies individuals were identified through a signature and massed together through serial numbers, in what Deleuze calls the control society, individuals are sliced into dividual transactions through username/password combinations. From this angle, the condividual "Luther Blissett" is nothing but the recursive name of an assemblage of dividual uses of the same name. One of the functions of this book is to analyze the social codes that modulate access to assemblages of enunciation like Luther Blissett. See Deleuze, "Postscript on the Societies of Control," *October* 59 (Winter 1992): 3–7.

3 Michel Foucault, *Society Must Be Defended: Lectures at the Collège de France 1975–1976,* trans. David Macey (New York: Palgrave Macmillan, 2003), 8.

4 Ibid., 7.

5 Michel De Certeau, *The Practice of Everyday Life,* trans. Steven Rendall (Berkeley: University of California, Press, 1984).

6 Pierre Bourdieu, *Language and Symbolic Power,* trans. Gino Raymond and Matthew Anderson (Cambridge, Mass.: Harvard University Press, 1991), 75. By noting how Austin's reflections on the conditions that make a performative utterance successful are essentially social, Bourdieu writes that "the person who wishes to proceed *felicitously* with the christening of a ship or of a person must be entitled to do so, in the same way that, to be able to give an order, one must have a recognized authority over the recipient of that order" (73). The possession of symbolic capital, understood as the possession of a socially recognized competence, is thus a precondition for the magic of words to act on the social world. The difference between

symbolic capital and symbolic power is that the former is a competence that has been accumulated over time, whereas the latter is the active exercise of this competence.

7 Michael Hardt and Antonio Negri, *Commonwealth* (Cambridge, Mass.: Harvard University Press, 2009), 338–39.

8 In an assemblage, write Deleuze and Guattari, "the whole not only coexists with all the parts; it is contiguous to them, it exists as a product that is produced apart from them and yet at the same time is related to them." Gilles Deleuze and Félix Guattari, *Anti-Oedipus: Capitalism and Schizophrenia,* trans. Robert Hurley, Mark Seem, and Helen R. Lane (Minneapolis: University of Minnesota Press, 1983), 43–44.

9 J. R. Maddicott, "The Birth and Setting of the Ballads of Robin Hood," *English Historical Review* 93 (1978): 276–99.

10 For Poor Konrad, see Friedrich Engels, *The Peasant War in Germany* (New York: International, 1966). For Captain Swing, see Eric Hobsbawm and George Rudé, *Captain Swing* (London: Lawrence and Wishart, 1969). For Rebecca, see David Williams, *The Rebecca Riots: A Study in Agrarian Discontent* (Cardiff: University of Wales Press, 1978).

11 Kevin Binfield, *Writings of the Luddites* (Baltimore: Johns Hopkins University Press, 2004).

12 For *The Pseudonym Library,* see Troy J. Bassett, "T. Fisher Unwin's Pseudonym Library: Literary Marketing and Authorial Identity," *English Literature in Transition, 1880–1920* 47, no. 2 (2004): 143–60. For the Anonyma series, see Rachel Sagner Buurma, "Anonymity, Corporate Authority and the Archive: The Production of Authorship in Late-Victorian England," *Victorian Studies* 50, no. 1 (2007): 15–42.

13 Maurice Mashaal, *Bourbaki: A Secret Society of Mathematicians,* trans. Anna Pierrehumbert (Providence, R.I.: American Mathematical Society, 2006).

14 André Weil, "Appendix to Part One: On the Algebraic Study of Certain Types of Marriage Laws," in Claude Lévi-Strauss, *The Elementary Structures of Kinship,* trans. James H. Bell, John Richard von Stunner, and Rodney Needham, 221–32 (1949; repr., Boston: Beacon Press, 1969). For the encounter between Weil and Lévi-Strauss, see A. Weil, *The Apprenticeship of a Mathematician,* trans. Jennifer Gage (Basel: Birkhäuser, 1992), 185.

15 Andrew Sarris, *The American Cinema: Directors and Directions 1929–1968* (1968; repr., New York: Da Capo Press, 1992).

16 See Jeremy Braddock and Stephen Hock, eds., *Directed by Allen Smithee* (Minneapolis: University of Minnesota Press, 2001); Jacques Derrida, "Signature, Event, Context," in *A Derrida Reader: Between the Blinds,* ed. Peggy Kamuf, 80–112 (New York: Columbia University Press, 1991).

17 Deleuze and Guattari develop the notion of minor literature in *Kafka:*

Towards a Minor Literature, trans. Dana Polan (Minneapolis: University of Minnesota Press, 1986).

18 Michel Foucault, "What Is an Author?," in *Language, Counter-memory, Practice: Selected Essays and Interviews by Michel Foucault,* ed. and trans. Donald F. Bouchard, 113–38 (Ithaca, N.Y.: Cornell University Press, 1977).

19 Franco Berardi, *The Soul at Work: From Alienation to Autonomy,* trans. Francesca Cadel and Giuseppina Mecchia (Los Angeles, Calif.: Semiotext(e), 2009).

20 Jacques Derrida, *Given Time: I. Counterfeit Money,* trans. Peggy Kamuf (Chicago: University of Chicago Press, 1992).

21 See Chuck Welch, ed., *The Eternal Network: A Mail Art Anthology* (Calgary: University of Calgary Press, 1995).

22 See Laura Kaplan, *The Story of Jane: The Legendary Underground Feminist Abortion Service* (New York: Pantheon Books, 1995).

23 See Gilbert Simondon, *Du mode d'existence des objets techniques* (Paris: Aubier, 1958–89). A partial English translation of this text is available at https://english.duke.edu/uploads/assets/Simondon_MEOT_part_1.pdf.

24 "Indeed, precisely because talent isn't abundant in a minor literature, there are no possibilities for an individuated enunciation that would belong to this or that 'master' and that could be separated from a collective enunciation. Indeed, scarcity of talent is in fact beneficial and allows the conception of something other than a literature of masters; what each author says individually already constitutes a common action, and what he or she says or does is necessarily political, even if others aren't in agreement." Deleuze and Guattari, *Kafka,* 17.

25 Nicholas Thoburn, *Deleuze, Marx, and Politics* (London: Routledge, 2003).

26 Stevphen Shukaitis, *Imaginal Machines: Autonomy and Self-Organization in the Revolutions of Everyday Life* (London: Minor Compositions, 2009), 66–67.

27 De Certeau, *Practice of Everyday Life,* xix.

28 Ibid.

29 Ibid., 36.

30 Jean-François Lyotard, *The Differend: Phrases in Dispute,* trans. Georges Van Den Abbeele (Minneapolis: University of Minnesota Press, 1988), 42.

31 Plato, *Cratylus,* in *Complete Works,* ed. John M. Cooper (Indianapolis, Ind.: Hackett, 1997), 101–56.

32 Aristotle, *Metaphysics* 1043a12–1043b32, in *The Complete Works of Aristotle: The Revised Oxford Translation,* vol. 2, ed. Jonathan Barnes (Princeton, N.J.: Princeton University Press, 1991).

33 Ludwig Wittgenstein, *Tractatus Logico-Philosophicus* (New York: Harcourt, Brace, 1922), 4.12.

34 Betrand Russell, introduction to Wittgenstein, *Tractatus Logico-Philosophicus,* ix.
35 Wittgenstein, *Tractatus,* 3.322, 3.323.
36 Gottlob Frege, "On Sense and Reference," in *Meaning and Reference,* ed. Alan W. Moore, 23–42 (Oxford: Oxford University Press, 1993).
37 Bertrand Russell, "On Denoting," *Mind* 14, no. 56 (1905): 479–93.
38 Saul Kripke, *Naming and Necessity* (Oxford: Basil Blackwell, 1980), 135.
39 Michel Foucault, *Security, Territory, Population: Lectures at the Collège de France 1977–1978* (New York: Palgrave Macmillan, 2007), 104.
40 Slavoj Žižek, *The Sublime Object of Ideology* (London: Verso, 1989), 94–95.
41 Ernesto Laclau, *On Populist Reason* (London: Verso, 2005), 108.
42 Gilles Deleuze and Félix Guattari, *A Thousand Plateaus,* trans. Brian Massumi (Minneapolis: University of Minnesota Press, 1984), 502, 504.

1. NED LUDD, THE MACHINE BREAKER

1 E. P. Thompson, *The Making of the English Working Class* (New York: Vintage Books, 1966), 553.
2 The story has been handed down in two slightly different versions. The first, originally reported by the *Nottingham Review* on December 20, 1811, and cited by J. L. Hammond and Barbara Hammond, says that Ludlam's master complained about his apprentice's poor performance to a magistrate, who ordered a whipping. Ludlam in response demolished the hated frame. The second version, originally reported by John Blackner, a radical contemporary historian of Nottingham, and cited by Thomis and others, says that Ludlam was ordered to square his needles by his father. See J. L. Hammond and Barbara Hammond, *The Skilled Labourer: 1760–1832* (London: Longmans, Green, 1919), 259; Malcolm Thomis, *The Luddites: Machine-Breaking in Regency England* (Newton Abbott, U.K.: David and Charles 1970), 11.
3 The Hammonds quote an article published in the *Nottingham Review* on December 6, 1811, that details the technical differences between the wide frames and the traditional knitting machines. See Hammond and Hammond, *Skilled Labourer,* 226–27.
4 Ibid., 169.
5 Eric Hobsbawm, *Labouring Men: Studies in the History of Labour* (London: Weidenfeld and Nicolson, 1964), 9.
6 Adrian Randall, preface to Binfield, *Writings of the Luddites,* xvi.
7 Karl Marx, *Capital: A Critique of the Political Economy,* vol. 1, trans. Ben Fowkes (New York: Penguin, 1976), 554.
8 See Thompson, *Making of the English Working Class,* 556.

9 Ibid., 485–500.

10 Binfield, *Writings of the Luddites,* 36.

11 E.g., George Rudé and Eric Hobsbawm have labeled the 1830 Swing riots against the mechanization of agriculture in the South and East of England as an episode of "agricultural Luddism." See Hobsbawm and Rudé, *Captain Swing,* 17. Even nowadays, an attitude of radical refusal of technological innovation is generally labeled as Luddism. See, e.g., Steven E. Jones, *Against Technology: From the Luddites to neo-Luddism* (London: Routledge, 2006).

12 See Frank Peel, *Risings of the Luddites, Chartists, and Plug-Drawers,* 3rd ed. (Brighouse, U.K.: J. Hartler, 1895), and D. F. Skyes and G. H. Walker, *Ben O' Bill's, the Luddite: A Yorkshire Tale* (United Kingdom: Simpkin, Marshall, Hamilton, Kent, 1898).

13 See Hammond and Hammond, *Skilled Labourer,* 168.

14 Thompson, *Making of the English Working Class,* 575–76. Likewise, 1930s historian Frank Darvall treats machine breaking as an issue of public order and crowd control, denying the Luddites any political intention. Darvall goes as far as saying that "there was no movement, or even tendency, of revolt against the established system as such; no disposition to see in the system the cause of the many very grave evils from which grave bodies of the people were suffering." F. Darvall, *Popular Disturbances and Public Order in Regency England* (1934; repr., New York: Augustus M. Kelley, 1969), 317.

15 See Eric J. Hobsbawm, *Primitive Rebels: Studies in Archaic Forms of Social Movement in the Nineteenth and Twentieth Centuries* (Manchester, U.K.: Manchester University Press, 1959).

16 Hobsbawm, *Labouring Men,* 9.

17 See Thompson, *Making of the English Working Class,* 138–66, for Thomas Spence and the Spenceans, and 220–31, for William Cobbett.

18 The economic liberalism of the two parties emerged clearly in 1812 when the United Committee of Framework Knitters of Nottingham tried to introduce a bill to guarantee higher production standards by limiting the use of wide frames in workshops. This attempt also failed, leaving the legalistic side of the workers' movement impotent and isolated. Ibid., 536–41.

19 The actual efficacy of Napoleon's continental system is disputed by historians. Owing to overwhelming superiority of the Royal Navy, the enforcement of the blockade was difficult and spotty. Although the British exports to Continental Europe undoubtedly declined during this period, trade with the overseas colonies increased, opening up new markets for the textile industry.

20 Thompson, *Making of the English Working Class,* 551–52.

21 Ibid., 553.

22 Thomis's criticism of Thompson's use of oral sources (recorded by local historian Frank Peel) regarding the existence of a revolutionary underground is only partly convincing. As John Rule points out, "difficult as it is to evaluate, this oral evidence was recorded by an historian with no evident motive other than to record honestly a popular tradition. It cannot be simply dismissed because Peel got a date wrong or by disregarding authentic oral tradition as 'legend.'" Rule concludes that the interpretation of Luddism advanced by Thompson "may be unprovable," but "this is not the same thing as saying that it has been disproven." Rule, *The Labouring Classes in Early Industrial England, 1750–1850* (London: Longman, 1986), 374–75.

23 Thomis, *Luddites,* 172.

24 J. L. Dinwiddy, "Luddism and Politics in the Northern Counties," *Social History* 4, no. 1 (1979): 60. Dinwiddy adds the important proviso that the revolutionary impulse must not have been formidable if it is true that it withered by the end of the summer. "It did not apparently get beyond the formation of a few loosely connected conspiratorial groups, patchily supplied with arms" (59).

25 Adrian Randall, *Before the Luddites: Custom, Community, and Machinery in the English Woollen Industry, 1776–1809* (Cambridge: Cambridge University Press, 1991), 278–79.

26 Ibid., 133.

27 Ibid., 150–51.

28 Craig Calhoun, *The Question of Class Struggle: Social Foundations of Popular Radicalism during the Industrial Revolution* (Chicago: University of Chicago Press, 1982), 149–50.

29 Ibid., 205. In response to Calhoun, John Rule argues that "class conflict was at least latent in eighteenth-century labor disputes in manufacturing, while it has been recently suggested that in the southern counties a proletarianised agricultural workforce formed a separate 'community of labourers' from the end of the eighteenth century in contradiction to the paternalist model of social harmony." Rule, *Labouring Classes,* 159.

30 See Norman Simms, "Ned Ludd's Mummers Play," *Folklore* 89, no. 2 (1978): 166–78.

31 Ibid., 172.

32 Ibid.

33 Hobsbawm and Rudé, *Captain Swing,* 67–69.

34 See John Bohstedt, *Riots and Community Politics in England and Wales, 1790–1810* (Cambridge, Mass.: Harvard University Press, 1983); Alan Brooke and Lesley Kipling, *Liberty or Death: Radicals, Republicans, and Luddites 1793–1823*

(Honley, U.K.: Workers History Publications, 1993); and Adrian Randall, *Before the Luddites.*

35 See Kirkpatrick Sale, *Rebels against the Future: The Luddites and Their War on the Industrial Revolution: Lessons for the Computer Age* (New York: Basic Books, 1995), and Brian Bailey, *The Luddite Rebellion* (New York: New York University Press, 1998).

36 Thomis, *Luddites,* 173.

37 Binfield, *Writings of the Luddites,* 6.

38 In "The Crime of Anonymity," a study of 284 anonymous threatening letters published by authority in the *London Gazette* between 1750 and 1820, Thompson argues that such letters are a "characteristic form of social protest in any society which has crossed a certain threshold of literacy, in which forms of collective organized defence are weak, and in which individuals who can be identified as the organizers of protest are liable to immediate victimization." E. P. Thompson, "The Crime of Anonymity," in *Albion's Fatal Tree: Crime and Society in Eighteenth Century England,* ed. Douglas Hay (New York: Random House, 1975), 255.

39 Binfield, *Writings of the Luddites,* 6.

40 Ibid., 18.

41 Ibid., 23.

42 Ibid., 24.

43 "By the Frameworck Knitters, A+Declaration," Nottinghamshire Archives M 429, 31–32, in Binfield, *Writings of the Luddites,* 89–90. The editor also transcribes a heavily emended version of the "Declaration" preserved in the Home Office archive and labeled H. O. 42/119.

44 J. L. Austin argues that the insertion of the word "hereby" in formal or legal texts "serves to indicate that the sentence is, as it is said, the instrument effecting the act of warning, authorizing, &c. 'Hereby' is a useful criterion that the utterance is performative." Austin, *How to Do Things with Words* (Cambridge, Mass.: Harvard University Press, 1962), 57.

45 "By the Frameworck Knitters, A+Declaration," 32.

46 It is worth noting that the acceptation of Robin Hood as a paternalist figure—that is, a distressed lord or earl who steals from the rich to give to the poor—appears only in the sixteenth century. As Stephen Knight points out, the medieval Robin Hood that first appears in the fourteenth century ballads is consistently described as a "yeoman," that is, a free man who is not a bound serf but not even a member of the gentry. In these texts, Hood is a figure of social banditry who looks after himself and his close associates. As noted in the introduction, John Maddicott contends that Robin Hood may have originally functioned as an alias shared by fourteenth-century bandits—an argument disputed by Knight (196–97). Knight also shows how

the emergence of Robin Hood as the distressed aristocrat who has fallen in disgrace and usually aspires to return to noble rank is an invention of the sixteenth century. It is hard to know what kind of Robin Hood the Luddites had in mind when they compared his gestures to Ludd's. See S. Knight, *Robin Hood: A Mythic Biography* (Ithaca, NY: Cornell University Press, 2003), 196–97.

47 "General Ludd's Triumph," H. O. 42/119, January 27, 1812, in Binfield, *Writings of the Luddites*, 98–100.

48 *"Declaration; Extraordinary. Justice.* Death, or Revenge," H. O. 42/118, November 1811, ibid., 72–73. Binfield notes that the signature, in particular the last word, "Death," is almost illegible and may not be correctly transcribed.

49 Binfield notes how "legal forms and models of writs and warrants for all varieties of offenses were readily available . . . in books written specifically for magistrates and clerks" (ibid., 26). Both "Declaration; Extraordinary" and the aforementioned "By the Framework Knitters, A Declaration" share many rhetorical features with a "Proclamation" issued by the Prince Regent and published in several newspapers, which required local sheriffs and other civil officers "to discover, apprehend, and bring to Justice" the Luddites of Nottingham (ibid., 27).

50 By "institution," Bourdieu does not necessarily mean a particular organization but, as John B. Thompson points out in the introduction to *Language and Symbolic Power,* "to any relatively durable set of relationships which *endows* the speaker with the authority to carry out the utterance which his or her utterance claims to perform" (8).

51 Randall, *Before the Luddites,* 131–32.

52 Binfield, *Writings of the Luddites,* 53.

53 Randall, *Before the Luddites,* 279. Binfield supplements Randall's point, noting that the absence among the clothiers of a constitutive charter made "Paine's attack on the constitutions that supported a government that denied protection to the trade" particularly relevant. Binfield, *Writings of the Luddites,* 61.

54 "Letter from 'Ned Ludd Clerk' addressed to 'To Mr Smith Shearing Frame Holder at Hill End Yorkshire,' Hill End near Leeds," Leeds University Manuscripts 193, Gott Papers, vol. 3, 106, March 9 or 10, 1812. In Binfield, *Writings of the Luddites,* 209.

55 Ibid., 210.

56 Ibid.

57 See, e.g., "The Cropper's Song," a song supposedly sung by a Luddite at the Shears Inn, Hightown, which celebrates cropper potency by eulogizing the "Great Enoch," the large hammers used by the Luddites to destroy the shearing framers. "The hammers were named after Enoch Taylor, a

metalsmith from the Marsden area who produced not only hammers but also the shearing frames that threatened the croppers' trade," writes Binfield in *Writings of the Luddites.* "The choice . . . to name the hammers 'Enoch' marks a discourse of local containment and internal regulation—that is, the idea that both problems and solutions can come from within the community" (54–55). The song is reproduced in its entirety ibid., 201–3.

58 "Letter from 'Peter Plush' purporting to write from Nottingham to 'Mr Edward Ludd' at Huddersfield," Radcliffe Papers, 126/46, May 1, 1812. Ibid., 224.

59 Thompson, "Crime of Anonymity," 322.

60 "Letter from 'Peter Plush,'" 224.

61 Thompson, "The Crime," 322.

62 "Letter from 'Peter Plush,'" 223.

63 Thompson, "The Crime," 273.

64 Posted notice "To Whitefield Luddites," H. O. 42/112, and transcribed in "Hay's letter to Ryder," April 27, 1812. In Binfield, *Writings of the Luddites,* 175–76.

65 Ibid., 33.

66 Hammond and Hammond, *Skilled Labourer,* 49.

67 Cited in Thompson, *Making of the English Working Class,* 276.

68 Thompson effectively describes this dynamic: "When markets were sluggish, manufacturers took advantage of the situation by putting out work to weavers desperate for employment at any price, thereby compelling them 'to manufacture great quantities of goods at a time, when they are absolutely not wanted.' With the return of demand, the goods were then released on the market at cut price; so that each minor recession was succeeded by a period in which the market was glutted with cheap goods thereby holding wages down to their recession level." Ibid., 277–78.

69 Hammond and Hammond, *Skilled Labourer,* 61.

70 Ibid., 63.

71 "Letter from Holywell, Flintshire, to Mr. Douglas and others at Manchester" May 5, 1812, H. O. 40/1/1. In *Writings of the Luddites,* 181–82.

72 Thompson, *Making of the English Working Class,* 595.

73 Binfield, *Writings of the Luddites,* 36.

74 See Bohstedt, *Riots and Community Politics.*

75 "Letter ('A') to Mr. Simpson, Manchester," H. O. 40/1/1, April 30, 1812, and enclosed in Hay's correspondence with Home Office secretary Richard Ryder. In Binfield, *Writings of the Luddites,* 178–79.

76 Darvall, *Popular Disturbances,* 93–95. The old reformer is Archibald Prentice, author of *Historical Sketches and Personal Recollections of Manchester Intended to Illustrate the Progress of Public Opinion from 1792 to 1832* (London: C. Gilpin,

1851). Cited in Thompson, *Making of the English Working Class,* 567.

77 Thompson, *Making of the English Working Class,* 568.

78 According to E. P. Thompson, Manchester boasted a grammar school as well as private schools where the sons of artisans and masters could learn Latin. Ibid., 714.

79 Binfield, *Writings of the Luddites,* 46–47.

80 See Roman Jakobson, "Two Types of Language and Two Types of Aphasic Disturbances," in Roman Jakobson and Moris Halle, *Fundamentals of Language* (1956; repr., Berlin: Walter de Gruyter, 2002), 69–90.

81 Hayden White, *Metahistory: The Historical Imagination in Nineteenth-Century Europe* (Baltimore: Johns Hopkins University Press, 1973), 35.

82 Ibid., 36.

83 See Ernesto Laclau, "Why Do Empty Signifiers Matter to Politics?," in *Emancipation(s),* 36–46 (London: Verso, 1996).

84 Ibid., 43.

85 Ernesto Laclau and Chantal Mouffe, *Hegemony and Socialist Strategy: Towards a Radical Democratic Politics* (London: Verso, 1985), xiii. It is worth noting that Laclau and Mouffe reject the distinction between discursive and nondiscursive practices and maintain, against Foucault, that "every object is constituted as an object of discourse, insofar as no object is given outside every discursive condition of emergence" (107). This does not mean that the material world cannot exist outside of thought but rather that meaning is socially constructed through discursive formations (here the two follow Foucault), which are governed by a principle of "regularity in dispersion." In other words, a discursive formation is a configuration in which an "ensemble of differential positions" appear both dispersed and in relation to one another. Thus "the practice of articulation, as fixation/dislocation of a system of differences, cannot consist of purely linguistic phenomena; but must instead pierce the entire material density of the multifarious institutions, rituals and practices through which a discursive formation is structured" (109).

86 Laclau, *Emancipation(s),* 43.

87 Ibid., 52.

88 "In deconstructive terms: the conditions of possibility of the system are also its conditions of impossibility." Ibid., 53.

89 Here Laclau makes the example of Perón. As a leader in exile of the Argentinean opposition to the military regime, Perón was in perfect position to become an empty signifier "incarnating the moment of universality in the chain of equivalences which unified the popular camp." Ibid., 55. But as soon as he returned to power in 1973, he had to carry out a specific politics that could not satisfy and keep together the left- and right-wing factions of the Peronist movement.

90 Thompson, *Making of the English Working Class,* 10.
91 Ibid.
92 Rosa Luxemburg, *The Mass Strike, the Political Party, and the Trade Unions,* trans. Patrick Lavin (Detroit, Mich.: Marxist Educational Society of Detroit, 1925).
93 Laclau, *Emancipation(s),* 40–41.
94 Thompson, *Making of the English Working Class,* 569.
95 Ibid.
96 Marx, *Capital,* 1:554–55.
97 Laclau and Mouffe, *Hegemony and Socialist Strategy,* 137.
98 In *A Thousand Plateaus,* 504, Deleuze and Guattari write that "it is necessary to ascertain the content and the expression of each assemblage, to evaluate their real distinction, their reciprocal presupposition, their piecemeal insertions."
99 Thoburn, *Deleuze, Marx, and Politics,* 29.
100 This nonlinear development of class consciousness is also evident from the fact that Ludd continued to release its imaginal power even after the end of the Luddite riots and the repeal of the Combination Acts, a measure that partly favored the development of modern trade unionism. It is certainly no accident that the impoverished rural workers who destroyed thousands of threshing machines in the South and East of England in 1830 were also led by a mythic figure, Captain Swing, whose signature was appended to the threatening letters sent to wealthy landlords, magistrates, and parsons. For the Swing riots, see Hobsbawm and Rudé, *Captain Swing.*

2. ALLEN SMITHEE, THE ANTI-AUTEUR

1 The Copyright Act of 1842 made authors less dependent on patronage and charity by extending the copyright term to forty-two years from a work's first publication or the author's lifetime plus seven years, whichever was longer. See Catherine Seville, *Literary Copyright Reform in Early Victorian England: The Framing of the 1842 Copyright Act* (Cambridge: Cambridge University Press, 1999). On the economics of the Victorian publishing industry, see Alexis Weedon, *Victorian Publishing: The Economics of Book Production for a Mass Market, 1836–1916* (Burlington, Vt.: Ashgate, 2003).
2 Mark Rose, *Authors and Owners: The Invention of Copyright* (Cambridge, Mass.: Harvard University Press, 1993), 16–17.
3 E.g., as early as 1545, the Venetian Council of Ten issued a public edict that established that no book was to be printed or sold without prior consent of the author and his heirs. In the same period, the Parliament of Paris accorded to various authors the exclusive right to print their work against that of the publisher. Rose argues that these measures are not to be

confused with modern copyright in that while they enabled some authors to retain control over their publications and encouraged publishers to secure the author's permission before printing his manuscript, they still identified ownership with publishing, not authorship. In seventeenth-century British common law, there is not a single case in which the author is identified as the owner of a book. Ibid., 18–25.

4 As Dallas Liddle has pointed out, these writers prevailed over the supporters of journalism's traditional anonymity, not in virtue of their arguments, but because the reading public effectively rewarded the emerging signature system. "Signed journals tended to succeed, anonymous ones to fail, and that was all publishers knew and all they needed to know." Liddle, "Salesmen, Sportsmen, Mentors: Anonymity and Mid-Victorian Theories of Journalism," *Victorian Studies* 41, no. 1 (1997): 62.

5 See Alexis Easley, *First-Person Anonymous: Women Writers and Victorian Print Media, 1830–70* (Aldershot, U.K.: Ashgate, 2004).

6 Michel Foucault, "The Discourse on Language," in *The Archeology of Knowledge and The Discourse on Language,* trans. A. M. Sheridan Smith, 215–37 (London: Tavistock, 1972).

7 Genette writes that once the reader becomes aware of the alias, "the pseudonym is included in his image, or idea, of that particular author, so that inevitably (although in varying degrees from reader to reader) he considers pseudonym or patronymic together, or in alternation; and thereby, no less inevitably, he distinguishes within his idea or image the figure of the author from the figure of the private man." Gérard Genette, *Paratexts: Thresholds of Interpretation,* trans. Jane E. Lewin (Cambridge: Cambridge University Press, 1997), 50.

8 Here I follow Pierre Bourdieu's definition of symbolic capital as a socially recognized competence that is accumulated by a group or an individual over time. See introduction, note 6.

9 The story is reported in Don Siegel, *A Siegel Film: An Autobiography* (London: Faber and Faber, 1993), 320–21. According to DGA board member John Rich, the first name proposed was Alan Smith, but the DGA eventually opted for Allen Smithee to make clear that the name was artificial and to avoid possible confusion with existing directors. See Amy Wallace, "Name of Director Smithee Isn't What It Used to Be," *Los Angeles Times,* January 15, 2000, and the documentary *Directed by Alan Smithee* (dir. Lesli Klansberg, United States, 2002).

10 Allen Smithee is the first pseudonym chosen by the DGA. Beginning in the 1980s, the variation "Alan Smithee" becomes more frequently used than Allen Smithee—a sign of the growing impropriety of the name. I preserve this ambiguity by using Allen Smithee when referring to the circumstances

of the alias's baptism, the work of the Allen Smithee Group, and the DGA's control over the name. I rely instead on Alan Smithee when referring to unauthorized uses of the name, specific film credits, and the circumstances of the alias's demise.

11 For a complete list of Smithee's works, see "Alan Smithee," http://www.imdb.com/.

12 See Wallace, "Name of Director Smithee."

13 Leonard J. Leff and Jerold L. Simmons, *The Dame in the Kimono: Hollywood, Censorship, and the Production Code* (Lexington: University Press of Kentucky, 2001), 85–86.

14 Only five (Fox Film, Loews/MGM, Paramount, RKO Radio Pictures, and Warner Bros.) of the Big Eight owned significant distribution chains. The "Little Tree" (Universal Pictures, Columbia Pictures, and United Artists) owned only small theater circuits.

15 The demise of the Hays Code was anticipated by *Joseph Burstyn, Inc. v. Wilson* (1952), another landmark Supreme Court ruling, which established that cinema was a form of art and as such was entitled to First Amendment protection. Repeated violations of the Hays Code throughout the 1960s showed that the system had become obsolete. Thus, in November 1968, the MPAA introduced the Classification and Rating Administration (CARA), which is currently in charge of the rating system.

16 Cited in Peter Biskind, *Easy Riders, Raging Bulls: How the Sex-Drugs-and-Rock 'n' Roll Generation Saved Hollywood* (New York: Simon and Schuster, 1998), 20.

17 Ibid., 18–22.

18 See Douglas Gomery, *The Hollywood Studio System: A History* (London: BFI, 2005), 198–223.

19 Ibid., 191.

20 Truffaut, in Barry Keith Grant, ed., *Auteurs and Authorship: A Film Reader* (Malden, Mass.: Blackwell, 2008), 9–18.

21 Andrew Sarris, "Notes on the Auteur Theory in 1962," *Film Culture,* no. 27 (Winter, 1962–63): 1–8. In Gerard Mast, Marshall Cohen, and Leo Braudy, eds., *Film Theory and Criticism: Introductory Readings* (New York: Oxford University Press, 1992), 561–64.

22 Sarris groups directors into hierarchical categories such as "Pantheon Directors," "The Far Side of Paradise," "Expressive Esoterica," and "Lightly Likeable." See A. Sarris, *The American Cinema: Directors and Directions 1929–1968* (New York: Dutton, 1968); 2nd ed. (New York: Da Capo Press, 1996).

23 Timothy Corrigan, *A Cinema without Walls: Movies and Culture after Vietnam* (New Brunswick, N.J.: Rutgers University Press, 1991), 102.

24 Peter Bart, "In Hollywood, the Name Is the Game," *Variety* 21 (March

1980): 3. Cited in Jessie Labov, "Smithee in *The Twilight Zone: The People v. John Landis et al.* and Other Trials of Authorship," in Braddock and Hock, *Directed by Allen Smithee,* 112.

25 Directors Guild of America, *The Creative Rights Handbook 2011–2014,* 3, http://www.dga.org/Contracts/Creative-Rights.aspx.

26 Jeremy Braddock, "Smithee's Incorporation," in Braddock and Hock, *Directed by Allen Smithee,* 155.

27 Ibid., 156.

28 Jonathan P. Eburne, "The Cheerless Art of Industry: Marcel Duchamp and the Smithee Readymade," in Braddock and Hock, *Directed by Allen Smithee,* 230–31.

29 Ibid., 232.

30 Jeremy Braddock, "Smithee's Incorporation," 159.

31 Invited by producer Michael de Luca to attend a clarifying meeting at New Line, Kaye brought with him a rabbi, a priest, and a monk. Even though the three had not seen the movie, Kaye thought that their presence would have somehow helped his cause. He also managed to get the movie pulled from the Toronto Film Festival and hired an intermediary to answer all his phone calls. See Tony Kaye, "Losing It: Tony Kaye Falls Out with Hollywood Film," *The Guardian,* October 25, 2002, http://www.theguardian.com/film/2002/oct/25/artsfeatures.advertising, and Benjamin Svetkey, "X Marks the Spat," *Entertainment Weekly,* October 23, 1998, 28–36.

32 The story of the DGA's counteroffer is reported by Craig Saper, whom Kaye hired as an expert witness in the suit. See Craig Saper, "Artificial *Auterism* and the Political Economy of the Allen Smithee Case," in Braddock and Hock, *Directed by Allen Smithee,* 43–46.

33 Cited in David Robb, "American History X: Kaye Pleading the First in 'X' Credits Dispute," *Hollywood Reporter,* October 2, 1998.

34 During the first round of negotiations to obtain the director's cut in 1964, the DGA had offered producers to fly in at its own expense one of twelve top-notch directors to complete a film if a director failed to produce his own cut. Although this proposal, formulated by Frank Capra, was rejected by the producers, it shows that the DGA was ready to invest significant economic resources into obtaining higher creative control. See Lyndon Stambler, "Director's Cut," *DGA Quarterly,* Spring 2011, http://www.dga.org/Craft/DGAQ/All-Articles/1101-Spring-2011/Feature-Creative-Rights.aspx.

35 Adam Higginbotham, "I Did Abominable Things," *The Telegraph,* June 10, 2007, http://www.telegraph.co.uk/culture/3665724/I-did-abominable-things.html.

36 Cited in Svetkey, "X Marks the Spat."

37 Saper, "Artificial *Auterism,*" 45.

38 Jeremy Braddock and Stephen Hock, "The Specter of Illegitimacy in an Age of Disillusion and Crisis," in Braddock and Hock, *Directed by Allen Smithee,* 13.

39 See André Bazin, "La Politique des auteurs," *Cahiers du cinéma* 70 (1957). In Peter Graham, ed., *The New Wave* (New York: Doubleday, 1968), 154.

40 Braddock and Hock, "Specter of Illegitimacy," 16.

41 See Christian Keathley, "*Signateurism* and the Case of Allen Smithee," in Braddock and Hock, *Directed by Allen Smithee,* 121–42.

42 Saper, "Artificial *Auterism,*" 41–42.

43 Jacques Derrida, *Signsponge,* trans. Richard Rand (New York: Columbia University Press, 1984), 70.

44 For the deconstruction of Hegel and Genet's surnames, see Jacques Derrida, *Glas,* trans. John P. Leavey and Richard Rand (Lincoln: Nebraska University Press, 1986). For Kant, see Jacques Derrida, *The Truth in Painting,* trans. Geoff Bennington and Ian McLeod (Chicago: University of Chicago Press, 1987).

45 Keathley, "*Signateurism,*" 134.

46 See Labov, "Smithee in *The Twilight Zone,*" 101–20.

47 Stuart Black, "Danger on the Film Set," *New York Times Magazine,* December 4, 1983, 124.

48 Randall Sullivan, "Death in the Twilight Zone," *Rolling Stone,* June 21, 1984. Cited in Labov, "Smithee in *The Twilight Zone,*" 104. The *Rolling Stone*'s attack on Landis prompted a letter of response from fourteen directors—including Billy Wilder, Francis Ford Coppola, George Lucas, and John Houston—who claimed that although the director must have artistic control, he cannot be in control of all technical aspects of a film. Labov notes that "Steven Spielberg, who co-executive produced *Twilight Zone* with Landis, was noticeably absent" (104).

49 Labov, "Smithee in *The Twilight Zone,*" 103–5.

50 See "Film Crew Reports Reprisals for Testifying," *New York Times,* August 10, 1983, http://www.nytimes.com/1983/08/10/arts/film-crew-reports-reprisals-for-testifying.html.

51 Labov, "Smithee in *The Twilight Zone,*" 107.

52 See Jeffrey Smith, "'A Good Business Proposition': Dalton Trumbo, *Spartacus,* and the End of the Blacklist," *The Velvet Light Trap* 23 (Spring 1989): 75–100. In Matthew Bernstein, *Controlling Hollywood: Censorship and Regulation in the Studio Era* (London: Athlone Press, 2000), 206–37.

53 Bernstein, *Controlling Hollywood,* 215.

54 The Stout interview with Dalton Trumbo was aired by CBS on April 10, 1957, and was titled "Who Is Robert Rich?"

55 Trumbo, cited in Patrick Goldstein, "When Writers Really Were Nobody," *Los Angeles Times*, March 13, 2001.

56 Smith, "A Good Business Proposition," 217.

57 Dalton Trumbo, *Additional Dialogue: Letters of Dalton Trumbo, 1942–1962*, ed. Helen Manfull (New York: M. Evans, 1970), 408.

58 Ceplair, cited in Labov, "Smithee in *The Twilight Zone*," 112.

59 Ibid., 116.

60 See "Box Office/business for *An Alan Smithee Film: Burn Hollywood Burn*," http://www.imdb.com/title/tt0118577/business.

61 The Golden Raspberry Awards, also known as "Razzies," have been held in Los Angeles the day before the Academy Awards ceremony since 1981.

62 See Wallace, "Name of Director Smithee."

63 Slavoj Žižek, *In Defense of Lost Causes* (London: Verso, 2008), 411.

64 Ibid., 390–91.

65 Slavoj Žižek, *The Parallax View* (Cambridge, Mass.: MIT Press, 2006), 17.

66 Ibid.

67 The Internet Movie Database (IMDb) attributes more than twenty directing credits and even a few writing and acting credits to Smithee since 2000. The Smithee movies of the post-DGA era include comedies, horrors, documentaries, short films, and episodes of TV series. See "Alan Smithee," http://www.imdb.com/.

3. MONTY CANTSIN, THE OPEN POP STAR

The first epigraph to this chapter is plagiarized from Tristan Tzara's famous lecture on Dada: "Dada is a state of mind. That is why it transforms itself according to races and events. Dada applies itself to everything, and yet it is nothing, it is the point where the yes and the no and all the opposites meet." See Tristan Tzara, "Lecture on Dada," 1922, in *The Dada Painters and Poets: An Anthology*, ed. Robert Motherwell (Boston, Mass.: G. K. Hall, 1981), 251.

1 This definition appears in several texts and is probably attributable to Michael Tolson aka tENTATIVELY a CONVENIENCE, who first used it in 1984 in a mail correspondence. Stewart Home recycled it to describe "the magazine of multiple origins" *SMILE* and the "open context" Karen Eliot. See Monty Cantsin, "Neoist Correspondence Script," *SMILE*, no. 7 (1985), http://www.stewarthomesociety.org/neoism/corscript.htm, and Karen Eliot, "Orientation for the Use of a Context and the Context for the Use of an Orientation," *SMILE*, no. 8 (1985). The text has been reprinted in N. O. Canstin, *A Neoist Research Project* (London: Openmute.org, 2010). It is also available from Seven by Nine Squares, http://www.thing.de/

projekte/7:9%23/karen_eliot.html, a nonlinear archiving project of Neoist texts managed by Florian Cramer since 1995.

2 The main proponent of this cognitive nihilism is the U.S. philosopher and avant-garde musician Henry Flynt. In 1961, Flynt coined the expression "concept art" to refer to "a kind of art of which the material is language." Rather than using concepts as building blocks, Flynt empties them of any objective relation to the names of which they are the attributes. By admitting only "a subjective relation between a name and its intension," Flynt soon recognizes that there are no cognitively valid bases to endow art with a social function. As such, art can only be pure self-gratification and recreation. See Flynt, "Concept Art," in *Anthology of Chance Operations,* ed. La Monte Young (New York: La Monte Young and Jackson Mac Low, 1963). Also available at http://henryflynt.org/. On the notion of art as pure recreation, see the chapters from *Against "Participation": A Total Critique of Culture* published at http://henryflint.org/. Although Flynt did not have a direct influence on the early stages of Neoism, he influenced later Neoists such as John Berndt and, to a lesser extent, Florian Cramer. In this sense, the Neoist refusal to subject Cantsin to any ethical guidelines or "instruction for use" can be seen as broadly inspired by Flynt's notion of an incommunicable art.

3 Stewart Home, *The Assault on Culture: Utopian Currents from Lettrism to Class War* (Edinburgh: AK Press, 1991), 75; 1st ed. (London: Aporia Press/Unpopular Books, 1988). Home claims that Blitzinformation had drawn inspiration from the Christus GmbH or Christ Ltd., an imaginary company cofounded by Berlin Dada artists Johannes Baader and Raoul Hausmann in 1917 to protect World War I deserters by allowing them to claim the identity of Jesus Christ to feign madness. The anecdote regarding the imaginary foundation of the company is originally reported by Raoul Hausmann, *Courrier Dada* (Paris: Le Terrain Vague, 1958), 75.

4 Ibid.

5 See Daniel Baird, "Istvan Kantor with Daniel Baird," *Brooklyn Rail,* June 2004, http://www.brooklynrail.org/2004/06/art/istvan-kantor.

6 Istvan Kantor, "The Poetical Plunderground of Neoism?! (from 1976 to date)," http://ccca.concordia.ca/performance_artists/k/kantor/kantor_perf18/neoism/neoist_plunder.rtf.

7 David "Oz" Zack, "Letter to Graf Haufen," June 1986. Reprinted as "One Thing I Did Invent . . ." in N. O. Cantsin, *A Neoist Research Project.* Also available from Seven by Nine Squares, http://www.thing.de/projekte/7:9%23/cantsin_index.html.

8 See John Held Jr., "Interview with Al Ackerman," *N D Magazine,* no. 15 (1991).

9 Al Ackerman, "Origins of Neoism Illuminated," *Photostatic*, no. 38 (October 1989): 1416.

10 The original spelling of the name "Cantsins" suggests that Zack may have simply conflated the surnames "Kundzins" and "Kantor" in the same way as he collaged his letters. However, this hypothesis would contradict Zack's own account, which states that Kantor was contacted via mail only after he and Kundzins had developed the name. See Zack, "Letter to Graf Haufen."

11 The lack of financial resources surfaces in various accounts of the period. In an interview with the author (Baltimore, December 15, 2009), Ackerman said, "I cannot stress enough that all I was trying to do is to keep Zack away from my fridge." And Kantor recalls how "every few months Zack organized the Unpaid Bills Poetry Festival, using up accumulated unpaid bills as basic material to make collage poems. Participants brought their own unpaid bills to make poster size, collective works. Accompanied by cello or tenor guitar, Zack recited the long list of numbers printed on hydro bills and the last notices of raging landlords." See Cantsin, "Poetical Plunderground."

12 Ackerman, "Origins of Neoism."

13 Home, *Assault on Culture*, 76. In a different text, Home provides a slightly different account, claiming that the Portland group's original antimovement was called "No Ism." See Home, "Neoism as Negation and the Negation of Neoism," in *Neoism, Plagiarism, and Praxis* (Edinburgh: AK Press, 1995), 96.

14 Kantor claims of the *Brain in the Mail* show, "Mostly it is considered to be the beginning of Neoism. Even though I came up with the name only a couple of months later and typed the word Neoism for the first time on a Smith-Corona typewriter on May 1, 1979, in Apt. 215, at 1100 McGregor Street, to be really exact." Cited in Baird, "Istvan Kantor with Daniel Baird."

15 John Berndt, interview with the author, Baltimore, December 15, 2009. Berndt adds, "This group of juvenile delinquents recognized in Kantor a guy who was pretending to be a fascist leader and took him seriously, in a way." The term *fascist* is not to be understood in a strictly political sense, but rather as a rebellious attitude toward the (art) system, which occasionally took on a violent or vandalic character. In the same interview, Berndt explains that the "[Montreal Neoists] would go into an art gallery, enter the bathroom, set steam irons on fire, and torch the paintings in the gallery." From that time, the flaming iron became an iconic Neoist object. Even though Berndt was never part of the Montreal group and joined Neoism only in the late 1980s, like Florian Cramer, he belongs to a second wave of Neoists who were not directly involved in the many diatribes that plagued the network in the 1980s.

16 According to Berndt, "there was a fairly clear division of responsibility in this gang. Kiki was the wild man and sort of the most dangerous, he had a place called the Peking Pool Room. Tristan was the musician, he made all of Monty's early music. Boris was the video guy, Napoléon was the theorist, and Alan Lord the noise guitarist. There were another ten to fifteen hangers-on in this group, including a lot of very New Wave girls." Ibid.

17 Cited in Baird, "Istvan Kantor with Daniel Baird."

18 Monty Cantsin, "Neoist Chair and Neoist Chair Action," in Cantsin, *A Neoist Research Project.*

19 Home, *Assault on Culture,* 88.

20 In an e-mail to the author, Florian Cramer writes, "I am practically 100% sure that *nobody* of the early Neoists was substantially influenced by Futurism. Neither have I encountered any reference to Italian futurism in early Neoist zines and pamphlets. . . . Canada has a long tradition of robotic art (and also video art, with Western Front in Vancouver), and Istvan and some of the Neoists had contacts to that scene. Bill Vorn, for example, an early Canadian Neoist who produced Istvan's electro pop records, was a robotic artist and continues to work as one." March 20, 2014.

21 Home writes that "the most important of these events were the 'Red Supper' held at Véhicule Art, Montreal, on 30 June 1979, and the 'Hallowmass and Supper,' held at the Motivation 5 Gallery on 31 October 1979. There were a number of other 'suppers' in which the food motif played an important part." Stewart Home, "Critique of International Neoism," *SMILE,* no. 8 (1985). Reprinted in *YAWN: Critique of Culture,* no. 38 (March 1993): 1860–61.

22 See Baird, "Istvan Kantor with Daniel Baird."

23 Other expressions of this radical anti-art attitude are the aforementioned vandalic actions committed in art galleries by the Montreal Neoists involving the use of steam irons.

24 See Julia Dault, "X Marks the Spot—Istvan Kantor: Two Decades of Bloodletting," January 24, 2006, http://www.cbc.ca. Now offline and archived at http://archive.org/web.

25 The impossibility of determining whether the Neoists take themselves (and are to be taken) seriously is reinforced by other surreal interventions of the same period, such as Kiki Bonbon's notorious video *The Flying Cats.* In this video, two men dressed in white uniforms stand on top of a tower block from which they allegedly throw a number of cats to their deaths while repeating the phrase "the cat has no choice." See Home, *Assault on Culture,* 94. Home admits of not having seen the video.

26 E.g., Guy Debord's *Society of the Spectacle* echoes in the "First Manifesto of

Neoist Performance and the Performance of Neoism," a text authored by Stewart Home in 1984, "Rather than being concerned with images, Neoist performers are interested in the social relation between people whose lives are mediated by images. Neoism has more to do with the social uses of myth, than the means by which individual myths are created." In Stewart Home, *Neoist Manifestos* (Edinburgh: AK Press, 1991), 25–26. This text is bound back to back with *The Art Strike Papers* edited by James Mannox. The first version of this manifesto was signed by Monty Cantsin and appeared in *SMILE,* no. 6 (1984). See also Guy Debord, *Society of the Spectacle,* trans. Ken Knabb (London: Rebel Press, 2004). The French version was originally published in 1967.

27 Home, *Neoism, Plagiarism, and Praxis,* 98.

28 tENTATIVELY a CONVENIENCE is a well-known figure of the Baltimore underground art scene. At the time, he was a liaison between the Neoists, the Krononauts, and the Church of the SubGenius. The Church of the Subgenius is a faux cult founded in 1979 that mocks conspiracy theories, Scientology, ufology, and other New Age phenomena. The mythic founder and central figurehead of the Church is the "world's greatest salesman" J. R. "Bob" Dobbs, whose image is a smiling pipe-smoking man based on style of clip art from the 1950s. With its cult of weirdness and pursuit of "total slack"—perceived as an indispensable attitude for original free thinking—the Church has recruited members of "Subgenii," especially among college students and young hackers. According to Stewart Home, the Church "bears a certain conceptual similarity to The College of Pataphysics, but with a popularist rather than intellectual approach. It is this lowest common denominator attitude that accounts for its success. Similar cults, such as the Krononauts—who among other things have held a 'Party For The People Of The Future' with the intention of attracting time travelers—are too *rigorously intellectual* to appeal to the average male college student." Home, *Assault on Culture,* 93–94.

During the 1983 World SubGenius Convention, tENTATIVELY executed one of the most well-known stunts of the Church, the "Pee Dog and Poop Dog Copright [*sic*] Violation Ritual." He invited forty SubGenii to follow him from the convention center in Baltimore to a no-trespassing railway tunnel where, naked and covered only in white greasepaint, he beat the carcasses of two dead dogs hanging from the ceiling. Shortly thereafter, he was arrested by more than twenty cops, granting the Church the highest media visibility to date. The ritual also granted Tolson a probation order and a place in the Church as a saint. See Reverend Ivan Stang, "The Church of the Subgenius: The Greatest Joke (?) Ever Told," http://www.subgenius.com/.

29 tENTATIVELY a cONVENIENCE, "The APT Project, the Practice of a

Common Cause," in *What Is a uh uh Apartment Festival??????* (Montreal: Centre de Recherche Néoiste, 1981). Reprinted in Home, *Assault on Culture,* 89.

30 Alain Napoléon Moffat, "The Legitimacy of Akademgorod," read at the Fifth Neoist Apartment Festival, New York, March 1982, http://www.thing.de/projekte/7:9%23/akademgorod_legitimacy.html.

31 The "it's always six o' clock" motto was added to the Neoist Akademgorod in the late 1980s. It was lifted from Lewis Carroll's *Alice in Wonderland,* where Time has decided to mark always six o' clock (tea time) in revenge for the Hatter's manipulation of a song meter.

32 An example of PP performance is Horobin's "Seven Scripts for One Week of Neoist Activity," which consists of a set of instructions: "NEODAY ONE The principle player does not think about art for twentyfour hours. NEODAY TWO The principle player does not eat for twentyfour hours. NEODAY THREE The principle player makes a pot of tea in the traditional manner . . . NEODAY SEVEN The principle player sifts the ashes of the dead Neofire. Taking out the lumps of charcoal. The fire ash is put into a container. Samples from this container are put into plastic bags which are sealed. Labelled. Stamped. Dated. And mailed to known Neoist sympathisers." See Home, *Assault on Culture,* 90–91.

33 Lewis & Dr. Dubord (with Monty Cantsin), "Monty Cantsin Interviewed by Lewis & Dr. Dubord," http://www.thing.de/projekte/7:9%23/cantsin_15.html.

34 In *Assault on Culture,* 88, Home writes, "In Kantor's hands, the Monty Cantsin concept regressed rather than developed. During the course of what were often violent performances, he would offer 'his' neoist chair to anyone who wanted to take on the 'open pop-star' identity. The aggressive way in which this was done intimidated those who might have taken up the offer. When, in the mid-1980s—due to the intervention of a number of European neoists—the Cantsin identity was taken up widely for the first time since Zack left Portland in '79, Kantor circulated letters claiming to be the 'real' Monty Cantsin."

35 tENTATIVELY a cONVENIENCE, "Neoist Guide Dog," in *A Mere Outline for One Aspect of a Book on Mystery Catalysts, Guerrilla Playfare, booed usic, Mad Scientist Didactions, Acts of As-Beenism, So-Called Whatevers, Psychopathfinding, Uncerts, etc.*, 3rd ed. (privately printed, July 1995). The text-only version is available at http://www.thing.de/projekte/7:9%23/tent_mere_outline.html.

36 See Brian Morton et al., "Vanishing Point: Gustav Metzger and Self-Cancellation," roundtable discussion, *Art&Research: A Journal of Ideas, Contexts, and Methods* 3, no. 1 (2009–10): 7.

37 For example, tENTATIVELY a CONVENIENCE openly accused Home

of having, like Kantor, "careerist motives" and of using Neoism only as "a springboard for his success." In a text in which Home is referred to as David A. Bannister, tENTATIVELY writes, "The historian's position was perfect for Bannister's purposes. He could write about something that very few people had any direct experience with—thusly avoiding conflicting history. He could write about the activities of the Neoasts [*sic*] without much fear of contradiction from them—knowing that they were either too busy with other activities to take time off to write to refute him (after all, 'History begins where Life ends')." tENTATIVELY a CONVENIENCE, "History Begins Where Life Ends," http://www.thing.de/projekte/7:9%23/tent_history_begins.html.

38 Some of the materials published on the Seven by Nine Squares website, which first went online as a BBS in 1994, were previously published in Monty Cantsin, *Neoism Now* (Berlin: Artcore, 1987). The editor of this two-hundred-page book is the Berlin Neoist Graf Haufen, who also ran the Artcore Gallery—an exhibition space dedicated to mail art, copy art, and Neoism—from his apartment. Other materials are taken from *SMILE* magazines edited by Stewart Home and John Berndt and preexisting texts by Berndt, tENTATIVELY, and Ackerman. The icons were originally designed by Jean Joseph Rolland Dubé for the Societé de Conservation du Present, a Montreal conceptual art group that was connected to the early 1980s Neoist scene. Florian Cramer, e-mail to the author, March 20, 2014.

39 See Stewart Home and Florian Cramer, *The House of Nine Squares: Letters on Neoism, Psychogeography, and Epistemological Trepidation* (London: Invisible Books, 1997). An edited web version of this text is available at http://www.stewarthomesociety.org/neoism/ninesq.htm.

40 Ibid (web version).

41 Peter Bürger, *Theory of the Avant-Garde,* trans. Michael Show (Minneapolis: University of Minnesota Press, 1984), 78.

42 Craig J. Saper, *Networked Art* (Minneapolis: University of Minnesota Press, 2001), 5.

43 See Ray Johnson Estate, "Ray Johnson's Biography," http://www.rayjohnsonestate.com/.

44 On Ray Johnson's mailing activities, see Ray Johnson, *Please Add to and Return* (Barcelona: MACBA, 2010); Anna Boschi, *Ray Johnson e la Mail Art: Retrospettive e Testimonianze* (Bologna: Biblioteche Comunali di Castel San Pietro Terme, 2008); and the documentary *How to Draw a Bunny* (dir. John W. Walter, United States, 2002).

45 William S. Wilson, "NY Correspondance School," *Art and Artists* 1, no. 1 (1966): 54.

46 Ina Blom, "'Every Letter I Write Is Not a Love Letter': Inventing Sociality

with Ray Johnson's Postal System," *Quaderns Portàtils* (Barcelona: MACBA, 2010): 21:14.

47 Deleuze and Guattari, *Anti-Oedipus,* 77–78.

48 John Durham Peters, *Speaking into the Air: A History of the Idea of Communication* (Chicago: University of Chicago Press, 1999), 7.

49 Blom, "Every Letter I Write," 13.

50 See Marcel Mauss, *The Gift: The Form and Reason for Exchange in Archaic Societies,* trans. W. D. Halls (New York: W. W. Norton, 1990).

51 See Jacques Derrida, *Given Time: I. Counterfeit Money,* trans. Peggy Kamuf (Chicago: University of Chicago Press, 1992).

52 Ibid., 30.

53 Ibid.

54 Ibid., 54.

55 Johnson's letter to Wilson consists of a series of ironic annotations on a forwarded letter originally sent from Frederick St. Abyn to Johnson on October 6, 1958. Quoted in Blom, "Every Letter I Write," 12.

56 Johnson organized at least two Nothings. The first, held in July 1961 at AG Gallery—a space operated by George Maciunas—was a gathering of artists and friends attending in anticipation of a performance, which never took place. Invited guests gathered inside the gallery, and after a short waiting period, Johnson threw a box of wooden spindles down the staircase leading up to the gallery. The second Nothing took place at Maidman Playhouse, New York, 1962. See "Ray Johnson's Biography."

57 Johnson was assaulted and mugged on June 3, 1968—the same day Andy Warhol was shot by Valerie Solanas. Shaken and frightened, he left the city and moved to Glen Cove in Long Island and then to Locust Valley, New York, where he died in 1995.

58 Blom, "Every Letter I Write," 9.

59 One of the earliest Fluxus postal works was Ben Vautier's *The Postman's Choice.* Started in 1965, it consisted of a blank postcard with two different addresses and stamps on each side of the card, with the final destination to be determined by the mailman. In 1968, Vautier's postcard was included in a *Flux Post Kit* assembled by George Maciunas, which included rubber stamps, artist-made postage stamps, cancellation marks, and other postal ephemera. Saper refers to these sociopoetic experiments as "intimate bureaucracies." See Saper, *Networked Art,* 113–48.

60 Higgins published the first book of correspondence art, a collection of Johnson's mailings titled *The Paper Snake* (New York: Something Else Press, 1965). In 1966, Friedman began distributing the *International Contact List of the Arts,* a directory that was essential for the early-1970s emergence of the Mail Art network. In 1973, he also organized the Omaha Flow System,

a mail art exhibition that linked museums, public schools, colleges, and shopping malls in a global networking exchange. In the early 1970s, "two Canadian-funded artist publishing projects, *FILE Magazine* and Image Bank's *International Image Exchange Directory* became decentralized clearing houses that introduced correspondence art to a global audience." Chuck Welch, "Corresponding Worlds: Debate and Dialogue," in Welch, *Eternal Network,* 188.

61 Robert Filliou, "Research on the Eternal Network," *FILE,* September 1973, 7. Cited in John Held Jr., "Networking: The Origin of Terminology," in Welch, *Eternal Network,* 17.

62 *VILE* was published between 1974 and 1980 and released the collection book *About VILE* in 1983. The magazine frequently addressed pornography and sexual politics and dedicated a whole issue to "Fe-Mail-Art" in 1978. These two magazines were inspirational for *SMILE.*

63 Cited in Welch, "Corresponding Worlds," 191.

64 Ibid., 189.

65 Zack, "Letter to Graf Haufen."

66 Dault, "X Marks the Spot."

67 Monty Cantsin, "Monty Cantsin ISM," in *A Neoist Research Project.*

68 E.g., all Kantor's and Home's writings about Neoism are published on their personal websites, de facto defeating the purpose of using a pseudonym. Notable exceptions are the cited Seven by Nine Squares website and the collection of Neoist texts *A Neoist Research Project.*

69 In 1994, Home resuscitated the Neoist label for the Neoist Alliance, a self-promotional banner aimed at endowing pamphlets and other publications with corporate authority.

70 Tatiana Bazzichelli, *Networked Disruption: Rethinking Oppositions in Art, Hacktivism, and the Business of Social Networking* (Aarhus: Digital Aesthetics Research Center, Aarhus University, 2013), 85.

71 Ibid.

72 Karen Eliot, "Orientation for the Use of a Context."

73 The Festival of Plagiarism was opened by an exhibition of found objects at the Bedford Hill Gallery. The Eliot signature was used by twenty-seven individuals who plagiarized images and texts at the Community Copy Art and showed them under the title "Karen Eliot—Apocrypha." Other chapters of the festival were simultaneously held in Madison, Wisconsin, and San Francisco, and later in the year in HBK Braunschweig, West Germany. For a detailed account of the event, see Stewart Home, *The Festival of Plagiarism* (London: Sabotage Editions, 1989). Available at http://www.stewarthomesociety.org/festplag.htm.

74 Home, *Neoist Manifestos,* 4–5.

75 Baroni's letter is dated May 7, 1987. Cited in Home, *Assault on Culture,* 76–77.

76 In few circumstances the Mind Invaders released conceptual and silent pieces that were performed by other bands. The Mind Invanders band had two imaginary members: Tom Mix and Chris Lutman. See Piermario Ciani, *Dal Great Complotto a Luther Blissett* (Udine, Italy: AAA Edizioni, 2000).

77 See Piermario Ciani, Vittore Baroni, and Massimo Giacon, eds., *Last TRAX: Final Report of the TRAX Project* (privately published book and record, 1987).

4. LUTHER BLISSETT, THE MYTHMAKER

1 The Free Art Campaign website was hosted by Geocities.com, a popular free web-hosting service owned by Yahoo! It remained online until October 2009, when Yahoo! decided to shut down the service.

2 The titles of the eight performances were *Jung, Va' Pensiero, Beata Mariae Vergini, Skinned Rembrandt, Deposition, Eurotic, Garbage,* and *Ecce Homo.* Maver's hermetic manifestos *Aforagenetica* and *The Dimension of the Extrabodies* were also archived on the Geocities website mentioned in note 1.

3 Free Art Campaign, "Darko Maver è stato incarcerato per aver esercitato il diritto alla libertà di espressione" [Darko Maver has been imprisoned for having exercised the right to freedom of expression], *Tema Celeste,* no. 73, March–April 1999; Antonio Caronia, "Darko Maver," *Flesh Out,* no. 3 (April–May 1999).

4 The press release was archived at the aforementioned Geocities website; see note 1.

5 Andrea Natella, "Manichini di Guerra" [War mannequins], *Modus Vivendi,* July–August 1999.

6 0100101110101101.org and Luther Blissett, "The Great Art Swindle: Do You Ever Feel You're Being Cheated? A Disclosure by 0100101110101101.ORG and Luther Blissett," February 6, 2000, http://www.lutherblissett.net/.

7 *The Great Rock 'n' Roll Swindle* (United Kingdom, 1980) is a mockumentary on the Sex Pistols directed by Julien Temple.

8 Among the accomplices that first devised the Luther Blissett strategy were the mail artists Alberto Rizzi and Piermario Ciani and the Bolognese group of writers (Roberto Bui, Giovanni Cattabriga, Federico Guglielmi, and Luca di Meo) who would later go on to found the collective of novelists Wu Ming. See Ciani, *Dal Great Complotto a Luther Blissett,* 148–49. Rizzi's seminal role has been subsequently acknowledged by the Wu Ming, who have granted his name cameo appearances in all their novels.

9 The most comprehensive archive of English, Italian, and Spanish texts by

and about Luther Blissett is archived on the LBP "official" website, http://www.lutherblissett.net.

10 Paul Doyle, Shaikh Sajit, and Georgina Turner, "Did AC Milan Sign Luther Blissett by Mistake?," *The Guardian*, January 5, 2005.

11 BBC, "Luther Blissett: Anarchist Hero," *BBC Sport: Football*, March 9, 1999.

12 In the 1970s, Harry Kipper was the handle used by Martin von Haselberg and Brian Routh, a two-man performance group known as the Kipper Kids. In the mid-1970s, the Kipper Kids ran a show called *The Boxing Match* in which one Harry acted as a boxer and the other as referee. As recalled by Genesis P-Orridge, "the idea was that whichever Harry was the boxer had boxing gloves on and boxed himself. So he would be punching himself in the face, as hard as possible. Because the performance did not end until Harry Kipper the boxer had knocked himself out, it was a very bloody sight." Cited in Jon Savage, *England's Dreaming: Anarchy, Sex Pistols, Punk Rock, and Beyond* (New York: St. Martin's Press, 2001), 250. See also C. Carr, *On Edge: Performance Art at the End of the Twentieth Century* (Middletown, Conn.: Wesleyan University Press, 1993), 148–53.

13 Vittore Baroni, "Leggende Urbane, Nomi Multipli e Calcio a Tre Porte" [Urban legends, multiple names, and three-sided soccer], *Rumore*, nos. 42–43 (July–August 1995).

14 See Luther Blissett, *Mind Invaders, Come Fottere i Media: Manuale di Guerriglia e Sabotaggio Culturale* [Mind invaders, how to fuck the media: Handbook of guerrilla and cultural sabotage] (Rome: Castelvecchi, 1995). This book has little in common with the homonymous volume edited by Stewart Home, *Mind Invaders: A Reader in Psychic Warfare, Cultural Sabotage, and Semiotic Terrorism* (London: Serpent's Tail, 1997). Although Home's book does feature some translations from the Italian companion, it is largely a collection of articles written by Home himself under various pseudonyms.

15 Baroni, "Leggende Urbane."

16 "In a very short letter to Vittore Baroni . . . Johson [*sic*] dropped the line: 'By the way, who is Luther Blissett?' The receiver (whoever he was) suddenly remembered the calamitous footballer, and started laughing. In a letter he diverted the question to Stewart Home of the Neoist Alliance. On February 15th 1994, . . . Stewart Home joined his fellows of the London Psychogeographical Association for a planned psychogeographical 'drift' in Greenwich. There the party found . . . Blissett Street. In the following days the LPA discovered that it was named after Rev. George Blissett, a Victorian do-gooder. 'Luther Blissett' went to London as a funny story and came back to Italy as an infectious multiple name." See Luther Blissett, "Selected Excerpts from *Mind Invaders, Come Fottere i Media: Manuale di Guerriglia e Sabotaggio Culturale,* Rome: Castelvecchi, 1995," http://www.lutherblissett.net/.

17 See Blissett, *Mind Invaders,* 46–50. Coleman Healy is presented as a U.S. radical performance artist. According to another foundation myth, Healy would have conceived the LBP together with Ray Johnson during the Pan-American Meeting of Subversion in 1992, a fictional gathering supposedly attended by various revolutionaries, including the Subcomandante Marcos. In fact, Healy is himself a fictional character, the name of a serial killer in James Ellroy's *Big Nowhere.*

18 It is to be noted that "Luther Blissett Project" is a signature that was mostly used by the Bolognese faction and occasionally by Roman and Viterbese activists. The mail artists and other activists who wanted to emphasize the decentralized character of Luther Blissett kept using only the multiple-use signature. I remain faithful to this distinction by using the LBP diction to denote interventions that were devised by the more organized and political wing of Luther Blissett and LB to denote more spontaneous and less "strategic" uses.

19 Baroni, cited in Home, *Neoist Manifestos,* 76–77.

20 As previously noted, one of the most divisive events of the Neoist network was Istvan Kantor's choice to adopt Monty Cantsin as his permanent pseudonym. Furthermore, in 1994, Home founded the Neoist Alliance in London to mark his distance from the international Neoist network. In the same year, he established the first contact with the Bolognese branch of the LBP.

21 The book reviews novels and movies that focus on subversive naming and linguistic practices. For instance, as discussed in the chapter on Allen Smithee, in Stanley Kubrick's *Spartacus,* the revolting slaves captured and defeated by Crassus refuse to identify their leader and shout out, "I am Spartacus!" In John Shirley's proto-cyberpunk novel *Transmaniacon,* the hero Ben Rackey surfs a telematic network of sorts, taking on different names and identities with the goal of inciting revolt and destroying the invisible ionic barrier that separates the United States from the rest of the world.

22 Aired September 28, 1991.

23 Luther Blissett, *Totò, Peppino e la Guerra Psichica 2.0* [Totò, Peppino, and the psychic warfare 2.0] (Torino: Einaudi, 2000), 4, translation mine. This book is a compendium of two previous volumes: the aforementioned *Mind Invaders,* of which the Einaudi version excerpts about forty pages, and the integral reprint of *Totò, Peppino e la Guerra Psichica: Materiali dal Luther Blissett Project* (Udine: AAA Edizioni, 1996), an anthology of materials from the LBP edited by Vittore Baroni and Piermario Ciani. Subsequent citations of *Totò, Peppino* are from the Einaudi volume.

24 Ibid., 3–5. See also the Wikipedia article "Darmok," http://en.wikipedia.org/wiki/Darmok.

25 See Giorgio Agamben, *The Coming Community,* trans. Michael Hardt (Minneapolis: University of Minnesota Press, 1993).

26 In the *Grundrisse,* Marx writes, "Monetary greed, or mania for wealth, necessarily brings with it the decline and fall of the ancient communities [*Gemeinwesen*]. Hence it is the antithesis to them. It is itself the community [*Gemeinwesen*], and can tolerate no other standing above it. But this presupposes the full development of exchange value, hence a corresponding organization of society." Karl Marx, *Grundrisse: Foundations of the Critique of Political Economy,* trans. Martin Nicolaus (New York: Penguin, 1973), 223. Marx's reflections on capital's tendency to realize itself as material community, or capital-community, form the departure point of the philosophy of Jacques Camatte, another inspirational figure to the LBP.

27 Karl Marx, "Comments on James Mill, *Elements of Political Economy* (1821)," in *The Collected Works of Karl Marx and Friedrich Engels: Vol. 3. 1843–44* (New York: International, 1975), 126–27.

28 This view is shared by the collective of novelists Wu Ming, the main offshoot of the Bolognese LBP. In an interview on their novel *1954,* Wu Ming says, "The making of pop culture (we don't draw a clear distinction between the 'underground' and the 'mainstream' here) was a collective process during which the borders of ever-changing open communities were constantly re-traced, subcultures constantly re-shaped themselves around myths. We'd better understand what 'pre-requisites of communism' were at work in that process, instead of believing that millions of people were being brainwashed." See Snafu and Wu Ming, "1954: A Pop-Autonomist Novel," *Make Worlds,* no. 2 (2002). Available online at http://www.wumingfoundation.com/.

29 See Ernst Bloch, *The Principle of Hope,* vol. 1, trans. Neville Plaice, Stephen Plaice, and Paul Knight (Cambridge, Mass.: MIT Press, 1995). In this respect, the LBP anticipated a tendency in contemporary media and cultural studies that emphasizes the ability of Internet-based participatory culture to reuse, recontextualize, and remix mainstream media narratives for progressive purposes. I am thinking here of the work of Henry Jenkins, Stephen Duncombe, Siva Vaidhyanathan, and Francesca Coppa, among many others.

30 Naomi Klein, "Squatters in White Overalls," *The Guardian,* June 8, 2001.

31 For a detailed account of the Bolognese LBP, see Luca Muchetti, *Storytelling: L'informazione secondo Luther Blissett* [Storytelling: Newsmaking according to Luther Blissett] (Milano: Arcipelago Edizioni, 2007).

32 Four issues of *River Phoenix* were printed, in runs of eight hundred to one thousand copies, between November 1993 and June 1994. In summer 1994, the editors discontinued the magazine and announced their confluence in

the LBP. The three coeditors of *River Phoenix* were Giovanni Cattabriga (later on Wu Ming 2), Federico Guglielmi (Wu Ming 4), and Enrico Brizzi (soon to become a popular novelist with the best seller *Jack Frusciante Has Left the Band*).

33 Roberto Bui, *Transmaniacalità e Situazionauti* (Bologna: Synergon, 1995), 10, translation mine.

34 Ibid., 12.

35 "The Spectacle is a system of simulacra which are neither true nor false. By which I mean that the 'frontal assault' and the molar clash with the media spin is useless. We need to enter the vortex, learn how to sabotage in a fluid manner the dominant codes, in the most fluid and unpredictable way." Ibid., 14.

36 Created by Tom Jennings in 1984, FidoNet allowed users to exchange e-mails and data packages among different BBSs over the direct-dial telephone network. BBSs were typically managed by the users themselves, and thanks to the UUCP gateways to the Internet, FidoNet users could exchange e-mails across different nations and continents. It is estimated that by 1993, FidoNet had more than twenty thousand nodes and more than two million users worldwide. See Randy Bush, "FidoNet: Technology, Use, Tools, and History," http://www.fidonet.org/inet92_Randy_Bush.txt. In Italy, the first node of FidoNet had been opened by Giorgio Rutigliano in 1986. By the mid-1990s, the network counted roughly three hundred nodes.

37 Roberto Bui (aka Wu Ming 1), interview with the author (via Skype), October 9, 2008. In the same interview, Bui acknowledges the shortsightedness of Bordiga's reading of fascism as a regime that was not qualitatively different from liberal democracy but just an extension of the capitalist system.

38 Ibid.

39 Gilberto Centi, ed., *Luther Blissett: L'impossibilità di possedere la creatura una e multipla* [Luther Blissett: The impossibility of owning the one and multiple creature] (Bologna: Synergon, 1995), translation mine.

40 Cited in Muchetti, *Storytelling*, 202, translation mine.

41 See Muchetti, *Storytelling*, 57–61.

42 Actors' training consisted of recording environmental stimuli in various urban spaces, such as streets, squares, public buses, and malls. On the basis of the gathered information, the actors prepared a performance and enacted it in the appropriate areas with the purpose of transforming the social perception of a specific space. Video documentation of one of the Teatro Situazionautico's performances has been uploaded to YouTube by WoT4 under the titles "Teatro Situazionautico Luther Blissett pt 1," and "Teatro Situazionautico Luther Blissett pt 2," https://www.youtube.com/.

43 Situationist International, "Definitions," June 1958, in *Situationist International Anthology*, ed. Ben Knabb, trans. Nadine Bloch and Joel Cornuault (Berkeley, Calif.: Bureau of Public Secrets, 1981), 45.

44 See Stewart Home, "On the Mind Invaders Anthology: A Talk Originally Entitled 'Mind Bending, Swamp Fever, and the Ideological Vortext: How Avant-Bard Satire Blisters the Cheeks of the Aparatchiki,'" lecture at Public Netbase, Vienna, April 29, 1998, http://www.stewarthomesociety.org/. Home's influence on the early phases of Luther Blissett is evident from his regular correspondence with Vittore Baroni and Roberto Bui. The latter recalls how, after contacting the Neoist Alliance for information, Home "sent [me] back a lot of stuff, and I mean A LOT. That was at the beginning of '94. The package I received contained a copy of his book *The Assault on Culture,* a copy of his novel *Red London,* all the issues of the London Psychogeographical Association newsletter, and more stuff by the Neoist Alliance, e.g., a report of their 'psychic attack' on a Stockhausen concert in Brighton. That's how we got to know Monty Cantsin and Karen Eliot." Interview with the author.

45 Andrea Natella, interview with the author, Rome, July 15, 2008.

46 Ibid.

47 Home, *Mind Invaders,* xii.

48 Hakim Bey, *T.A.Z.: The Temporary Autonomous Zone, Ontological Anarchy, Poetic Terrorism* (New York: Autonomedia, 1991), 102.

49 Ibid., 106.

50 A collection of essays by Hakim Bey, some of which were authentic and some of which were apocryphal, the book *A Ruota Libera* (Roma: Castelvecchi, 1996) sold two-thirds of its first run in two months, after receiving positive reviews by leftist newspapers such as *Il Manifesto* and *Liberazione,* and after the Shake editorial collective, which had published *T.A.Z.* in Italy, attacked Castelvecchi for copyrighting the text. When Luther Blissett claimed to be the real author of the apocryphal, Castelvecchi withdrew the text from the bookstores. It is to be noted that the book editor is Fabrizio P. Belletati, a pseudonym frequently used by Roberto Bui. On the reasons why Blissett tried to undermine Bey's popularity, see Luther Blissett, "Why I Wrote a Fake Hakim Bey Book and How I Cheated the Conformists of Italian 'Counterculture,'" August 1996, http://www.lutherblissett.net/. In 1996, the young writer Giuseppa Genna borrowed the multiple-use name to author *Net.gener@tion,* a book that was published by Mondadori, the largest Italian publishing house, owned by Silvio Berlusconi. After attacking the book for the copyright clause and as a compilation of trite post-Situationist commonplaces, the LBP decided to claim that Genna had been manipulated by Blissett itself, which provided him with the

materials for the book. On March 8, 1996, the day before *Net.gener@tion* hit the bookstores, Blissett sent out a press release disowning the book. Like Castelvecchi, Mondadori was forced to withdraw the volume from distribution. For the press release, see Luther Blissett, "La Grande Truffa alla Mondadori" [The Great Mondadori Swindle], press release, March 8, 1996, http://www.lutherblissett.net/. For Genna's reply, see Giuseppe Genna, "Di chi ha paura Luther Blissett" [Whom is Luther Blissett afraid of], *Letture* 51, no. 527 (1996): 18–19. Available at http://www.lutherblissett.net/. For an English account from Blissett's perspective, see Luther Blissett, "How Luther Blissett Turned a Corporate Attack on the Multiple Name into a Marvelous Prank on a Major Publishing House," undated, http://www.lutherblissett.net/.

51 Luther Blissett, "Della guerra psichica nella metropoli traiettoriale," in Blissett, *Totò, Peppino e la Guerra Psichica,* 148.

52 Ibid., 159.

53 De Certeau, *Practice of Everyday Life,* xix.

54 Shake's political reading of cyberpunk is articulated in Raf "Valvola" Scelsi, ed., *Cyberpunk: Antologia di Testi Politici* (Milan: Shake, 1990). Although it was mostly translated from English, this collection of essays had no English counterpart and unexpectedly sold more than twenty thousand copies, laying the foundations of the publishing house as a commercial enterprise. Sterling and Gibson subsequently acknowledged that the Italian political reading of cyberpunk was an original interpretation of their literary work.

55 AvANa is an acronym for Avvisi ai Naviganti ("Warnings to the Sailors" or "Warnings to the Web Surfers").

56 Andrea Natella, interview with the author.

57 The Rizoma Autogestione Metropoli (RAM) was a research group on the relationship between urban development and social conflict that saw the participation of Daniele Vasquez, Andrea Tiddi, Fabrizio Carli, and Antonio Conti, among others. This group contributed important theoretical insights to the Roman LBP, in particular with the previously cited reflections on the mutated function of psychogeography in the postmodern metropolis.

58 See Sandrone Dazieri, ed., *Italia Overground* (Rome: Castelvecchi, 1996).

59 A book that summarizes the terms of this debate is Primo Moroni, Daniele Farina, and Pino Tripodi, eds., *Centri Sociali, Che Impresa!* [Social centers, what an enterprise!] (Rome: Castelvecchi, 1995). Another volume that tackles the issue by focusing on two Milanese case studies is a social inquiry conducted by Consorzio Aaster, CSOA Cox 18, CSOA Leoncavallo, and Primo Moroni, eds., *Centri Sociali: Geografie del Desiderio* [Social centers: Geographies of desire] (Milan: Shake, 1996).

60 Mario Tronti, *Operai e Capitale* [Workers and capital] (Torino: Einaudi, 1966).

61 Tronti's Copernican revolution is clearly articulated in the article "Lenin in England," which was originally published in the first issue of *Classe Operaia*: "We too have worked with a concept that puts capitalist development first, and workers second. This is a mistake. And now we have to turn the problem on its head, reverse the polarity, and start again from the beginning: and the beginning is the class struggle of the working class. At the level of socially developed capital, capitalist development becomes subordinated to working class struggles; it follows behind them, and they set the pace to which the political mechanisms of capital's own reproduction must be tuned." M. Tronti, "Lenin in England," *Classe Operaia*, no. 1 (January 1964): 1. Reprinted in Tronti, *Operai e Capitale*, 89–95, as "A New Style of Political Experiment."

62 Thirty years later, Hardt and Negri reiterated this key concept of workerism in *Multitude*: "Even though common use of the term might suggest the opposite—that resistance is a response or reaction—*resistance is primary with respect to power.*" Michael Hardt and Antonio Negri, *Multitude: War and Democracy in the Age of Empire* (New York: Penguin, 2004), 64.

63 Antonio Negri, "Archaeology and Project: The Mass Worker and the Social Worker (1982)," in *Revolution Retrieved: Writings on Marx, Keynes, Capitalist Crisis, and New Social Subjects (1967–83)* (London: Red Notes, 1988).

64 Harry Cleaver, introduction to *Marx beyond Marx: Lessons on the Grundrisse*, by Antonio Negri, trans. Harry Cleaver, Michael Ryan, and Maurizio Viano (New York: Autonomedia, 1991), xxv.

65 Marx, *Grundrisse*, 705.

66 Ibid., 709.

67 Ibid.

68 Paolo Virno, *A Grammar of the Multitude*, trans. Isabella Bertoletti, James Cascaito, and Andrea Casson (Los Angeles, Calif.: Semiotext(e), 2004), 63.

69 Ibid., 60.

70 Mariarosa Dalla Costa and Selma James, *The Power of Women and the Subversion of the Community* (Bristol, U.K.: Falling Wall, 1972); Silvia Federici, "Wages against Housework," in *The Politics of Housework*, ed. E. Malos (London: Allison and Busby, 1980); Leopoldina Fortunati, *The Arcane of Reproduction: Housework, Prostitution, Labor, and Capital*, trans. H. Creek (New York: Autonomedia, 1995); Silvia Federici, *Revolution at Point Zero: Housework, Reproduction, and Feminist Struggle* (New York: PM Press / Common Notions, 2012).

71 Leopoldina Fortunati, "Immaterial Labor and Its Machinization," *Ephemera: Theory and Politics in Organization* 7, no. 1 (2007): 145.

72 Ibid.

73 Michael Hardt and Antonio Negri, *Labor of Dionysus: A Critique of the State-Form* (Minneapolis: University of Minnesota Press, 1994), 9.

74 Hardt and Negri, *Multitude,* 66.

75 Ibid., 146.

76 Michael Hardt and Antonio Negri, *Empire* (Cambridge, Mass.: Harvard University Press, 2000), 403.

77 See Sergio Bologna and Andrea Fumagalli, eds., *Il lavoro autonomo di seconda generazione: Scenari del postfordismo in Italia* [The second-generation autonomous labor: Post-Fordist scenarios in Italy] (Milan: Feltrinelli, 1997); Andrea Fumagalli and Maurizio Lazzarato, *Tute Bianche: Disoccupazione di massa e reddito di cittadinanza* [White overalls: Mass unemployment and citizenship income] (Rome: DeriveApprodi, 1999); Christian Marazzi, *Capital and Language,* trans. Gregory Conti (Los Angeles, Calif.: Semiotext(e), 2008); and Christian Marazzi, *Capital and Affects: The Politics of the Language Economy,* trans. Giuseppina Mecchia (Los Angeles, Calif.: Semiotext(e), 2011).

78 Luther Blissett, "Dichiarazione dei diritti di Luther Blissett," in *Totò, Peppino e la Guerra Psichica,* 83–84, translation mine.

79 Ernesto Assante and Wu Ming, "Excerpts from the 10th Anniversary Interview with La Repubblica," August 24, 2004, http://www.wumingfoundation.com/.

80 Henry Jenkins and Wu Ming 1, "How Slapshot Inspired a Cultural Revolution: An Interview with the Wu Ming Foundation (Part One)," *Confessions of an Aca/Fan: The Official Weblog of Henry Jenkins,* October 5, 2006, http://www.henryjenkins.org/. Emphasis mine.

81 See Henry Jenkins, *Convergence Culture: Where Old and New Media Collide* (New York: New York University Press, 2006).

82 Wu Ming 1, "Why Not Show Off about the Best Things? A Few Quick Notes on Social Conflict in Italy and the Metaphors Used to Describe It," *Infopol,* no. 7 (December 2002), http://www.wumingfoundation.com/.

83 In *The Eighteenth Brumaire of Louis Bonaparte* (1897; repr., New York: International, 1994), Marx notes how in epochs of revolutionary crisis, human beings "anxiously conjure up into their service the spirits of the past, assume their names, their battle cries, their costumes to enact a new historic scene" (1). In the Bonapartism of Louis-Napoléon, Marx saw a contemporary form of Caesarism that, with all its classical references, could block the upcoming proletarian revolution. To get rid of those mythic masks, Marx argued that "the social revolution of the nineteenth century can not draw its poetry from the past," but only "from the future" (3).

84 Roland Barthes, *Mythologies,* trans. Annette Lavers (New York: Hill and Wang, 1972), 146–48.

85 Luther Blissett, "Well Begun Is Half Done: A Phone Prank Pulled by Luther

Blissett in January 1997," January 16, 1997, http://www.lutherblissett.net/.

86 Instead of treating the symptom directly, homeopathic medicine contends that by supplying the human body with a diluted substance that generates a symptom of a lesser intensity, the body enhances the immune system's ability to overcome the disease.

87 In Viterbo, a town of sixty thousand residents, the institution of a public university in 1991 had attracted students from different parts of the country, setting in motion new energies in an otherwise stagnant cultural landscape. Even though most of the Viterbese LBP members were native, they were immersed in this sparking cultural climate of the early 1990s. See Fango and Algernon, interview with the author, Viterbo, August 9, 2008.

88 See Luther Blissett Project, Comando Unificato dell'Etruria Meridionale, "Viterbo un anno vissuto satanicamente. Un resoconto completo della maxi-beffa scritto dai suoi autori" [Viterbo, a satanically lived year: A full report of the maxi-swindle written by its authors], in Luther Blissett, *Lasciate che i bimbi: Pedofilia: un pretesto per la caccia alle streghe* [Let the children: Pedophilia as a pretext for a witch hunt] (Rome: Castelvecchi, 1997). Also available at http://www.lutherblissett.net/.

89 Loredana Lipperini and Gianluca Nicoletti showed the extended version of the video on *TV7*, a RAI 1 weekly news magazine, on March 2, 1997.

90 Two weeks before the unveiling of the hoax, *Il Messaggero* finally begun doubting the truthfulness of the story and questioning the professionalism of the local press (but not its own). Conversely, *Il Corriere di Viterbo* never expressed any doubt, nor apologized to its readers, and continued asserting the existence of the Satanists and of the CoSaMo even after the RAI revelations.

91 Marco Dimitri, Pier Giorgio Bonora, Gennaro Luongo, and three other members of the sect were fully acquitted on June 20, 1997, after four hundred days of detention awaiting trial. Two other trials confirmed the innocence of the Satan's Children. In 2004, Luongo and Dimitri were finally granted compensation by a court as victims of unjust detention.

92 Simonetta accused the Satan's Children of every sort of crime, including being necrophiles, committing human sacrifices, entertaining relations with the Mafia, using swords and skulls in the course of sexual rituals, and so on.

93 See Luther Blissett, *Lasciate che i bimbi.*

94 The complete list of press articles regarding the *Musti v. Bambini di Satana* trial is available at http://www.lutherblissett.net/.

95 Luther Blissett, "Italian Crackdown: The Shit Hit the Fan," *Nettime,* April 24, 1998, http://www.nettime.org/archives.php. The Atto di Citazione (Certificate of action at law) filed by Musti is available at *La Repubblica's*

website, "L'atto di citazione del tribunale di Bologna," http://www.repubblica.it/.

96 It is worth noting that the "defamation" concerns the strong wording used in the book to describe Musti's person and does not dispute the merit of Blissett's allegations.

97 Don Fortunato di Noto, at the time the head of the Associazione Telefono Arcobaleno (later renamed Associazione Meter), had already obtained the obscuration of the entire network in 1998 for the publication of another presumably Satanic article. The priest was known in his hometown for having organized crusades against Japanese cartoons and digital pets such as Sailor Moon, Dragonball, and the Tamagotchi. See Snafu, "The Thing Rome Censored Again," *Nettime*, October 10, 2000, http://www.nettime.org/archives.php/.

98 Luther Blissett Project, *Nemici dello Stato: Criminali, "mostri" e leggi speciali nella società del controllo* (Rome: Derive Approdi, 1999). For an English translation of the introduction, see Luther Blissett Project, "Introduction to Enemies of the State: Criminals, 'Monsters,' and Special Legislation in the Society of Control," http://www.lutherblissett.net/.

99 Ibid.

100 Fango and Algernon, interview with the author.

101 Loredana Lipperini, one of the two journalists who covered the Viterbo hoax for *TV7*, is a professional journalist and writer to whom various members of the LBP leaked information any time there was a need to unveil a hoax. Lipperini also authored several articles about Luther Blissett on *La Repubblica*.

102 Ibid.

103 Miriam Tola, interview with the author, Rome, June 20, 2009.

104 Luther Blissett, *Totò, Peppino*, 51.

105 Luther Blissett Project, "Seppuku!," September 6, 1999, http://www.lutherblissett.net/. Italian version in *Totò, Peppino*, vi–ix.

106 See Luther Blissett, *Q* (Torino: Einaudi, 1999). Translated by Shaun Whiteside as *Q* (London: William Heinemann, 2003).

107 Roberto Bui, Giovanni Cattabriga, Federico Guglielmi, and Luca di Meo revealed their names as the real authors of *Q* in an interview with Loredana Lipperini, "Luther Blissett Siamo Noi" [Luther Blissett is us], *La Repubblica*, March 6, 1999. English translation available at http://www.lutherblissett.net/. (Because of the Musti libel suit against *Lasciate che i bimbi*, in this interview Bui is still using the nom de plume Fabrizio P. Belletati.) In 2001, the four were joined by Riccardo Pedrini as part of the Wu Ming collective, which reverted to a quartet in 2008 after the departure of Luca di Meo. Since then, the five-four Wu Mings have authored four collective

novels, including *54*, *Asce di Guerra* (with Vitaliano Ravagli), *Manituana*, *Altai*, and *L'Armata dei Sonnambuli* [The army of the sleepwalkers] as well as several solo novels. The Wu Ming Foundation website (http://www.wumingfoundation.com/) includes a list of complete publications as well as the possibility of downloading all of Wu Ming's books for free.

108 Lippolis is referring here to the fact that in the aftermath of Debord's death, Blissett had authored a pamphlet titled *Guy Debord è morto davvero* [Guy Debord is really dead] (Feltre: Crash, 1995), which attacked the sectarian tendencies of the SI and of its leader, nicknamed here "The Bore." L. Lippolis, "'Togliti i baffi, ti abbiamo riconosciuto': La vera storia di un bluff (il Luther Blissett Project e i suoi padrini) e della sua cattiva coscienza (l'Internazionale Situazionista)" ["'Take your mustaches off, we have recognized you.' The true story of a bluff (the Luther Blissett Project and its godfathers) and its bad conscience (the Situationist International)], *Invarianti*, no. 34 (2000). The English version of the pamphlet, *Guy Debord Is Really Dead* (London: Sabotage, 1995), is available at http://www.lutherblissett.net/.

109 Wu Ming has presented the LBP as a five-year plan in countless texts and interviews. See, e.g., the cited interview with Henry Jenkins, "How Slapshot Inspired a Cultural Revolution."

110 Wu Ming is a collective of professional writers and at the same time a political enterprise that has had a significant cultural influence on Italian social movements and the Italian Left in general. In 2001, in the days leading up to the Genoa G8, Wu Ming circulated in several languages the manifesto/call-to-arms "From the Multitudes of Europe Rising Up against the Empire and Marching on Genoa (19–20 July 2001)," http://www.wumingfoundation.com/.

111 For instance, as late as 2007, Luther Blissett claimed to be the author of a successful media hoax regarding the purported theft of *Harry Potter and the Deadly Hallows*'s manuscript. A few days before the original manuscript was sent to press, "a self-declared group of Catholic hackers purportedly gave away the ending of the book, declaring they violated the computer systems of Bloomsbury (exclusive publisher of the Harry Potter books) to obtain it." See Wikipedia, "Luther Blissett (nom de plume)," http://en.wikipedia.org/. In 2008, the Madrid-based contemporary art space Otro Espacio curated a publication titled "La Triste Muerte de Luther Blissett" (The sad death of Luther Blissett), investigating the reasons for Blissett's purported assassination, proposing the creation of a commemorative monument, and suggesting the reincarnation of the condividual in other identities. See http://www.freewebs.com/otroespacio/Emailed/reenvioo.pdf.

112 Robert P. Baird, "Stories Are Not All Equal: An Interview with Wu Ming," *Chicago Review* 52, nos. 2–4 (2006): 258.

113 Co-curated by Vittori Baroni and Charlie Holmes, the DVD was distributed by the music label Wot4 together with an art catalog for an homonymous art installation that was exhibited at the Bargecchia Art Center of Lucca in 2005.

114 Associazione Psicogeografica Romana and Aliens in Roma, eds., *Luther Blissett: The Open Pop Star* [CD], Wot4, 2000, http://www.lutherblissett.net/.

115 By admission of the authors, *Q* was originally inspired by Dieter Forte's *Martin Luther und Thomas Münzer*, a tragicomedy that is a clear allegory of the German 1968 movement. See Wu Ming, "Dieci anni fa usciva Q" [Ten years ago *Q* was released], *Giap*, no. 6, IX Series (March 2009), http://www.wumingfoundation.com/. *Giap* was Wu Ming's monthly newsletter, which was sent via e-mail to thousands of subscribers throughout the 2000s. It is now a blog available at http://www.wumingfoundation.com/giap.

116 McKenzie Wark, "Luther Blissett, Q, William Heinemann, 2003," *Nettime*, July 29, 2003, http://www.nettime.org/archives.php.

117 Ibid.

118 The analogy acquires a sinister aura if we consider that at the time of the Dimitri trial, the cardinal Joseph Ratzinger was the head of the Congregation for the Doctrine of the Faith, an institution that dates back to the Holy Office of the Inquisition. The Roman Inquisition, which is not be confused with the Spanish Inquisition, was originally instituted by Paul III and presided over during its first twelve years (1542–55) by Gian Pietro Carafa. Once he became pope, Carafa expanded the Inquisition's powers, instituted the infamous List of Prohibited Books, and was able to destroy nearly every single copy of the *Benefit of Christ Crucified*, the most popular book of the short-lived Italian Reformation. After *Let the Children* was incinerated, Joseph Ratzinger ascended to the papacy with the name of Benedict XVI.

119 Jake Purbright and Randolph Carter, "Wu Ming: An Interview in Two Parts," *3AM*, July 2005, http://www.3ammagazine.com/.

120 Utter Bliss and Luther Blissett, "OUTRO: Seppuku," in *Luther Blissett: The Open Pop Star*, translation mine. The text was written by Wu Ming 1 and Wu Ming 2 and performed by Leo Mantovani. MP3 available at http://www.lutherblissett.net/. Aikido is a martial art whose techniques are based on the use of (wooden) swords, knives, and sticks but are ultimately aimed at disarming a foe without using a weapon.

121 Like their Bolognese and London counterparts of the Association of Autonomous Astronauts, the MIR theorized the necessity for humanity to

explore forms of "autonomous contactism" with alien races independent of governmental oversight. MIR ran a magazine and a radio program and organized exhilarating stunts, such as a fake landing of a UFO in Riccione, Italy. Their motto was "UFO to the People." See Men in Red, *Ufologia Radicale: Manuale di Contatto Autonomo con Extraterrestri* [Radical ufology: Handbook of autonomous contact with extraterrestrials] (Rome: Castelvecchi, 1999). After MIR disbanded, Andrea Natella went on to found guerrigliamarketing.it, a guerrilla-marketing company and autonomous political enterprise whose surreal motto was "Fuck the Market so as to Enter It."

5. ANONYMOUS, THE TRANSDUCER

1 See Gilbert Simondon, *L'individuation psychique et collective* [The psychic and collective individuation] (Paris: Aubier, 1989), 24–28. The English translation of these pages is available as G. Simondon, "The Position of the Problem of Ontogenesis," trans. Gregory Flanders, *Parrhesia,* no. 7 (2009): 11–12.

2 See http://boards.4chan.org/b/.

3 Marble cake is both an unsanitary sex act and the name of the IRC channel that was used by Project Chanology (see later discussion in this chapter) to coordinate the attacks against the Church of Scientology. "The Game" is a mind game (and a 4chan inside joke) that requires those who play it not to think about it.

4 An accurate description of how the autovoters functioned is provided by Paul Lamere, "Inside the Precision Hack," April 15, 2009, http://musicmachinery.com/.

5 reCAPTCHA is an acronym based on the word *capture* that stands for "completely automated Turing test to tell computers and humans apart." The textual version of the test consists of two words selected from a database of terms that cannot be identified by optical character recognition (OCR) software. The first term is known to the system and serves as a control word to tell the human apart from the machine (usually a spam bot). The second word is a text the OCR software cannot recognize. This term is submitted to thousands of users until it reaches a threshold of matches. Once the term is consistently recognized, it enters the list of known words. Currently owned by Google, reCAPTCHA not only keeps spam at bay but helps digitize old issues of the *New York Times* and books from Google Books. Thus the service constitutes an invisible form of unpaid labor as it requires humans to perform tasks that cannot yet be executed by digital scans.

6 See Paul Lamere, "moot Wins, Time Inc. Loses," April 27, 2009, http://musicmachinery.com/.

7 As of June 2013, 4chan.org claims to attract more than 1.5 million unique visitors per day. See http://www.4chan.org/advertise.

8 The randonmess of /b/ was neither novel nor unique. In fact, Poole simply imported this feature from the random board of the Futaba Channel, the Japanese board from which he derived an English version in 2003. According to Julian Dibbell, Poole copied the source code of Futaba and translated its menus and GUI with the help of the automatic translator Babel Fish. See Julian Dibbell, "Radical Opacity," *Technology Review,* September–October 2010, http://www.technologyreview.com/featuredstory/420323/radical-opacity/.

9 Judith S. Donath, "Identity and Deception in the Virtual Community," in *Communities in Cyberspace,* ed. Mark A. Smith and Peter Kollock, 29–59 (London: Routledge, 1999).

10 See Matthatias Schwartz, "The Trolls among Us," *New York Times Magazine,* August 3, 2008, http://www.nytimes.com/2008/08/03/magazine/03trolls-t.html?_r=0.

11 David Auerbach, "Anonymity as Culture: Treatise," *Triple Canopy,* no. 15 (February 9, 2012), http://canopycanopycanopy.com/issues/15/contents/anonymity_as_culture__treatise.

12 Dibbell, "Radical Opacity."

13 E. Gabriella Coleman, "Phreaks, Hackers, and Trolls: The Politics of Transgression and Spectacle," in *The Social Media Reader,* ed. Michael Mandiberg (New York: New York University Press, 2012), 112.

14 Cited in Auerbach, "Anonymity as Culture."

15 Cited in Cole Stryker, *Epic Win for Anonymous: How the 4Chan's Army Conquered the Web* (New York: Overlook Duckworth, 2011), 73.

16 Peter Sloterdijk, *Critique of Cynical Reason* (Minneapolis: University of Minnesota Press, 1987).

17 Franco "Bifo" Berardi, *After the Future,* ed. Gary Genosko and Nicholas Thoburn, trans. Arianna Bove et al. (Edinburgh: AK Press, 2011), 24.

18 Weev, cited in "Troll," Encyclopedia Dramatica, https://encyclopediadramatica.se/.

19 Anonymous troll cited in Schwartz, "Trolls among Us."

20 Gilles Deleuze, *Nietzsche and Philosophy,* trans. Hugh Tomlinson (New York: Columbia University Press, 1983), 61.

21 Auerbach, "Anonymity as Culture."

22 The best known of these sites was chanarchive.org. Taking archival requests directly from 4chan users, the website archived a thread when it obtained enough votes from reviewers, who accrued points by rating and tagging

submissions. Chanarchive began experiencing hosting problems in 2013 and has been offline since late 2014.

23 Henri Paget, "Interview: Encyclopedia Dramatica Moderator," *Ninesm*, March 9, 2010. The original URL of this article no longer exists. A mirror page is available at https://encyclopediadramatica.se/Australian_Media_ED_Interview.

24 Poole and other administrators of 4chan have handed over some users' IP numbers to law enforcement agencies in a number of circumstances. This policy is known to 4chan users, who are generally aware that they should have no expectation of privacy for posts that are connected to illegal behaviors.

25 The *-fag* suffix is widely used on 4chan and attached to several typologies of users, including newfags (newbies) and oldfags (seasoned 4channers), Eurofags (posters from Europe), Ponyfags (fans of the cartoon series *My Little Pony: Friendship Is Magic*), and drawfags (users who doodle original images). While some critics argue that the widespread use of the suffix epitomizes 4chan's homophobic culture, others claim that the usage is so common that it carries no fixed positive or negative connotation.

26 Poole made Shii a 4chan moderator after reading an article he had authored in 2004 on the advantages of complete anonymity. The untitled article is available at http://wakaba.c3.cx/shii. Not long after, Shii and moot came to a disagreement over the direction 4chan had to take, and the former was removed from the board after he implemented forced anonymity on /b/. See Striker, *Epic Win for Anonymous*, 144–47.

27 Hideki Furukawa, "Q & A with the Founder of Channel 2," *Japan Media Review*, August 22, 2003. Cited in Shii.

28 Christopher Poole described 4chan as a "place to be wrong" in "The Case for Anonymity Online," TED talk, February 2010, http://www.ted.com/. The definition of 4chan as "the id of the Internet" has multiple sources, according to Julian Dibbell. Jonah Peretti has added that if this is the case, "then Google is kind of like the ego, and Facebook the superego." See Dibbell, "Radical Opacity."

29 The 4chan system sets a limit on the number of bumps a thread can get. Given the high volume of posts in /b/, even the most popular threads expire within a few hours. Furthermore, not all replies renew the thread's position in the forum. In some cases, posters can reply to a thread without bumping it by inserting the word "sage" in the e-mail field. While in Japanese forums and culture saging is a form of courtesy—that is, a way of adding complementary information without placing more demands on the original poster—in Western forums, such as 4chan, it signifies disapproval.

30 Michele S. Bernstein, Andrés Monroy-Hernàndez, Drew Harry, Paul André, Katrina Panovich, and Greg Vargas, "4chan and /b/: An Analysis of Anonymity and Ephemerality in a Large Online Community," paper presented at the fifth international Conference on Weblogs and Social Media (ICWSM), Barcelona, July 17–21, 2011.

31 Richard Dawkins, *The Selfish Gene* (Oxford: Oxford University Press, 1976), 189–201.

32 Terrence W. Deacon, "Editorial: Memes as Signs," *Semiotic Review of Books* 10, no. 3 (1999): 2, http://projects.chass.utoronto.ca/semiotics.

33 Tomberry, "Pool's Closed," *Know Your Meme*, http://knowyourmeme.com/memes/pools-closed.

34 Although DDoS attacks can be used for a variety of purposes—including financial extortion and government censorship—there is a political strand dating back to the mid-1990s that has employed DDoSs to target corporate and governmental websites as a form of electronic civil disobedience. Among the more renowned groups to have organized large DDoS attacks or virtual sit-ins in the late 1990s to early 2000s are the Electronic Disturbance Theater, the Federation of Random Action, and the Electrohippies. On this strand of hacktivism, see Tim Jordan and Paul Taylor, *Hacktivism and Cyberwars: Rebels with a Cause?* (London: Routledge, 2004), and Rita Raley, *Tactical Media* (Minneapolis: University of Minnesota Press, 2009).

35 The filing documents of the court case are archived at http://dockets.justia.com/docket/new-jersey/njdce/2:2007cv00306/198438.

36 Jonathan Jenkins, "Man Trolled the Web for Girls: Cops," *Toronto Sun*, December 7, 2007, http://cnews.canoe.ca/CNEWS/Crime/2007/12/07/4712680-sun.html.

37 Schwartz, "Trolls Among Us."

38 Kevin Poulsen, "Hackers Assault Epilepsy Patients via Computer," *Wired*, March 28, 2008, http://archive.wired.com/politics/security/news/2008/03/epilepsy.

39 This is what is suggested by some activists affiliated with Project Chanology in the documentary film *We Are Legion: The Story of the Hacktivists* (dir. Brian Knappenberger, United States, 2012). According to Gabriella Coleman, Anonymous is unlikely to be responsible for this attack, which she attributes to the rival board eBaum's world. See Gabriella Coleman, *Hacker, Hoaxer, Whistleblower, Spy: The Many Faces of Anonymous* (London: Verso, 2014), 69.

40 Coleman notes that in January 2009, the New York City branch of Chanology organized Operation Slickpubes, a one-man-raid in which an Anon nicknamed Agent Pubit walked into a midtown Scientology church with his torso covered only in Vaseline and pubic hair. This action showed that

the moralfags also engaged in the "carnivalesque humor" typical of the lulz. See Coleman, *Hacker, Hoaxer,* 70–71.

41 Roger Caillois, *Man, Play, and Games,* trans. Meyer Barash (New York: Free Press of Glencoe, 1961).

42 Ibid., 27–32.

43 See Nick Denton, "The Cruise Indoctrination Video Scientology Tried to Suppress," *Gawker,* January 15, 2008, http://gawker.com/5002269/the-cruise-indoctrination-video-scientology-tried-to-suppress.

44 Ibid.

45 Chris Landers, "Serious Business: Anonymous Takes on Scientology (and Doesn't Afraid of Anything)," *Baltimore City Paper,* April 2, 2008, http://www2.citypaper.com/.

46 ChurchofScientology, "Message to Scientology," January 21, 2008, https://www.youtube.com/watch?v=JCbKv9yiLiQ.

47 Ibid. It is worth noting that Anonymous identifies as a specific target the Religious Technology Center (RTC), which owns Scientology's trademark and controls all Scientology's and Dianetics's materials. With the emergence of the Internet, this emphasis on trademark protection and control over technology began to conflict with the technolibertarian ethos that values freedom of information and freedom of access to information technology.

48 Parmy Olson, *We Are Anonymous: Inside the Hacker World of Lulzsec, Anonymous, and the Global Cyber Insurgency* (New York: Little, Brown, 2012), 67–81.

49 Guy Fawkes was involved in and executed for the Gunpowder Plot, a failed Catholic conspiracy to assassinate King James I and blow up the House of Lords on November 5, 1605. Since then, the failure of the Gunpowder Plot is commemorated in Britain with fireworks and bonfires that are used to burn Guy Fawkes effigies. Molly Sauter argues that Guy Fawkes first entered 4chan as a subthread of Epic Fail Guy, a meme depicting a guy trying to achieve status and failing over and over: "In late September 2006, one such thread appeared wherein Epic Fail Guy discovered what appeared to be a *V for Vendetta* film-type Guy Fawkes in a garbage can. Subsequently, Epic Fail Guy was often depicted wearing the mask. It's unclear whether this association had anything to do with the historical story of Guy Fawkes (whose Gunpowder Plot was, in fact, an EPIC FAIL), or whether it was due simply to the marketing blitz for *V for Vendetta*. Either way, the initial popularity of the mask within the Anonymous community was directly due to its association with Epic Fail Guy, and only indirectly (if at all) to political sympathy with either the historical Guy Fawkes or *V for Vendetta*." Molly Sauter, "Guy Fawkes Mask-ology," *HiloBrow.com,* April 30, 2012.

50 Gabriella Coleman, "Old and New Net Wars over Speech, Freedom, and

Secrecy or How to Understand the Hacker and Lulz Battle against the Co$," paper presented at the Radars and Fences Conference, New York University, March 7, 2008. See also Gabriella Coleman, "Our Weirdness Is Free," *Triple Canopy,* no. 15 (January 13, 2012), http://canopycanopycanopy.com/issues/15/contents/our_weirdness_is_free.

51 Gabriella Coleman, "Anonymous," in *Depletion Design: A Glossary of Network Ecologies,* ed. Carolin Wiedemann and Soenke Zehle (Amsterdam: Institute of Network Cultures, 2012), 12.

52 E.g., on January 21, 2008, the administrators of Partyvan put on hold the entire Chanology by first kicking out thousands of users from #xenu and then readmitting them after installing five new servers that could support the swelling crowds. See Olson, *We Are Anonymous,* 73.

53 As Alexander R. Galloway and Eugene Thacker point out, from a politicomilitary standpoint, the strength of the swarm lies in the fact that having "no 'front,' no battle line, no central point of vulnerability," the swarm is an amorphous and ever-evolving entity that cannot be faced and confronted as a single entity. Galloway and Thacker note that at the peak of its power, the swarm can reach a level of cohesion and unity that makes it recognizable as such. Yet it is precisely at the moment in which the swarm can be faced that it can also be de-faced, that is, confronted and possibly defeated. See Galloway and Thacker, *The Exploit: A Theory of Networks* (Minneapolis: University of Minnesota Press, 2007), 66, 69.

54 Ibid., 33–34.

55 Deleuze and Guattari, *A Thousand Plateaus,* 474–500.

56 This statement should be qualified as *seeking* personal notoriety—especially through the media—clashes with Anonymous's strong anticelebrity ethos. For example, Coleman describes the collective decision to ban from AnonOps a Washington, D.C.–based activist named AnonSapple, who had revealed details about his own life to the *Washington Post.* Likewise, prominent Anons like Barrett Brown and Christopher Doyon remained highly controversial figures within the community for their media exposure (Brown) and over-the-top public statements (Doyon). Nonetheless, if egomania is chastised within Anonymous, there is a positive reputation economy that is inextricably tied to individual competences and contributions (as in any online community). For the sanctioning of AnonSapple, see Coleman, *Hacker, Hoaxer,* 184–89.

57 Foucault, "The Discourse on Language," in *The Archeology of Knowledge and The Discourse on Language,* 215–37.

58 Divyesh Singh, "Hollywood Hiring Cyber Hitmen to Combat Piracy," *DNA,* September 5, 2010, http://www.dnaindia.com/entertainment/report-bollywood-hiring-cyber-hitmen-to-combat-piracy-1433621.

59 Ben Grubb, "Film Industry Hires Cyber Hitmen to Take Down Internet Pirates," *Sydney Morning Herald,* September 8, 2010, http://www.smh.com.au/technology/technology-news/film-industry-hires-cyber-hitmen-to-take-down-internet-pirates-20100908-14ypv.html.

60 See Coleman, *Hacker, Hoaxer,* 90–95.

61 Olson, *We Are Anonymous,* 102.

62 Molly Sauter notes that LOIC had been distributed and codeveloped through open source software repositories such as Github and SourceForge, to which individuals can contribute code, report bugs, and request features. In this respect, argues Sauter, the development of LOIC was "far more social" than previous hacktivist tools like the Zapatista FloodNet, which had been created by the Electronic Disturbance Theater to coordinate virtual sit-ins in the late 1990s. "By December of 2010, versions of LOIC could be run on Windows, Mac, and Linux PCs as well as Android phones and jailbroken iPhones. A version called JS LOIC, or JavaScript LOIC, ran, like the EDT's FloodNet application, from within a web browser; the user was not required to download or install anything." Molly Sauter, *The Coming Swarm: DDoS Actions, Hacktivism, and Civil Disobedience on the Internet* (New York: Bloomsbury, 2014), 117.

63 Enigmax, "4Chan DDoS Takes Down MPAA and Anti-Piracy Websites," *TorrentFreak,* September 18, 2010, http://torrentfreak.com/4chan-ddos-takes-down-mpaa-and-anti-piracy-websites-100918/.

64 Luis Corrons, "4chan Users Organize Surgical Strike against MPAA," *Pandalabs* (blog), September 17–November 28, 2010, http://pandalabs.pandasecurity.com/.

65 Enigmax, "ACS:Law Anti-Piracy Law Firm Torn Apart by Leaked Emails," *TorrentFreak,* September 25, 2010, http://torrentfreak.com/acslaw-anti-piracy-law-firm-torn-apart-by-leaked-emails-100925/.

66 Crossley made this announcement during a court hearing in January 2011. He claimed that his e-mail had been hacked and to have been subjected to death and bomb threats. See Jane Wakefield, "Law Firm ACS: Law Stops 'Chasing Illegal File-Sharers,'" BBC, January 25, 2011, http://www.bbc.co.uk/.

67 See Coleman, *Hacker, Hoaxer,* 105.

68 It is estimated that by November 22, Operation Payback had conducted 28 DDoS attacks, which had caused a total of 2,761 website service interruptions for a combined downtime of 37 days. See Sean-Paul Correll, "Operation: Payback Yielded 37 Days of Total Downtime," *Pandalabs* (blog), November 22, 2010, http://pandalabs.pandasecurity.com/.

69 See Luis Corrons, "4chan Users Organize Surgical Strike."

70 See Coleman, *Hacker, Hoaxer,* 102–4.

71 On the early stages of Operation Payback, see Sean-Paul Correll, "An Interview with Anonymous," *Pandalabs* (blog), September 29, 2010, http://pandalabs.pandasecurity.com/.

72 A spokesperson for Anonymous motivated such choice with the need for showing that Anonymous was a "reasonable" entity. See Ernesto, "Behind the Scenes at Anonymous' Operation Payback," *TorrentFreak,* November 15, 2010, http://torrentfreak.com/behind-the-scenes-at-anonymous-operation-payback-111015/.

73 See Enigmax, "Pirate Parties Use Influence to Halt Anonymous' Operation Payback," *TorrentFreak,* November 20, 2010, http://torrentfreak.com/pirate-parties-use-influence-to-halt-operation-payback-101120/.

74 On WikiLeaks, cryptography, and the politics of whistleblowing, see Andy Greenberg, *This Machine Kills Secrets: How Wikileakers, Cypherpunks, and Hacktivists Aim to Free the World's Information* (New York: Dutton, 2012).

75 Gabriella Coleman, "Our Weirdness Is Free." See also Olson, *We Are Anonymous,* 113.

76 See Olson, *We Are Anonymous,* 113.

77 Lucian Constantin, "Anonymous DDoS Tool Gets Botnet Capabilities," *Softpedia,* September 27, 2010, http://archive.news.softpedia.com/news/Anonymous-DDoS-Tool-Gets-Botnet-Capabilities-158163.shtml.

78 Olson reports that Civil and Switch employed thirty thousand and thirteen hundred zombie computers, respectively, for the DDoS on PayPal.com. See Olson, *We Are Anonymous,* 117. Sean-Paul Correll reports that the number of computers connected in the LOIC botnet oscillated between five hundred and seventeen hundred on December 7–8. See Correll, "'Tis the Season of DDoS—WikiLeaks Edition," *PandaLabs* (blog), December 4–15, 2010, http://pandalabs.pandasecurity.com/.

79 Olson, *We Are Anonymous,* 120–21.

80 In the United States, DDoS attacks are punishable by up to ten years in prison, according to the FBI. See FBI, "Search Warrants Executed in the United States as Part of Ongoing Cyber Investigation," January 27, 2011, http://www.fbi.gov/. The DDoS attacks on PayPal sparked an FBI investigation that led to the indictment of fourteen young hacktivists, known as the PayPal 14, on two counts of conspiracy and intentional damage to a protected computer. In December 2013, 11 of the 13 defendants (one case was handled separately) pled guilty to a felony count in exchange for a reduced sentence to three years probation and a $5,600 restitution to PayPal per defendant. See Alexa O'Brien, "Inside the 'PayPal 14' Trial," *The Daily Beast,* December 5, 2013, http://www.thedailybeast.com/articles/2013/12/05/inside-the-paypal-14-trial.html. A parallel investigation by the British police has led to sentences that range between sixty

hours of unpaid work and eighteen months in jail for four British hacktivists. Two of them, FenniC and Nerdo, were AnonOps operators and administrators. See Alex Ward, "'Hacktivists' Who Caused Multi-million Pound Losses to PayPal and Other Websites in Cyber Attacks Walk Free from Court," *MailOnLine*, February 1, 2013, http://www.dailymail.co.uk/news/article-2272064/Anonymous-Jake-Birchall-walks-free-court-multi-million-pound-losses-PayPal.html.

81 See untitled, December 10, 2010, http://pastebin.com/WzzJ1Jp3. Olson notes that even the IRC operators were not that cautious as "the overwhelming sense of camaraderie and accomplishment dominated reasonable argument," giving them a false sense of safety in numbers. Olson, *We Are Anonymous*, 127.

82 An analysis of Spamdot.biz—an underground web forum devoted to spam services and commerce—shows that in September 2010, the market value of one thousand infected machines was $13 in Asia, $35 in Europe, and $125 in the United States. See Brett Stone-Gross et al., "The Underground Economy of Spam: A Botmaster's Perspective of Coordinating Large-Scale Spam Campaigns," paper presented at the fourth USENIX Symposium on Large-Scale Exploits and Emergent Threats, Boston, March 29, 2011.

83 In *The Future of the Internet and How to Stop It*, Jonathan Zittrain worries that the uncontrolled proliferation of worms, viruses, spam, spyware, and botnets may pose such a threat to Internet security that it will ultimately force regulators to close down what he calls the open and "generative" Internet. Zittrain notes that security threats have increased with the exponential growth of a largely illiterate population of Internet users. Zittrain does not consider, however, that many Internet users enjoy the free and unregulated forms of exchange that expose their computers to security risks. See Zittrain, *The Future of the Internet and How to Stop It* (New Haven, Conn.: Yale University Press, 2008).

84 Matteo Pasquinelli, *Animal Spirits: A Bestiary of the Commons* (Rotterdam: NAi, 2008).

85 See Justin M. Rao and David H. Reiley, "The Economics of Spam," *Journal of Economic Perspectives* 26, no. 3 (2012): 87–110. In 2010, e-mail spam was estimated to account for 88 percent of the total e-mail traffic. Rao and Reiley note that an unintended consequence of spam has been to drive out of business small e-mail providers that cannot afford the high costs of antispam technologies. Another unintended effect is that when a computer gets infected and begins to function as a spam relay, its IP address can be blacklisted and, with it, entire blocks of IP addresses belonging to the same network or using the same e-mail provider.

86 Michel Serres, *The Parasite* (Baltimore: Johns Hopkins University Press,

1980), 79. Drawing from Claude Shannon, Serres, and others, contemporary media theorists such as Tiziana Terranova and Peter Krapp suggest that noise is not mere interference but plays an active role in shaping networked communication and culture. See Terranova, *Network Culture: Politics for the Information Age* (London: Pluto, 2004), and Krapp, *Noise Channels: Glitch and Error in Digital Culture* (Minneapolis: University of Minnesota Press, 2011).

87 Paradigmatic is the case of Ryan Cleary, a British teenager who was both an AnonOps operator and the owner of a massive botnet, which he controlled via IRC. In May 2011, following a dispute with other IRC operators, Cleary DDoSed and compromised AnonOps, dropping a list of 653 user credentials and associated IP numbers. This leak threw AnonOps in disarray and prompted other Anons to dox him. Arrested in June 2011, Cleary was accused of lending his botnet to the hacker group LulzSec for DDoSing the websites of the Serious Organised Crime Agency and the CIA, among others. He was sentenced by a British court to thirty-two months in jail in May 2013. See Olson, *We Are Anonymous,* 119–20, 228–30, 317–23, 334–37, and Danielle Walker, "Judge in London Sentences LulzSec Members," *SC Magazine,* May 16, 2013, http://www.scmagazine.com/. For the dispute internal to AnonOps over Cleary's takeover, see the untitled announcement on Pastebin dated May 9, 2011, http://pastebin.com/bgP2CyVm.

88 Kareem Fahim, "Slap to a Man's Pride Set Off Tumult in Tunisia," *New York Times,* January 21, 2011, http://www.nytimes.com/2011/01/22/world/africa/22sidi.html.

89 Yasmine Ryan, "How Tunisia's Revolution Began," *Al Jazeera,* January 26, 2011, http://www.aljazeera.com/indepth/features/2011/01/2011126121815985483.html.

90 The cables are available at http://tunileaks.appspot.com/.

91 Lina Ben Mhenni, "Tunisia Censorship Continues as WikiLeaks Cables Make Rounds," *Global Voices,* December 7, 2010, http://globalvoicesonline.org/.

92 Steve Ragan, "Tunisian Government Harvesting Usernames and Passwords," *The Tech Herald,* January 4, 2011, http://www.thetechherald.com/articles/Tunisian-government-harvesting-usernames-and-passwords/12429/.

93 According to Olson, the attack took place in two phases. In the first part, a New York–based hacker named Sabu used the servers of a London-based company to overwhelm the Tunisian government's websites with junk requests. The Tunisian government's countermove was to shut down all Internet requests from outside Tunisia. In response, a Tunisian Anon logged in to the #OpTunisia IRC channel made his machine remotely

available to Sabu, who hacked and defaced the president's website using a Tunisian IP address. See Olson, *We Are Anonymous,* 142–45, 449. Coleman's account is more nuanced and emphasizes the cooperation between the organizing abilities of the Anons meeting in #opdeface and the advanced technical skills of those meeting in #internetfeds. See Coleman, *Hacker, Hoaxer,* 157–65.

94 The plug-in is available at http://userscripts.org/scripts/review/94122.

95 Anonymii, "Anonymous—The Uber-Secret Handbook v. 0.2.1," April 9, 2011, 4. In *Anonymous Care Package Light 18032012,* zipped folder available for download at http://www.cyberguerrilla.org/. A different version of the package is available at http://youranonnews.tumblr.com/downloads.

96 Ibid.

97 Among the arrested there was Slim Amamou, a thirty-three-year-old blogger and programmer who was accused of being part of a conspiracy to "destroy" government websites. Released on January 13, Amamou was appointed Ministry of Youth and Sport in the coalition government that formed after the collapse of the Ben Ali regime. See Jasmine Ryan, "Tunisia Arrests Bloggers and Rapper," *Al-Jazeera,* January 7, 2011, http://www.aljazeera.com/news/africa/2011/01/20111718360234492.html, and Hisham Almiraat, "Tunisia: Slim Amamou Speaks about Tunisia, Egypt and the Arab World," February 11, 2011, http://globalvoicesonline.org/.

98 Steven Levy, *Hackers: Heroes of the Computer Revolution* (1984; repr., Sebastopol, Calif.: O'Reilly, 2010), 29.

99 E. Gabriella Coleman and Alex Golub, "Hacker Practice: Moral Genres and the Cultural Articulation of Liberalism," *Anthropological Theory* 8, no. 3 (2008): 260.

100 On this strand of hacking, see E. Gabriella Coleman, *Coding Freedom: The Ethics and Aesthetics of Hacking* (Princeton, N.J.: Princeton University Press, 2013).

101 Ibid., 265.

102 For a brief history of this strand, see Coleman, "Phreaks, Hackers, and Trolls," 95–119.

103 Chavala Madlena, "Telecomix: Tech Support for the Arab Spring," *The Guardian,* July 7, 2011, http://www.theguardian.com/technology/2011/jul/07/telecomix-arab-spring. See also Quentin Noirfalisse, "Telecomix: Hacking for Freedom," *Owni.eu,* August 11, 2011, http://owni.eu.

104 Andy Greenberg, "Meet Telecomix, the Hackers Bent on Exposing Those Who Censor and Surveil the Internet," *Forbes,* December 26, 2011, http://www.forbes.com.

105 Interviewed in Knappenberger, *We Are Legion.* Commander X (real name, Christopher Doyon) is the leader of the People's Liberation Front, a hacker

group founded in greater Boston in 1985. Though the group has its own identity, Commander X has participated in various Anonymous operations and cyberattacks, especially DDoSes. In 2012, Doyon fled to Canada to escape prosecution for a DDoS attack he had organized in 2010 to protest against the antihomeless law of Santa Cruz, California. See David Kushner, "The Masked Avengers," *New Yorker,* September 8, 2014, http://www.newyorker.com/magazine/2014/09/08/masked-avengers.

106 Judith Butler, *Precarious Life: The Powers of Mourning and Violence* (London: Verso, 2004), 134.

107 Ibid., 147.

108 E.g., in August 2011, Anonymous joined a wave of protests against police brutality in the BART transportation system of the Bay Area. Originally sparked by the BART police killing of a homeless man, the protests induced the transportation authorities to shut down cell phone service in selected train stations to disrupt the activists' ability to coordinate in real time. In response, Anonymous launched Operation BART, which initially combined forms of civil disobedience such as a (failed) DDoS attack on the BART network, e-mail bombing, and the transmission of black faxes. On August 14, Anonymous breached a BART database and leaked the personal information of twenty-four hundred BART customers, including their telephone numbers, e-mail addresses, and home addresses. A few days later, it hacked into the BART police union website and disclosed the personal information of 102 BART police officers and other agency employees. Anonymous also organized its own street protest at the Civic Center station in downtown San Francisco on August 15, 2011. See "Operation BART," *Know Your Meme,* http://knowyourmeme.com/memes/events/operation-bart, and "Disguised Member of Hacktivist Group 'Anonymous' Defends Retaliatory Action against BART," *DemocracyNow!,* August 16, 2011, http://www.democracynow.org/2011/8/16/disguised_member_of_hacktivist_group_anonymous.

109 Franco "Bifo" Berardi, *The Uprising: On Poetry and Finance* (Los Angeles: Semiotext(e), 2012), 144.

110 On the relationship between Anonymous and Occupy, see Sean Captain, "The Real Role of Anonymous in Occupy Wall Street," *FastCompany,* October 18, 2011, http://www.fastcompany.com/1788397/real-role-anonymous-occupy-wall-street, and Saki Knafo, "Occupy Wall Street and Anonymous: Turning a Fledgling Movement into a Meme," *Huffington Post,* October 20, 2011, http://www.huffingtonpost.com/2011/10/20/occupy-wall-street-anonymous-connection_n_1021665.html.

111 An SQL injection is a technique that consists of querying an SQL database to expose sensitive data and possibly allow the attacker to manipulate the

database. A smurf attack is a type of denial-of-service attack that exploits a vulnerability in the IP protocol. The attacker sends a large number of ICMP or "ping" packets to an IP broadcast address, which transmits the request to the machines of a local network, whose simultaneous responses to the request cause network congestion.

112 The six core members of the group that hacked HBGary Federal and went on to found the LulzSec were Hector Xavier Monsegur aka Sabu, Jake Davis aka Topiary, Ryan Ackroyd aka Kayla/KMS, Mustafa Al-Bassam aka Tflow, and Avunit. With the exception of Avunit, who has not been identified by the authorities, the other five members were all male and of an age between sixteen and twenty-eight. Monsegur, the more experienced hacker and the only member based in the United States, was arrested by the FBI in June 2011 and turned into an informant. Besides providing critical information for the arrest of other LulzSec members, Sabu reported Jeremy Hammond (aka Anarchaos) for hacking the Arizona Department of Public Safety and the intelligence company Stratfor as part of the AntiSec operation. The other four members of LulzSec were all based in the United Kingdom.

113 Joseph Menn, "Cyberactivists Warned of Arrest," *Financial Times,* February 5, 2011, http://www.ft.com/cms/s/0/87dc140e-3099-11e0-9de3-00144feabdc0.html.

114 Steve Ragan, "Data Intelligence Firms Proposed a Systematic Attack against WikiLeaks," *Tech Herald,* February 9, 2011, http://www.thetechherald.com/articles/Data-intelligence-firms-proposed-a-systematic-attack-against-WikiLeaks/12751.

115 Nelson D. Schwartz, "Facing Threat from WikiLeaks, Bank Plays Defense," *New York Times,* January 2, 2011, http://www.nytimes.com/2011/01/03/business/03WikiLeaks-bank.html.

116 IRC transcripts of the conversations among Aaron Barr, Greg Hoglund (HBGary's CEO), Penny Leavy (president of HBGary), and the Anons are excerpted in Coleman, *Hacker, Hoaxer,* 217–27, and Olson, *We Are Anonymous,* 22–25.

117 The AntiSec Operation of 2011–12 is not to be confused with the AntiSec movement of the late 1990s by which it was loosely inspired. Although both movements opposed the computer security industry, the original AntiSec mostly aimed at discouraging security experts and hackers from publicly disclosing network vulnerabilities and exploits. AntiSec reasoned that inexperienced hackers used this information to compromise anything at hand while the security industry commercialized it to turn an easy profit. (The original AntiSec manifesto is now archived at http://web.archive.org/web/20010301215117/http://anti.security.is.) Coleman argues that "the AntiSec revival was driven by a more general sense of justice. The point

was to own banks, governments, security firms, and other corporations in search of politically damning, leakable information." See Coleman, *Hacker, Hoaxer,* 286.

118 McKenzie Wark, *A Hacker Manifesto* (Cambridge, Mass.: Harvard University Press, 2004), section 074.

119 Paolo Gerbaudo, *Tweets and the Streets: Social Media and Contemporary Activism* (London: Pluto Press, 2012), 155–56.

120 McKenzie Wark, *Telesthesia: Communication, Culture, and Class* (London: Polity, 2012), 115.

121 Berardi, *Uprising,* 64.

122 Rodrigo Nunes, "Pack of Leaders: Thinking Organisation and Spontaneity with Deleuze and Guattari," in *Deleuze and Guattari and Occupy,* ed. A. Conio and C. Colebrook (Ann Arbor, Mich.: Open Humanities Press), forthcoming.

123 Simondon, *Du Mode d'Existence des Objets Techniques,* 11, translation mine.

CONCLUSION

1 Simondon, *L'individuation psychique et collective,* 205.

2 Paolo Virno, "Angels and the General Intellect: Individuation in Duns Scotus and Gilbert Simondon," trans. Nick Heron, *Parrhesia Journal* 7 (2009): 64.

3 Ibid., 63.

4 See Jean-Luc Nancy, *The Inoperative Community,* trans. Peter Connor, Lisa Garbus, Michael Holland, and Simona Sawhney (Minneapolis: University of Minnesota Press, 1991); Maurice Blanchot, *The Unavowable Community,* trans. Pierre Joris (Barrytown, N.Y.: Station Hill, 1988); Roberto Esposito, *Communitas: The Origin and Destiny of Community,* trans. Timothy Campbell (Stanford, Calif.: Stanford University Press, 2010); Giorgio Agamben, *The Coming Community,* trans. Michael Hardt (Minneapolis: University of Minnesota Press, 1993); Alphonso Lingis, *The Community of Those Who Have Nothing in Common* (Bloomington: Indiana University Press, 1994); Jean-Luc Nancy, *Being Singular Plural,* trans. Robert Richardson and Anne O'Byrne (Stanford, Calif.: Stanford University Press, 2000). Of course, this debate does not really begin in the 1980s. Its main twentieth-century precursors and referents are George Bataille, Martin Heidegger, and Emmanuel Levinas.

5 Nancy, *Inoperative Community,* xxxvii.

6 Esposito, *Communitas,* 3.

7 Blanchot, *Unavowable Community,* 25.

8 Kuisma Korhonen, "Textual Communities: Nancy, Blanchot, Derrida,"

Culture Machine 8 (2009), http://www.culturemachine.net/index.php/cm/article/view/35/43.

9 Jacques Derrida, *Given Time*, 28.

10 Nancy, *Inoperative Community*, 58.

11 Ibid., 62.

12 See Martin Heidegger, "The Question Concerning Technology," in *The Question Concerning Technology and Other Essays*, trans. William Lovitt, 3–35 (New York: Harper and Row, 1977). On the effects that the ordering and "enframing" of modern technology have on the shift from a proper to an improper relationship of Being to itself (according to Heidegger), see Timothy Campbell, *Improper Life: Technology and Biopolitics from Heidegger to Agamben* (Minneapolis: University of Minnesota Press, 2011).

13 Gerald Raunig, "Eventum et Medium: Event and Orgiastic Representation in Media Activism," *eipcp*, June 2007, http://eipcp.net.

14 Rodrigo Nunes, *Organisation of the Organisationless: Collective Action after Networks* (London: Mute Books, 2014), 33.

15 See, e.g., David Graber, *The Democracy Project: A History, a Crisis, a Movement* (New York: Spiegel and Grau, 2013); Nathan Schneider, *Thank You, Anarchy: Notes from the Occupy Apocalypse* (Los Angeles: University of California Press, 2013); and Marina Sitrin and Dario Azzellini, *They Can't Represent Us! Reinventing Democracy from Greece to Occupy* (New York: Verso, 2014).

16 For example, Not an Alternative, a Brooklyn-based collective that was involved with Occupy Wall Street, notes that the OWS Direct Action group organized itself as a tight-knit affinity group. Concerned that the group could be infiltrated by undercover police, the activists decided to plan many of their actions behind closed doors and without seeking approval of the General Assembly—the deliberative body that was meant to coordinate the activity of the working groups. "As a result, throughout the duration of the movement, accusations have been fired at groups for organizing actions in the name of Occupy that were not agreed to by the General Assembly," writes Not an Alternative. "In a sense, a mindset was operative in the movement that simultaneously encouraged people to act autonomously and condemned them when they succeeded for not having secured approval in advance." Not an Alternative, "Counter-Power as Common Power: Beyond Horizontalism," *Journal of Aesthetics and Protest*, no. 9 (2014), http://www.joaap.org/.

17 Markus Miessen, *The Nightmare of Participation (Crossbench Praxis as a Mode of Criticality)* (Berlin: Sternberg Press, 2010), 15.

INDEX

MARCO DESERIIS is assistant professor of media and screen studies at Northeastern University. He is the coauthor of *Net.Art: L'arte della Connessione*, the first Italian book on Internet art.